GLOBAL CITIZENSHIP
AND THE UNIVERSITY

GLOBAL CITIZENSHIP AND THE UNIVERSITY

Advancing Social Life and Relations in an Interdependent World

Robert A. Rhoads and Katalin Szelényi

Stanford University Press
Stanford, California

Stanford University Press
Stanford, California

©2011 by the Board of Trustees of the Leland Stanford Junior University.
All rights reserved.

Printed in the United States of America on acid-free, archival-quality paper

Library of Congress Cataloging-in-Publication Data

Rhoads, Robert A., author.
Global citizenship and the university : advancing social life and relations in
an interdependent world / Robert A. Rhoads and Katalin Szelényi.
    pages   cm
Includes bibliographical references and index.
ISBN 978-0-8047-7541-0 (cloth : alk. paper) — ISBN 979-0-8047-7542-7
(pbk.: alk. paper)
  1. Education, Higher—Political aspects—Case studies.   2. Education,
Higher—Social aspects—Case studies.   3. Education and globalization—
Case studies.   4. Universities and colleges—Case studies.   5. World
citizenship.   6. Guangdong wa yu wai mao da xue.   7. University of
California, Los Angeles.   8. Universidad de Buenos Aires.   9. Central
European University.   I. Szelényi, Katalin, 1974- author.   II. Title.
  LC171.R56 2011
  306.43'2—dc22

                                                        2010050155

Typeset by Westchester Book Services in 10.5/15 Adobe Garamond

CONTENTS

ACKNOWLEDGMENTS

I acknowledge the hard work of my doctoral students, past and present, whose dedication and intellectual vitality help to continually inspire and energize me. Also, a special thanks goes out to my family for their support over the years. Finally thanks to Simon Marginson, Carlos Alberto Torres, and Fazal Rizvi for their intellectual support on this project and others as well. They are superb role models for countless scholars working in the areas of international comparative education, higher education, and sociology.

Robert A. Rhoads

I am grateful to my husband, Balázs Szelényi, for his unending emotional and intellectual support in this work and my other academic endeavors. My thanks also go to my daughter, Hanna Szelényi, for her patience when I was writing and her good spirits when I was taking a break. I am thankful to my family in Hungary for their encouragement and support. And my special thanks go to Rob Rhoads, for his guidance, wisdom, and inspiration over the past ten years. His words of encouragement and intellectual support have meant an incredible amount to me in completing this project.

Katalin Szelényi

And from both of us, we are indebted to the participants in our case study research at Central European University, Guangdong University of Foreign Studies, the University of Buenos Aires, and the University of California, Los Angeles (UCLA). Their experiences and insights have served as the most important source of inspiration in the writing of this book. And we offer our deepest thanks to Stanford University Press Executive Editor Kate Wahl for her support throughout this project.

CHAPTER I

GLOBALIZATION, CITIZENSHIP, AND THE UNIVERSITY

INTRODUCTION: GLOBALIZATION, OTHERING, AND HYBRIDISM

Globalization is not a recent phenomenon. The influence of individuals and groups on others has steadily increased throughout human history, reaching a point some five hundred years ago that could reasonably be described as "global" in nature. As means of transportation advanced over time, so did the power of one society to influence another. This was becoming increasingly evident by the sixteenth century with the rise of the great European powers and their ability to dominate parts of nearly every region of the world. Arguably, the origins of globalization are located in this period, for it marked the rise of the great navies, global shipping and trade industries, extensive transoceanic migration, and, of course, expansive colonization by Europeans.

Increased human interaction as a consequence of globalization added to the strength and intensity of "us-versus-them" thinking. Othering native inhabitants of distant lands was central to waging the kind of exploitative relationships critical to empire building. Imperialism depended on such an idea, as Edward Said clearly articulated in his book *Culture and Imperialism*: "Throughout the exchange between Europeans and their 'others' that began systematically half a millennium ago, the one idea that has scarcely varied is that there is an 'us' and a 'them,' each quite settled, clear, unassailably self-evident. . . . [T]he division goes back to Greek thought about barbarians, but whoever originated this kind of 'identity' thought, by the nineteenth century it had become the hallmark of imperialist cultures as well as those cultures trying to resist the encroachment of Europe."[1]

Conceptions of "us" and "them" historically have been embedded in cultural differences linked to geography, religion, ethnicity, race, and nationality. In the context of colonialism, views of us and them largely were shaped by xenophobia tied to these differences, with perceptions of race in particular often at the core of such beliefs.[2] History is replete with examples of empire building and its impact on a particular people defined as racialized others by citizens of a colonial power. European colonizers brought certain cultural and religious views to North America that ultimately transformed the physical landscape and decimated the indigenous population. Early European settlers, for example, saw the native population as "heathens" and sought to save them from their "savage" ways by introducing Christian-based forms of education.[3] The French, despite liberal philosophical claims to humanism, colonized Algeria by reducing the native inhabitants to less-than-human status. Colonialism hardly could have succeeded otherwise, for it depended on overseas soldiers and officials to enact cruelties upon the locals. As Frantz Fanon pointed out in *The Wretched of the Earth*, orders were given "to reduce the inhabitants of the annexed country to the level of superior monkeys in order to justify the settler's treatment of them as beasts of burden."[4] Violence enacted against the colonized had as its aim "the keeping of these enslaved men at arm's length."[5] The goals were to dehumanize them and erase their traditions, substitute their language with that of the colonizers, and in time "destroy their culture."[6]

There are other examples of us-and-them distinctions being employed for the purposes of subjugation and violence. The widespread enslavement of

Africans and their subsequent imprisonment and deportation to the so-called New World was most insidious and depended on race-based distinctions constructed primarily by Europeans deploying advanced technologies in service of their financial interests. There is the example of the Holocaust and the Nazi death camps in Germany, when the "us" was defined as defenders of the Aryan race and the "them," principally defined as Jews (along with gays, Gypsies, prisoners of war, Catholic priests, and Jehovah's Witnesses, among others), were sentenced to death as part of the "Final Solution of the Jewish Question." Us-and-them distinctions in the latter instance were quite complex, with religion and ethnicity of course being of central importance. Us-and-them distinctions also have been used as part of the justification for military invasion. In many of these instances, the process of othering inhabitants of a particular geographic region was grounded in conceptions of national identity but was also conflated with matters of race, ethnicity, and religion. For example, under former U.S. Presidents George H.W. Bush and George W. Bush, two wars were waged against Iraq with much support from the U.S. general public (at least in the beginning), largely the consequence of the vilification and demonification of Saddam Hussein in particular and Iraqis in general.[7] David Harvey noted, for example, that Saddam Hussein was portrayed as "an incarnation of evil that had to be combated as if war in the Middle East was an episode in some long-running medieval morality play."[8] In this case, race, religion, and nationality all played a role in leading, or rather misleading, a large percentage of the U.S. citizenry to support violence on a massive scale to be waged against Iraq, resulting of course in thousands of deaths among the civilian population.

Although the age of classic imperialism has passed, the mentality of colonialism has not fallen by history's wayside. Beliefs of "us as superior" and "them as inferior" prevail to a great extent and are reflected in the way subsequent generations are taught to see themselves and their homeland by comparison to others. Here again, Said is insightful: "The wonder of it is that the schooling for such relatively provincial thought and action is still prevalent, unchecked, uncritically accepted, recurringly replicated in the education of generation after generation. We are all taught to venerate our nations and admire our traditions: we are taught to pursue their interests with toughness and disregard for other societies."[9]

Perhaps what is most striking about contemporary forms of globalization is the ubiquitous nature of how one group is brought to bear on another, largely the consequence of the world, in Fazal Rizvi's terms, "becoming increasingly interconnected and interdependent."[10] Fortunately, the outcome of contemporary forms of cultural contact—increased exponentially by mass media, advanced communication systems, and information technology— more often than not—is less violent. Surely cultural influence is not entirely dependent on the butt of a rifle.

At their worst, less-violent forms of cultural influence may be seen as forms of imperialism—some have described this sort of influence as the Mc-Donaldization or Americanization of the world, at least when the United States is the source of influence.[11] At their best, cultural influences may be more reflective of local opportunism, as when members of a particular society develop new ways of interacting with their environment by borrowing provocative forms from another culture and modifying those forms to suit their local needs and interests. Emphasis on local opportunism stresses a multi-directional view of global influence, which in essence situates globalization as "both a differentiating [and] a homogenizing force."[12] Such a view is akin to the position adopted by Allan Luke and Carmen Luke, who see "hybridity" as a "social and cultural formation born out of complex and intersecting histories."[13] They argued for a more multidirectional understanding of globalization, whereby peripheral countries and cultures are not simply positioned as the passive recipients of "Euro-American authored 'capitalocentrism,'" but in fact there are "two-way, mutually constitutive dynamics of local-global flows of knowledge, power, and capital."[14] Luke and Luke posited that local histories are always embedded in the adoption of cultural elements and conditions. In supporting their case, they pointed to Thai popular music and how the country's musicians borrowed from the West but also incorporated Thai traditional folk music. The result is a cultural form hybrid in nature and yet unique and influential within the youth culture of Thailand.[15]

Another example of the hybridization of popular music and youth culture comes from China. In Shanghai, rapper Blakk Bubble points to the influence of U.S. popular culture and the ways in which rap is changing the Chinese music scene in urban settings such as Beijing and Shanghai.[16] A surface-level interpretation might suggest another case of the Americanization of the world through the increasing power and influence of U.S. media and popular culture. Certainly, there is likely to be some truth to such a position. But this argument is incomplete. For example, if we look further into the emergence of rap in China, we also see local innovation and adaptation; in the words of Luke and Luke, "local and regional force and power"[17] act upon U.S.-based versions of rap music. Thus, in adapting rap to their own localized context, Chinese youth do not rap about "gansta" life, but in "rah-rah" or "reformed" rap the messages are softer, gentler, and, of course, more censored by the government. As a Beijing disc jockey explained, "They can't curse, they basically have to say life is great, life is beautiful, nothing's wrong. It's not hip-hop."[18] So, although the United States and China share rap music as a common cultural form, the cultural distinctiveness of this music genre in the two countries remains evident.

The signs of hybridization are everywhere, from the obvious case of foreign companies and stores transplanted to other regions of the world, where they are refashioned to better fit local preferences (e.g., Toyota in the United States, Starbucks in China), to the more subtle ways in which forms of language, architecture, agricultural practices, beliefs, and so forth emerge in distant places, similar in content and form but modified according to local custom (Toyota had to modify some of its assemblage practices when transplanted to the United States, and Starbucks had to account for preferences for tea when transplanted to China). Hybridity also surfaces at the level of identity. A clear example is the way in which nationality is less and less tied to a particular race or ethnicity, as a consequence of the growing influence of migration and interracial marriage.

Hybridization, then, is another aspect of globalization and in some sense offers resistance to forms of othering, as the elements of culture that once separated one group from another are increasingly diffused and cultural identities more and more reflect a creolized mixture of global influences. Certainly, us-versus-them thinking continues to dominate in contemporary times, but many cultures and identities resist such dualistic terms, simply because cultural diffusion is so widespread that identifying us and them is not always so easy. And although it is fairly clear that the oppressive influence of cultural imperialism and othering is still quite real, nonetheless, when we look at the world today, it is hard to ignore the reality of hybridity and the vast influence of globalization.

THE ESSENCE OF OUR PROJECT

Said's work is particularly helpful to the line of thinking we advance in this book. Although his attention to cultural hybridity focused to a great extent on empire building and the lives of the colonizers and the colonized (as revealed in the literature, and mostly fiction at that), his notion of a contrapuntal global analysis has many implications for how we read identities and cultures within an increasingly global world. Most important to this book, we see the need to complicate and challenge us-versus-them thinking, as well as the forms of citizenship that spring forth from such frames of reference. Educational institutions in general and universities in particular, as key sites for perpetuating particular notions of identity, nationalism, and citizenship, must be critically analyzed for the ways in which they foster the othering of a "them." We see educational processes associated with the othering of various social groups (including nationalities), while ignoring the hybridity of contemporary life, as a key facet to a complex process that contributes to sustaining global instability. In a very real sense, this is the central mission we take on in this text, as we explore universities around the world and the ways in which more global and hybrid notions of social life and citizenship may be advanced. In essence, we argue that notions of citizenship have lagged behind the cultural realities of a hybridized world.

Our purpose to this point is to paint a portrait of a changing world, a world that is increasingly framed by global connections and transnational penetrations. It is a world in which the technological innovations of the most brilliant minds of our time seem to have outpaced the development of the human side of life. In fact, there continues to be a dominant line of thought that situates science and technology as the only source of insight capable of saving humankind, when in reality we surely have neglected the social imagination and our ability to construct societies and social relations in a manner consistent with promoting world peace. We can destroy the world with weaponry that the best scientific minds have produced, but we cannot seem to build transnational relationships in which such weapons are rendered useless. Martin Luther King, Jr. made a similar point some forty years ago, noting, "When we look at modern man we have to face the fact that modern man suffers from a kind of poverty of the spirit, which stands in glaring contrast to his scientific and technological abundance. We've learned to fly the air like birds, we've learned to swim the seas like fish, and yet we haven't learned to walk the earth as brothers and sisters."

We believe the technological advances of today have fundamentally changed the nature of social relations and that such changes call for new forms of citizenship. We see citizenship as a form of identity linked to complex rights and responsibilities that increasingly must be understood in terms of the local and the global as well as individualist versus collectivist objectives. Us-and-them tensions of a global world, complexities associated with hybridization, the challenges of cultural imposition, the expansiveness of global capitalism, and the growing transnational political spheres and interpenetrations all suggest the need for new forms of identity, especially new and innovative conceptions of citizenship. If we cannot advance more complex and expansive forms of citizenship, then we might as well abandon the tremendous advances associated with science and technology, for it is quite likely the case that the one thing we certainly will advance is our own doom and that of the planet.[19]

With the preceding in mind, we are concerned about the ways in which us-versus-them thinking continues to exist to this day, in the face of an increasingly global world. Despite rapid cultural exchange and increased hybridity, local identities are still constructed in significant ways on the basis of an us-versus-them ideological foundation. This can be seen nearly every day as different conflicts break out in various parts of the world; some of these conflicts are nationalistic in nature, others ethnic or religious, and still others a mixture of the three. We see the idea of citizenship, and what constitutes citizenship, as key to understanding today's world and the growing influence of globalization. Furthermore, we believe universities have a central role to play in challenging the foundations of us-versus-them thought and in forging more expansive notions of citizenship. We say this because of the central role universities play in preparing tomorrow's leaders and the place they occupy as a social conscience for society. The latter idea is particularly important when one recognizes the fundamental role universities play in the production, management, and application of knowledge, a role Simon Marginson argued is even more critical given today's "global connections" and "global flows of people, ideas, knowledge, and capital."[20] Accordingly, universities have an obligation to use their knowledge capacities to advance social life and to better the human condition. Just as we have used our sharpest university minds to advance science and technology, we must do the same in terms of advancing global social relations. Hence, we see the lives of students and faculty as a key context for exploring the possibility of more innovative and expansive conceptions of citizenship.

Although we can say a great many things about today's world, it is certainly clear that increased international integration and global ties are a driving force shaping contemporary lives. What do the changes that globalization brings mean to students and faculty learning and working in the context of the university? How are their experiences similar and different, depending on their location within an ever-changing global landscape that maintains and produces massive economic and political imbalances? How are their lives as citizens, as academic citizens, as global citizens, being reframed by increasing global ties and international integration? Most importantly, in what ways can us-versus-them forms of citizenship be challenged in the context of globalization? These questions are at the heart of this book as we examine faculty and students at four universities around the world: Guangdong University of Foreign Studies (GDUFS) in The People's Republic of China; the University of California, Los Angeles (UCLA) in the United States; the University of Buenos Aires (UBA) in Argentina; and Central European University (CEU) in Hungary. We select these four universities to explore academic life and the issue of global—or globally informed—citizenship in part because of the important global cities in which they reside: Guangzhou, Los Angeles, Buenos Aires, and Budapest. Furthermore, the geopolitical location of each university and the city in which it exists represents one or more key issues arising from complex relationships spawned by globalization. GDUFS and the city of Guangzhou reflect China's growing world engagement and the opening of China in the post-Mao era and help us consider the increasing impact of global capitalism and its far-reaching influence. UCLA and Los Angeles exist in the context of significant international scholarly exchange and massive immigration, respectively, and help us consider the growing impact of cultural globalization and the role of the United States as a source of cultural influence. UBA and Buenos Aires call to mind the growing North-South divide and increasing resistance arising in the South to hegemonic versions of globalization advanced by powerful countries and the intergovernmental institutions they helped to found. CEU and Budapest, by virtue of Hungary's recent incorporation in the European Union, help us consider the ways in which regionalization emerges within the context of globalization, as well as ongoing struggles that universities in peripheral and semiperipheral countries face in light of a world increasingly shaped by the dictates and decision making of central countries. The preceding cases, taken as a whole, help us consider complex and emerging forms of citizenship in light of globalization and the growing power of global capitalism.[21]

METHODOLOGICAL CONSIDERATIONS

We adopt a case study approach and anchor our analysis to an interpretive tradition informed by critical social science.[22] Our line of thought is comparable to arguments advanced by Clifford Geertz about the nature of social science inquiry and the quest for knowledge. For Geertz, social inquiry is not so much about "discovering the Continent of Meaning and mapping out its bodiless landscape" as it is "guessing at meanings, assessing the guesses, and drawing explanatory conclusions from the better guesses."[23] We, like Geertz, are interested in the ways in which human actors construct meaning from their experiences. This involves a serious focus on culture and the ways in which individuals become "suspended in webs of significance" that they in fact help to construct. Unraveling such webs of significance is less "an experimental science in search of law" than it is "an interpretive one in search of meaning."[24] Accordingly, we see ourselves not so much as hard-core scientists testing hypotheses but as adventurers in a quest for meaning, seeking to understand how different individuals at diverse universities in varying parts of the world experience and define citizenship in a global age. When we suggest that we are not following the common hypothesis-testing model of social science, this is not to imply that we reject other key elements of rigorous social science inquiry. Indeed, we place great emphasis on face-to-face, time-consuming data collection strategies involving extensive field work and numerous site visits. We also embrace a rigorous analytical process grounded in multiple methodologies for ensuring the authenticity of our findings, including engaging some of our research participants in extended conversations about preliminary conclusions.

As a model for presenting our work, we find Frances FitzGerald's book *Cities on a Hill: A Journey Through Contemporary American Cultures* inspirational. FitzGerald's provocative book detailed the inner workings of four unique American communities: San Francisco's Castro district; Reverend Jerry Falwell's Liberty Baptist community in Lynchburg, Virginia; a retirement community in Sun City, Florida; and the Oregon community constituted by the followers of guru Bhagwan Shree Rajneesh. Although each community offers a different portrait of an American way of life, including the efforts of individuals and groups to create a meaningful existence, FitzGerald nonetheless weaves a narrative that reveals some of the underlying commonalities that constitute the American vision of "a City Upon a Hill," where "the eyes of all people are upon us," as the Puritan John Winthrop once noted in helping to found the Massachusetts Bay Colony.[25] We, too, select diverse communities, more precisely universities as communities, and look at varying circumstances and issues helping to shape contemporary notions of globalization and citizenship. But as FitzGerald did in *Cities on a Hill*, we see some pivotal connections that we believe can help us better understand the challenges of citizenship in an increasingly global world.

THE ROLE OF GLOBAL CAPITALISM

The central construct framing this book is *globalization*, which has been defined by Anthony Giddens in *The Consequences of Modernity* as "the intensification of worldwide social relations which link distant localities in such a way that local happenings are shaped by events occurring many miles away and vice versa."[26] Similarly, David Held described globalization as the reduction of time and space such that events in one part of the world have the potential to influence events in another part of the world.[27] Most scholars of globalization locate its origins in the sixteenth century, when, as Held argued, "a dense pattern of global interconnections began to emerge with the initial expansion of the world economy and the rise of the modern state."[28] But a second phase of globalization is also identified and dated to around the middle of the twentieth century, following World War II. This phase of globalization typically is that to which most social theorists point when they discuss the rise of international, transnational, and multinational organizations, advances in technology and information sciences, the emergence of a worldwide division of labor, and the increase in human mobility through improved and more affordable transportation. We see these changes primarily driven by the steady march of capitalism toward the goal of global domination to the extent that by the early 1980s one might realistically speak of "global capitalism."

From our perspective, one cannot examine globalization without looking at its economic features and the increasing role that capitalism and free-market ideology play around the world. Furthermore, we see global capitalism as the driving force in escalating cultural contact, whether the results of such contact represent cases of hybridization (including elements of local empowerment) or imperialism (both violent and nonviolent). We see the United States, as the world's largest and most dominant economy and the only remaining superpower, militarily speaking, leading the way in shaping economic forms of globalization.

In her provocative book *World on Fire*, Amy Chua made an excellent case for the problematic ways in which the United States shapes the rest of the world through the spread of global markets and democracy "American style." U.S. political and economic leaders accomplish their international economic agenda by shaping a variety of transnational and multinational organizations with the stated goal of advancing democracy and freedom (defined mostly as free markets) around the world. As Chua noted,

The fact is that in the last two decades, the American-led global spread of markets and democracy has radically transformed the world. Both directly and through powerful international institutions like the World Bank, International Monetary Fund, and World Trade Organization (WTO), the United States government has helped bring capitalism and democratic elections to literally billions of people. At the same time, American multinationals, foundations, and nongovernmental organizations (NGOs) have swept the world, bringing with them ballot boxes and Burger Kings, hip-hop and Hollywood, banking codes and American-drafted constitutions.[29]

Chua went on to argue, "The prevailing view among globalization's supporters is that markets and democracy are a kind of universal prescription for the multiple ills of underdevelopment."[30] But her book reveals that this is not necessarily the case, as free-market democracy often leads to antidemocratic movements, a consequence of clashes between a market-dominant minority and an economically disenfranchised majority. Furthermore, and at a global level, Americans are seen as a market-dominant minority relative to the rest of the world. Thus, although Americans benefit tremendously from the country's economic superiority and dominance throughout the world—and the ways in which the U.S. government "spreads" free-market ideology—they also become the target of massive resentment, including terrorist attacks such as what we witnessed on September 11, 2001.

The spread of global capitalism has produced innumerable governing bodies that span the boundaries of nation-states and suggest new forms of political organizing. As Chua pointed out, intergovernmental organizations (IGOs) such as the International Monetary Fund (IMF), the World Bank (WB), and the World Trade Organization (WTO) exert power and influence over transnational interactions and relations. Furthermore, regional partnerships and trade agreements such as the Association of Southeast Asian Nations (ASEAN), European Union (EU), Mercosur (a trade agreement among Argentina, Brazil, Paraguay, and Uruguay), North American Free Trade Agreement (NAFTA), and Central America Free Trade Agreement (CAFTA) all produce forms of transnational and multinational governance. Beyond trade, IGOs and international governing bodies such as the United Nations, North Atlantic Treaty Organisation (NATO), the African Union, and the G-8 all add to the complexity of global, transnational politics.

For many social theorists, the advance of global capitalism and its related international governing bodies and organizations are best understood in terms of the expansion of neoliberal ideology to a global level.[31] Neoliberalism essentially reflects the view that the best way to advance societies (and democracy as well), most notably developing societies, is by liberalizing trade (hence the new liberalism or neoliberalism). The liberalization of trade involves the elimination of state subsidies, tariffs, and other forms of protectionism. Some recognize this philosophy as taking a strong hold on the West during the reigns of Ronald Reagan in the United States and Margaret Thatcher in the United Kingdom; in essence, powerful conservatives (in the United States they have been described as the Washington Consensus) have successfully advanced the capitalist project to such an extent that it has achieved hegemony throughout much of the world. One result is the "internationalization of production and the internationalization of financial transactions" largely under the jurisdiction and control of multinational corporations.[32]

In some sense, then, neoliberalism is a confusing descriptor, since what we see today in terms of global economics is a near total victory of conservatism and the power of neoconservative geopolitical influence. Michael Apple clarified some of this when he described the ways in which neoliberalism and neoconservatism have produced a conservative restoration in the case of the United States, erasing many of the reforms of or deriving from the progressive movements of the 1960s, including extensive attacks against affirmative action in higher education.[33] Some argue that the conservative restoration is reflected in the influence of the "angry white man" trope in film and literature throughout the 1980s and into the 1990s, including the creation of the likes of "Rambo."[34]

A central goal of neoliberalism is to transfer numerous public functions, assets, and roles to the private sector—the belief being that a free market ultimately yields a greater return and through fair competition produces cheaper and better products and services. From the perspective of neoliberalism, citizens stand to benefit from reduced taxes and less expensive services, albeit funded by user fees; such user fees in part contribute to the weakening if not the elimination of a progressive tax code, because everyone pays the same price for a particular service, regardless of their extreme wealth or poverty. In part, neoliberalism reflects the teachings of Adam Smith and the general views held by diehard capitalists, whose central mission over the past forty years or so has been to cripple and then eliminate the Keynesian welfare state, primarily through deregulation and privatization. Although the global economic recession of the latter part of the first decade of the twenty-first century should have been a wake-up call to the ills of neoliberalism, little in fact has changed. Wall Street still remains relatively unregulated, as free-market ideology has found numerous ways of reinventing and reinserting itself.

Neoliberalism also seeks to eliminate any notion of the broader public good, including institutions such as public schools and public universities. In essence, there is nothing beyond the free market, and social programs meant to improve the lives of others, especially the most economically disenfranchised, violate the basic premise of neoliberalism and its corporate mentality. Hence, one sees pervasive assaults waged by conservatives and neoconservatives against public schools and public universities, not to mention social systems such as social security and public works and welfare programs. Under the banner of neoliberalism, the nation-state is redefined to serve the needs of the corporate sector, whose interests are seen to be in line with the interests of the society and free-market democracy. Corporations are to serve themselves, and in so doing they will quite naturally benefit the broader society; the power and vitality of neoliberalism depend on individuals and corporations acting in their own self-interest, not the interest of others or of the commonweal. Along these lines, Joel Bakan argued that corporations are by their nature pathological in their pursuit of self-interests, defined mostly in terms of profit: "As a psychopathic creature, the corporation can neither recognize nor act upon moral reason to refrain from harming others. Nothing in its legal makeup limits what it can do to others in pursuit of its selfish ends, and it is compelled to create harm when the benefits of doing so outweigh the costs."[35] Bakan added, "The corporation, like the psychopathic personality it resembles, is programmed to exploit others for profit. That is its only legitimate mandate."[36] We are left to ponder in light of the growing power of corporate capitalism, what is to become of a world in which such an ideology goes unchecked at a global level? Indeed, what kind of citizenry can we expect a corporate-driven global capitalism to fashion?

As a consequence of markets providing the governing mechanism for societies, the role of the nation-state is redefined as monitoring and advancing whatever policies are necessary to ensure free trade and to work toward the elimination of public services in favor of privatization. Thus, around the world we see widespread sell-offs of public services, including sources of energy, along with pernicious attacks waged against long-standing social programs (e.g., social security in the United States).

Privatization thus has become the mantra of the neoliberalists. And why not? The wealthy stand to gain a great deal if social programs are eliminated in favor of private pay-as-you-go services, because, after all, the philosophy in the Keynesian welfare state was that those who are the best off have some social responsibility to the downtrodden, the underclass, the unemployed, the underemployed, the persecuted, and so forth. But such idealism has become sinful in the context of neoliberal ideological domination and the die-hard conservatives who seek to fashion a new vision of society and citizenship—citizens as individualists geared for economic competition. We can only conclude that Milton Friedman was not joking when he asked, "What kind of society isn't structured on greed?"

With the expansion of global capitalism we have witnessed the rise of governing bodies that in part assume some of the former functions of the nation-state. This is why numerous authors have discussed the so-called decline of the nation-state.[37] In part what we see today is a confounding of two interrelated interests that David Harvey linked to a new form of imperialism. Harvey argued that "capitalist imperialism" represents "a contradictory fusion" of the political goals and aspirations of the state (he called this "the politics of state and empire") and complex intersecting processes associated with capital accumulation (he described this facet as "the molecular processes of capital accumulation in space and time").[38] The politics of state and empire center on "the political, diplomatic, and military strategies invoked and used by a state," while the molecular processes of capital accumulation center on "ways in which economic power flows across and through continuous space, towards or away from territorial entities through the daily practices of production, trade, commerce, capital flows, money transfers, labour migration, technology transfer, currency speculation, flows of information, cultural impulses, and the like."[39] Harvey maintained that the capitalist seeks individual gain (for herself or himself or a company), "while the statesman seeks a collective advantage"[40] and is responsible to some assemblage of citizens, albeit often a group of economic elites. The processes associated with the state often are open to debate and have the potential to be democratic, whereas those tied to the work of the capitalist are more private and closed in nature and more or less antidemocratic. The condition that arises when the interests of the capitalist take precedence over those of the state is what some describe as the disappearing or fading nation-state. Of course, the rise of neoliberalism has brought the state into greater alignment with the interests of capital, and in this sense neoliberalism clearly advocates a weak state; the one exception, of course, is that the state must act aggressively to advance and maintain global free markets and the interests of corporations.[41] Given the important role of the state in supporting global markets, claims that the state has in fact disappeared or faded to the background seem somewhat overstated.[42]

The kinds of changes we see taking place globally—involving politics, economics, and culture—are keys to understanding the changing context of societies and the citizens who occupy them.[43] Our position is that conceptions of citizenship have not kept pace with the changing complexities of global societies. In the context of global capitalism of the neoliberal variety, we see the need for new and more compelling conceptions of citizenship.

CITIZENSHIP AS A FRAMEWORK

We use the concept of citizenship, more specifically global citizenship, to frame our analysis of academic life and the changing context of the world's universities. By citizenship, we refer to a particular facet of identity—a subset, so to speak, of the broader idea of identity—that relates primarily to sets of rights and responsibilities linked to one's geographic locale and the global penetrations that in part help to define the range and limits of one's life across the key dimensions of social experience, namely, the political, economic, and social. From a traditional perspective, and absent the reality of globalization, the nation-state played a pivotal role in shaping individuals' rights and responsibilities. However, globalization adds much complexity to how we presently think about rights and responsibilities, given that the nation-state is challenged in many ways by three powerful realities: (1) the massive mobility of peoples, (2) the rapid and extensive exchange of information and knowledge, and (3) the intervention of other complex organizations, agencies, and movements in advancing notions of rights and responsibilities. Thus, for us, citizenship as a subset of identity is no longer bound solely by the logic of the nation-state but takes on added complexity in a social environment that is increasingly porous and amorphous; part of our goal in this project is to complicate and confound notions of citizenship that in the past have been overly embedded in the local geographic and national context. Consequently, we advance a view of citizenship in which the geographic reference point for one's sense of rights and responsibilities is broadened and in some sense complicated by a more expansive spatial vision and understanding of the world.

The concept of citizenship tends to be associated with the political/civic dimension of social life, perhaps because the field of political science has had such a huge impact on the scholarly work on citizenship. But such a view ignores the larger complexities of life as a citizen, and the fact that individuals occupying particular locales (increasingly globalized locales) have rights and responsibilities extending far beyond simply the political and civic dimension of life. Most notably, individuals also exist within economic and social dimensions that, like the political/civic dimension, suggest various rights and responsibilities. Put another way, the engagement of individuals as citizens reflects understandings of rights and responsibilities across three basic dimensions of social life: the political (including civic aspects), the economic (including occupational aspects), and the social (including cultural aspects). The political dimension speaks to one's engagement in the civic and governmental aspects of particular organizations, social groups, and societies (this dimension also may be considered as the political/civic dimension). The economic dimension primarily references the ways in which one generates a livelihood—the occupational facets to one's life. The social dimension points to the shared experiences one has within various social collectivities (e.g., families, friendship groups, organizations, and so forth) and derives to a great extent from the kind of social life one leads (the social dimension thus includes cultural aspects and may also be thought of as the social/cultural dimension). All three dimensions of citizenship may encompass experiences rooted in the local context as well as those operating at a more global level. What separates our notion of citizenship as delineated here from the broader concept of identity is that we limit citizenship to issues specifically relating to rights and responsibilities—the basic components of an individual's relationship to particular locales (again, locales that are increasingly influenced by global processes).

We contend that notions of citizenship are much more confounding than typically is acknowledged. Indeed, a dominant line of thinking about citizenship in the United States tends to stress the civic and political aspects of one's status as a "legal" citizen of a particular nation.[44] Citizens are granted certain rights, such as the right to vote, and as citizens they inherit a variety of responsibilities, such as obeying the laws of the land. But this rather legalistic notion of citizen bound by the context of a nation-state and its related nationalism ignores the fact that an individual occupying a particular geographic space, but not possessing legal status as citizen, also has rights and responsibilities. For example, Yasemin Soysal noted that guestworkers without legal status as citizens, nonetheless are "incorporated into various aspects of the social and institutional order of their host countries."[45] She explained, "The participation of guestworkers in the host polity as social, political, and

economic actors with a wide range of rights and privileges contests the foundational logic of national citizenship."[46] The solution to this conceptual dilemma for Soysal is a "postnational" definition of citizenship in which one's
rights and responsibilities are not rooted in the nation-state but instead are
tied to one's personhood: "What were previously defined as national rights
become entitlements legitimized on the basis of personhood."[47]

Soysal's point about the participation of guestworkers in the "social, political, and economic" facets of the polity also suggests an expansion of the
concept of citizenship by noting the relevance of the social and economic
dimensions, as opposed to only the political/civic. More times than not, citizenship is discussed in terms of civic responsibilities, typically ignoring the
fact that when individuals occupy a particular geographic space they also
participate in social and economic dimensions of society. The relevance of the
social dimension (again, perhaps best understood as the social/cultural dimension) of citizenship is also stressed in the work of Richard Guarasci, who
criticized views of citizenship focused only on civic-oriented rights and
responsibilities—"the citizen as simply voter and taxpayer."[48] Guarasci stressed
the importance of "interculturalism" and the reality that citizens in today's
world must "reconcile the social realities of an intercultural and multicentric
society."[49] Similarly, both Robert Rhoads and Carlos Alberto Torres advanced
the idea of "democratic multicultural citizenship" in which education helps
students to develop the dispositions and abilities to work across social and cultural differences in a quest for solidarity.[50] They argued that such skills are essential to citizenship in a multicultural, global environment.

As Soysal made clear, there are economic dimensions to citizenship as
well. When we occupy a particular locale as a resident of some type, be that
permanent or otherwise, we face the challenges of generating an income, a
livelihood, a means of subsistence. The range of options available to us are
limited to a certain extent by the society in which we find ourselves, although
increasingly we are less and less bound by the local conditions. But even if we
make our living in a more global manner, by engaging in e-commerce
through an Internet-based business, for example, local conditions may place
limits on the feasibility of our work; in some countries, for example, Internet
connections may not be so easily accessible, and in others, legal limits may be
placed on how the Internet is utilized.[51] Our point is that the manner by

which individuals make a living varies to some extent by geographic location, just as the ways in which we interact socially and politically vary as well. Nonetheless, all three dimensions—political, economic, and social—are key to a more expansive vision of citizenship. For us, the three dimensions of citizenship provide a basic understanding of the broad contexts in which citizens think, act, and react; that is, thoughts and actions as citizens may be understood as existing across these three dimensions of life.

Additionally, actions as citizens concern issues relating to rights and responsibilities; the focus on rights and responsibilities helps us distinguish citizenship or citizenship identity from the broader concept of identity, which encompasses much more than simply rights and responsibilities. To be more clear, human actors express forms of identity within the context of the three main dimensions of society, but their identities as citizens are distinguished by those expressions relating to the enactment of rights and responsibilities (see Figure 1.1).

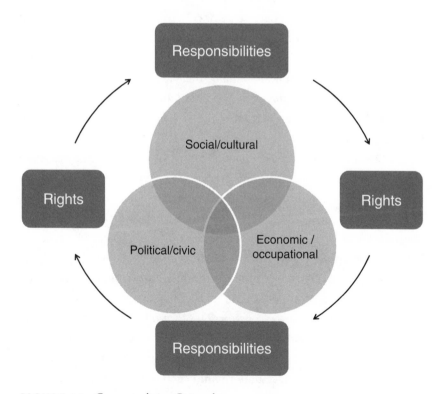

FIGURE 1.1. Conceptualizing Citizenship

Our conceptualization of citizenship here, and global citizenship in the next section, is formed by the interplay of theory and empirical data collected at the four universities we studied. Although in this chapter we stress the theoretical literature more than the empirical data, the upcoming case study chapters and concluding chapter clearly reveal the complex ways in which the academic lives of students and faculty contribute to more advanced understandings of citizenship—indeed, global citizenship.

In terms of citizenship in general, we see a university education contributing to one's ability to negotiate the political, economic, and social dimensions of human experience, and hence it is important to understand the role that universities play in advancing forms of citizenship. For example, a college degree confers certain economic and professional rights (perhaps better understood as occupational opportunities) as well as responsibilities. When one graduates with a degree from a college or university, certain professional expectations are likely to become central to one's life; these expectations can be no more separated from one's sense of citizenship than legal and political rights and responsibilities. Similarly, it is hoped that the kinds of experiences one has in college will contribute to a broader understanding of the world socially and culturally speaking. Finally, there are great expectations placed on college graduates in terms of their political and civic engagement within the societies in which they find themselves as well as across societies in an increasingly globalized world.

Additionally, university faculty and students, in their close proximity to the production, management, and application of knowledge, play unique roles in shaping how societies envision citizenship, primarily through their roles as academic citizens. Indeed, there is much scholarly literature on the role of professors as engaged scholars, whose work ideally is to contribute to the broader society.[52] Similarly, there is much written about the roles students play as agents of social change and their potential to contribute to the betterment of society as civic or political actors.[53] Consequently, we see faculty and students as key players in the construction of various notions of citizenship, and potentially, conceptions of global citizenship. For example, in their many roles as teacher, researcher, outreach worker, student leader, and even activist, professors and students enact and/or reinforce various models of citizenship grounded in their lived experiences at universities. Coming to terms with the ways in which these key actors conceptualize and embrace modalities of citizenship, especially in an increasingly globalized world, may be quite helpful in understanding the complexities of global citizenship. Consequently, we see the analysis of modern universities, and key actors within them, as critical to advancing a more globally oriented vision of citizenship.

EXPLORING GLOBAL CITIZENSHIP AND UNIVERSITIES

Many universities around the world make specific mention of an international or global mission in the areas of teaching, research, and service. In fact, it is hard to find a university Web site these days that does not in some way address the issue of increased international integration and the emergence of a global community. For example, we examined the Web sites of many universities around the world and noted the following messages (the italicized text represents our emphasis). The University of Melbourne in Australia seeks to prepare students "to contribute effectively to their communities wherever in the *world* they choose to live and work." The University of Guadalajara in Mexico seeks to foster students' holistic development, including increased tolerance and "the love of country and *humanity*," as well as a social conscience grounded in the values of democracy, justice, and liberty applicable around the world. Similarly, the University of Botswana seeks to "advance the intellectual and human resource capacity of the nation and the *international community*." Kyoto University in Japan "welcomes students from all over the *world* who aspire to learn and to foster their interest in taking an active part in *international society*."

Many university officials are quite explicit in connecting their institutions to a global environment. According to Tokyo University's president, Komiyama Hiroshi ("Message from the President"), his university aims to become the "World's Tokyo University" and strives to create "an institution that contributes to the benefit of *all human society*." He further explains, "The age of nations is coming to an end, and global competition has inspired a growing awareness of the need for a *collective human society*." The president of New York University, John Sexton ("Message from the President"), also claims "global university" status: "We have expanded our focus from New York, the world's capital city, to become a truly *global university*, with significant New York University Centers around the world." Another U.S. university, Michigan State University (MSU), seeks to reach out to the world as well. The text on its Web site highlights how MSU's land-grant and service mission now extends to international settings. Its mission statement directly addresses changes linked to globalization: "The evolution of this mission reflects the increasing complexity and cultural diversity of society, the *world's greater interdependence*, changes in both state and national economy, and the explosive growth of knowledge, technology, and communications." If nothing else, university leaders and their public relations staffs are quite aware of the growing prominence of international issues and the role universities are expected to play in advancing global relations.

Although many universities around the world rhetorically at least seek to advance a broader conception of citizenship (and social and civic obligation), reaching clarity on what such forms of citizenship actually entail is not so simple. In this regard, we find the construct of global citizenship helpful in framing the kinds of discourses and changes we see taking place around the world. But this term too can be confusing. Various conceptualizations of global citizenship in the literature are referred to as vacuous, incoherent, and vague.[54] Indeed, no clear definition of global citizenship—or as otherwise referred to, cosmopolitan or world citizenship—has been concisely articulated.[55] A dominant view of global citizenship suggests an economic model in which all the world's populations compete in some grand free market (based on a model of the market economy), with nation-states limiting their interventions or only intervening to further advance global capitalism (this relates to the model of neoliberalism that we discussed earlier).[56] Others place less emphasis on economics and examine additional facets of global citizenship. For example, Manuel Castells and Alain Touraine situated citizens more or less as actors within an ever-changing landscape of networks and social movements with the traditional concept of society playing a decreasing role in defining social experience.[57] Whereas Castells and Touraine saw the rise of social movements as a counterpoint to a changing global landscape, a more individualistic and conservative position (and consistent with neoliberalism as well) was advanced by Margaret Thatcher, who argued, "There is no such thing as society, only individual men and women and their families."[58]

In an alternative interpretation of global citizenship, Derek Heater identified a continuum from vague to more precise representations, the vaguest referring to "the sense of identity with the whole of humanity, of membership of the human race. Less vague is acceptance of some moral responsibility for the condition of the planet and its inhabitants, human and even non-human."[59] In its most precise form, "world citizenship is that which embraces the need for some effective form(s) of supra-national political authority and for political action beyond the nation-state."[60] In yet another account, Richard Falk delineated five categories of global citizens: (1) the "global reformer" and supporter of supranational government, (2) the elite class of globe trotters engaged in global business activities, (3) individuals committed to global economic and ecological sustainability, (4) supporters of regional governance structures as in the example of the European Union, and (5) transnational activists involved in grassroots organizations fighting for human rights and democracy.[61] Although the spectrum of definitions regarding global or cosmopolitan citizenship is vast, a major organizing principle is the notion of greater or lesser degrees of ethical responsibility toward human rights and other individual and community rights, as well as moving beyond the nation-state—in the form of transnational organizations and movements—in acting upon one's sense of responsibility.

Attempts to define global citizenship also have been limited by disputes within left-leaning intellectual circles, concerning the importance of the nation-state and the relevance of nationalism in a global era.[62] The debate, by and large, originates in the concurrent emphasis on nationalism and internationalism in different strains of socialist thought. As David Miller argued,

The internationalist strain stems philosophically from the Marxist belief (like most Marxist beliefs not held in its crude form by Marx himself) that national divisions are created artificially by the capitalist class to divide the proletariat, and politically from the belief that socialism in [only] one country could never be a feasible possibility. The nationalist strain derives first from the fact that all socialist projects, whether communist or social-democratic, have been national projects in the sense that they have been undertaken by parties and movements working within national borders; second from the fact that in order to carry these projects through, socialists have needed to invoke the idea of the nation.[63]

The ambivalence of the left is reflected in its simultaneous support and criticism of forms of transnational governance, such as the European Union.[64]

Fear of nationalism is a major force driving some scholars to embrace the importance of providing universal human rights beyond—while often also parallel to—the scope of the nation-state.[65] Supporters of a cosmopolitan democracy propose a focus on universal rights. The notion of cosmopolitan identity arises from concerns over the weakening of the nation-state in the global order and its perceived inability to cater to the rights of its citizens in the presence of global forces. As Anthony McGrew explained, "The fate of democratic communities across the globe is becoming ever more tightly interwoven by patterns of contemporary globalization with the result that established territorial models of liberal democracy appear increasingly hollow."[66] Some have argued that in order to compensate for a weakened nation-state, new forms of "cosmopolitan democracy" are needed.[67] Cosmopolitan democracy entails "a model of political organization in which citizens, wherever they are located in the world, have a voice, input, and political representation in international affairs, in parallel with and independent of their own governments."[68] The weakening of the nation-state is thus to be compensated for by the increased role of regional and global (nongovernmental) organizations that in essence take over some of the responsibilities of national governments. However, nation-states do not disappear completely, but their role is complemented—sometimes compromised—by regional and global organizations that are by and large independent of the governmental sectors of specific nation-states.[69]

A person espousing cosmopolitan citizenship in this sense is characterized by the acceptance of the weakening of state power in the context of globalization and the rejection of the continued relevance of nationalism.[70] Cosmopolitans work to promote human rights through the activities of nongovernmental organizations and social movements independent of specific nation-states and, in turn, place less emphasis on the preservation of strong states and exhibit limited recognition of certain responsibilities that might be regarded—by those favoring a strong state—as impossible to achieve without state intervention.

Opposing these ideals, other representatives of the left have launched a strong critique of arguments for attaining a cosmopolitan democracy.[71] These scholars highlight the continuing importance of the nation-state and nationalism—though importantly, not in the sense of ethnonationalism that often leads to ethnic conflict and war.[72] Doubtful of the adequacy of multinational states in the global order, Miller argued that only single nation-states, where people share linguistic and cultural backgrounds, are able to provide for the trust among various constituents necessary for the maintenance of democracy, and only such states can instill in people the social consciousness and self-sacrifice required for achieving social justice.[73] Additionally, left-leaning scholars concerned about the growing power and influence of corporations and neoliberal domination see the nation-state as a potential counter to unchecked global capitalism. It is important to note, however, that these same scholars often point to how democratic governments have failed to live up to professed ideals, siding more times than not with capital over people.[74]

In a similar vein, and critiquing Soysal's notion of postnational membership in nation-states, a form of membership affording noncitizen migrants universal human rights based on their fundamental rights of "personhood," Christian Joppke cautioned that the conferral of human rights to noncitizens—no matter how universally accepted they may be—continues to be tightly based in the power of the welfare state.[75] Rogers Brubaker reaffirmed the continuing relevance of the nation-state in our time by describing it as a system of "territorial," "domestic," and "ethnocultural closure," whereby noncitizens are essentially excluded from certain rights (for example, suffrage in the domestic closure domain) available only to citizens.[76] Importantly, even certain aspects of nationalism are defended against the notion of cosmopolitan democracy. As Craig Calhoun asserted, "To treat nationalism as a relic of an earlier order, a sort of irrational expression, or a kind of moral mistake is to fail to see both the continuing power of nationalism as a discursive formation and the work—sometimes positive—that nationalist solidarities continue to do in the world."[77]

Admittedly, nearly all of the preceding strains of thought regarding global citizenship and cosmopolitan democracy offer useful insights. On the one hand, how could we argue against the struggle for universal human rights in structures (supranational) that complement the reach of the nation-state or the emergence of a globally responsible identity able to go beyond the constraints of state boundaries in trying to solve problems in the world? On the other hand, the emphasis on strengthening the nation-state (or better put, the welfare state) against the increasing reach of global capitalism also has critical implications for the maintenance of individual and community rights. Can the two sides of the debate be reconciled with the acknowledgment of both contributing to the notion of responsible citizenship in the national as well as global realms? Perhaps it is possible to nurture a form of citizenship that, with a strong basis in ethical considerations, promotes concern and action for the resolution of societal problems on both local/national and global levels, while at the same time preserving the role of the nation-state (again, *welfare state* may be a better expression here) in regulating local/national as well as global processes and overseeing the rights of its citizens beyond national borders. Consequently, our view of global citizenship incorporates both local/national awareness with a growing sense of the interconnectedness of all nation-states and the importance of forging common ties and connections in terms of global rights and responsibilities.

As we move forward throughout this book, we seek to advance an understanding of new forms of citizenship that hold the possibility of reconciling key tensions between the local and the global as well as tensions between decisions and actions rooted in collectivism versus those more oriented toward individual interests.

Globalization poses new and complex possibilities for conceiving citizenship and the related rights and responsibilities as extending beyond the traditional boundaries of society and nation-state. Thus, we see the need to develop a particular notion of citizenship that incorporates a serious global component. Accordingly, we see global forms of citizenship as taking place within one or all dimensions of society or social life (better considered as social life given the context of globalization and its society-spanning potential), with their performative quality focused on rights and responsibilities, but informed by global understandings and oriented toward the collective good. Thus, the key to constituting various thoughts and actions as manifestations of global citizenship is reflected by the degree to which they are grounded in global understandings (versus being limited to only local understandings) and whether such thoughts and actions seek to serve broader collective concerns (versus being individualist in nature). In this regard, we may think of

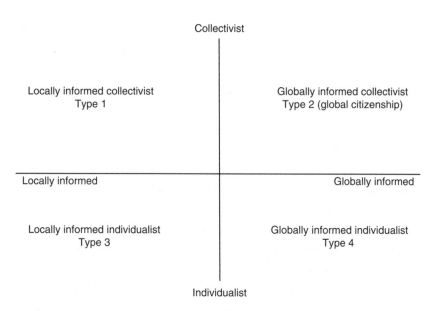

FIGURE 1.2. Citizenship/Global Citizenship Typology

citizenship as existing within the framework of two intersecting axes (see Figure 1.2): (1) ranging from individualist to collectivist and (2) ranging from locally informed to globally informed (in terms of the forms of understanding that frame one's thoughts and actions).

From our perspective, it is not simply the geographic scope of one's actions as a citizen that constitutes global citizenship, but rather it is the nature of one's understandings and the commitment to broader concerns that constititute global citizenship; thus, we see global citizenship as being marked by an understanding of global ties and connections and a commitment to the collective good. What this suggests is that even actions on the part of citizens aimed at addressing local concerns may still constitute forms of global citizenship when those actions are informed by global understandings and reflective of concerns beyond those of the individual (that is, they are collectivist in nature).

Throughout the case studies that follow this chapter, examples of faculty and student considerations and actions as citizens will mostly concern Type 2 and 4 forms of citizenship, as the goal of this book is to better understand how university actors may shed light on globally informed forms of citizenship. However, the majority of the examples will focus on globally informed collectivism (Type 2), as we see the challenges of today's world as requiring global citizens who value and are committed to a broader sense of the social good; in other words, they are globally informed and collectivist in orientation.

In our concluding chapter, Chapter 6, we return to our citizenship typology and offer clear examples from our four case studies. We do this to highlight how our conceptualizations of globally informed citizenship are in fact informed by the empirical data collected through our diverse cases. We see the academic lives of students and faculty, operating within the parameters of the contemporary university, as being key to the development of our thinking about global citizenship, given their relationship to the production, management, and application of knowledge. In other words, as the world increasingly moves in the direction of a global knowledge economy, the university and its key actors—its academic citizens—can help us to better understand the changing context of citizenship broadly conceived.

This brings us, then, to a discussion of the university and its vital role in framing particular visions of citizenship. Indeed, we see universities as one of the few remaining spaces in which unchecked global capitalism (neoliberalism) and the kind of citizenry it advances may still be challenged. We need academics, students, and graduates of universities who possess the dispositions and skills to resist the present movement toward corporate-driven self-interest and who see themselves as part of the struggle for a broader, more globally responsible citizenship. As Bakan astutely noted, we are heading down a pathological path toward our own destruction. What we need more than ever is *not* the elimination of the public sphere, but its strengthening: "Social groups and interests judged to be important for the public good or too precious, vulnerable, or morally sacred to subject to corporate exploitation, should be governed and protected by public regimes."[78] For us, the university is a crucial link in advancing such public regimes, and we see the university itself as an interest too precious to be subject to corporate control and domination. What we need is a powerful democratic space, and universities have a key role to play in advancing such a project. The problem is that the university itself has become a central target of the neoliberal assault.

GLOBALIZATION AND THE ASSAULT ON THE UNIVERSITY

Universities increasingly are called upon to do more with less. Indeed, universities often are expected to do more than one can imagine a single institution setting out to accomplish. For example, universities are expected to provide support for economic and technological development. In wealthy countries such as Germany, Japan, the United Kingdom, and the United States, billions of dollars are allocated by central governments to advance academic science and strengthen relationships between universities and industries. Additionally, universities and their faculty are expected to use their expertise to serve local and regional needs, not only in terms of economic and technological development but also through their work with various social institutions, including the government, corporations, and industry. Universities are expected to assume a vital role in preparing citizens for jobs and careers appropriate to the economic needs of a given society. In fact, universities face significant public criticism if academic programs and curricula are seen to be out of step with the training needs of employers. And although some within the academy often respond by pointing to the shortcomings of universities being overly vocationalized, it is hard to ignore the pressure they are under to meet the demands of an ever-changing labor market.

Given the monumental economic functions that universities must serve, the preparation of citizens capable of contributing to the political and social dimensions of a society often is relegated to a minor role, if acknowledged at all. Keeping in mind that when we think of citizens and the ways in which their lives intersect with societies, we see the political, economic, and social dimensions all as critical. But unfortunately, universities increasingly are called upon to pay greater attention to the economic, as in training graduates to enter the work force, while they often neglect the political and social dimensions of everyday life. The growing strength of neoliberalism—and the idea of placing economic needs and concerns at the center of public policy, as defined within the context of global capitalism—pushes universities toward preoccupation with the economic dimension of citizenship. A central concern that we bring to this work focuses on the ways in which universities might resist a reductionistic view of students and faculty—as cogs in the global capitalist machinery—and instead see them in more holistic ways, by recognizing the multiple dimensions of social life and citizenship.

Perhaps the most profound influence on universities today derives from neoliberal economics and the increasing push toward privatization. Although this trend is most obvious in the United States, it is also revealed around the world, as the work of Boaventura de Sousa Santos reveals.[79] Santos argued that the scientific and pedagogical autonomy of the public university in large part has been based on its financial dependency on the state. Just as a state-supported judicial system often has retained a sense of independence, in terms of the autonomy of its courts and decision making, so too the public university operated by and large as an autonomous body despite its support from the state. "However, contrary to the judicial system, the moment the state decided to reduce its political commitment to the universities and to education in general, converting education into a collective good that, however public, does not have to be exclusively supported by the state, an institutional crisis of the public university automatically followed."[80] Santos pointed to the past thirty years as the principal period during which states began disinvesting in universities, in part because universities lost their dominant position as educational and scientific institutions (he described this as the "crisis of hegemony"), as industry increasingly came to play a role in these areas. Given the private sphere in which most industries—and, of course, corporations—operate, as well as the intensification of global processes over the past thirty years or so, in which neoliberalism increasingly shaped state decision making, it should come as no surprise that movements arose to reduce support for public universities and turn them over to the interests of private capital and the needs of industry.

In aligning the public university ever more closely with the interests of capital and industry, two important results were achieved, especially in peripheral countries governed by antidemocratic regimes. First, the loss of autonomy led to "the elimination of the free production and diffusion of critical knowledge."[81] This strengthened the existing political regimes. Second, reforms "put the university at the service of modernizing authoritarian projects, opening the production of the university-as-public-good to the private sector and forcing the public university to compete under conditions of unfair competition in the emerging market for university services."[82] In more democratic countries (peripheral countries that had made the transition from dictator-ship to democracy), the second reason became the guiding rationale for university reform—"especially beginning in the 1980s, when neoliberalism was imposed as the global model of capitalism."[83]

By the 1990s, the economic restructuring of the university was well under way, and with the efforts of the World Bank and the WTO, higher education was that much closer to being just another service exchangeable on the world market to be governed by global trade policies. What had become clear to economic elites by this point was that much money was to be had within the arena of higher education, and so distancing the universities from the broader public good and resituating them within the context of the free market (and thus promoting privatization) were an absolute necessity. As Santos argued, "The two defining processes of the decade—the state's disinvestment in the public university and the mercantile globalization of the university—are two sides of the same coin. They are the two pillars of a huge global project of university politics destined to profoundly change the way the university-as-public-good has been produced, transforming it into a vast and vastly profit-able ground for educational capitalism."[84] And so, according to Santos, by the dawn of the twenty-first century the mercantilization of the public university, and universities in general, was well under way.

THE COMMERCIALIZATION OF THE U.S. UNIVERSITY

To understand the changes taking place at a global level, we find it helpful first to make sense of the case of the U.S. university (the structure with which we are most familiar) and its steady march to the beat of capital and capital-ism. Indeed, there is a vast and growing body of literature focused on how universities—primarily U.S. universities—became shaped by corporate and neoliberal influences. This literature varies considerably in quality, ranging from retired university presidents' reflections on the state of commercialized affairs in academe to more polemical works highly critical of the corporatiza-tion of the university to empirically grounded works examining the impact of academic capitalism and entrepreneurialism (commercialization). Here is just a sample of the books we explored in conducting research for this project: *The Knowledge Factory: Dismantling the Corporate University and Creating True*

Higher Learning by Stanley Aronowitz; *Universities in the Marketplace: The Commercialization of Higher Education* by Derek Bok; *Creating Entrepreneurial Universities: Organizational Pathways of Transformation* by Burton Clark; *Take Back Higher Education: Race, Youth, and the Crisis of Democracy in the Post-Civil Rights Era* by Henry Giroux and Susan Searls Giroux; *The University in a Corporate Culture* by Eric Gould; *The Enterprise University: Power, Governance, and Reinvention in Australia* by Simon Marginson and Mark Considine; *Academic Capitalism: Politics, Policies, and the Entrepreneurial University* by Sheila Slaughter and Larry Leslie; *Academic Capitalism and the New Economy: Markets, State and Higher Education* by Slaughter and Gary Rhoades; *Leasing the Ivory Tower: The Corporate Takeover of Academia* by Lawrence Soley; and *University Inc.: The Corporate Corruption of Higher Education* by Jennifer Washburn.[85]

The movement of the U.S. university to the beat of corporate interests actually may be traced back to the World War I and II eras, when extramural investment began to play a major role in shaping the university and its research commitments. No one has done a better job of documenting the development of the American research university than Roger Geiger,[86] who in his books *To Advance Knowledge: The Growth of American Research Universities, 1900–1940* and *Research and Relevant Knowledge: American Research Universities Since World War II* stressed how philanthropic foundations and private benefactors, business and industry, and the federal government became involved in complex and varying ways to fund university research for the purpose of advancing academic science. Geiger argued that the period around World War I was critical in the development of academic science in the United States, which essentially moved before the war from "a provincial outpost in the international world of science . . . [to] rough parity with other leading scientific nations well before events in Europe forced the intellectual migration of the 1930s."[87]

Initially, though, there were tensions between the interests of academic scientists and various individuals and organizations external to the university, which sought to shape the nature of knowledge produced. This tension revolved in part around debates over basic versus applied research. As one can easily imagine, a donor seeking to fund academic science held an interest in the nature of the outcomes and consequently was more likely to support researchers whose goals were to produce tangible and potentially income-generating scientific findings. Obviously, corporations provided funds for university research with a clear goal of using the knowledge generated to enhance their business activities. Corporations and industries were and continue to be in the business of making money, and the funding of academic science was for the express purpose of improving their bottom line. But, as Geiger noted, "University research . . . was wedded to the ideal of disinterested inquiry. The divergence in these outlooks held potential for conflict. There were important differences between the interested and the disinterested pursuit of knowledge in terms of what problems would be investigated and what use was to be made of the results."[88]

Of course, World War II and its aftermath dramatically altered the nature of academic science in the United States, as the role of the federal government dramatically increased and many research universities became increasingly tied to contracts with the Office of Scientific Research and Development (OSRD). In the pre–World War II period, there was a general reluctance of academic scientists to become entangled with the federal government and with any effort that might compromise the disinterested pursuit of knowledge. As Geiger noted, "They tended to fear government interference with the autonomy of science more than they welcomed its succor."[89] Nonetheless, representatives of academic science sought greater funding from the federal government by arguing for a New Deal for university research, hoping to tap into monies tied to the National Industrial Recovery Act, a piece of legislation designed to support industrial development in the aftermath of the Great Depression of 1929. Geiger argued that what New Deal appeals failed to muster, World War II pretty much guaranteed, as the federal government increasingly turned to academic science in the face of an international crisis and the need to organize the country's greatest minds. Thus, the relationship between academic science and extramural funding was changed forever: "It was only after an extensive federal role in support of university research had become an accomplished fact that it was possible to formulate a policy to rationalize and legitimate it. To this end President Roosevelt in 1944 directed the OSRD's director, Vannevar Bush, to advise him on how the wartime government experience in sponsoring scientific research could be applied after the cessation of hostilities."[90] Although Bush and other advocates of increased federal support for academic science emphasized the need for basic science as well as the desire to protect the autonomy of the research university, this was to become increasingly difficult as the twentieth century progressed.

In a certain sense, it was during the World War II period that the genie was released from the bottle. She could never be returned, because the flow of capital into academic science would only increase. In the face of escalating federal, corporate, and philanthropic investment in the post–World War II years, concerns about the disinterested pursuit of university research in particular and university autonomy in general were hushed to the back of the pews, mostly to be voiced from time to time by those most marginalized by a growing revenue-generating culture. Indeed, resistant voices were (and still are) more likely to come from those faculty operating in the hinterlands of academic capitalism—professors in the social sciences, humanities, or natural science programs at lesser-ranked universities, places where the flow of money was not so great or where teaching was held in higher regard. In other words, the greatest protests have come over the years from those most removed from the steady flow of revenue, while those capable of tapping into the flow have tended to do just that. In some cases, the pressure brought to bear on the latter group of faculty is so great that outright resistance to the capitalist model is practically unfathomable and at elite research universities surely untenurable.

When we think about Geiger's work and his extensive documentation of how various private, corporate, and federal forces came to shape the national project to advance knowledge, we cannot help but be reminded of Sandra Harding's feminist critique of science and the central question raised by her book and embedded in its title—*Whose Science? Whose Knowledge?*[91] These days, concerns about the place of interested versus disinterested research largely have faded to the background. Much funded research today clearly is not the kind of disinterested science that was once practiced. Instead, contemporary academic science is often tied to particular interests, much of which is directly connected to capital—and oftentimes, a lot of it. But whose interests are being served by university research that clearly is *interested* inquiry? Whose science and whose knowledge is it? Why are there seemingly so few critical questions raised about the role external revenues play in shaping academic life and the forms of academic knowledge seen as valuable? Along these lines, Harding likens the contemporary model of academic science to Mary Shelley's Frankenstein: "How the monster actually got created—and gets nourished and reproduced day after day—retreats into the shadows, as if there are no persons or institutional practices that we can hold responsible for the shape of the sciences and the kind of social order with which they have been in partnership."[92]

In raising these concerns, we are not calling for a return to pre–World War II forms of academic science and knowledge construction. Indeed, we are not calling for a return to disinterested academic science and disinterested universities. We believe, as Santos has so astutely argued, that the new challenges of a global world must be met with new responses. Falling back on a nostalgic sense of the university that was never so democratic or socially transformative in the first place is not the answer. We reject an overly romanticized view of the historic university, when so many groups were excluded and when so much of the educational and research capacity of the university was rarely invested in meeting the needs of the great mass of citizens. For example, women and minorities were by and large excluded from the university of old—which is partially Harding's point in raising questions about whose interests have been served by science. One can just as easily ask of the contemporary university: Whose interests are served by today's universities and the massive research projects undertaken by academic scientists? The answer is fairly self-evident: The interests served are tied to individuals and groups with large enough sums of money to fund university research (and researchers). Big money primarily shapes the direction of research and knowledge construction, and given what Warren Bennis and Hallam Movius called the "pay-your-own-way philosophy," in which faculty members must find their own revenue streams to support their work, they are best served when they connect their interests to "the big money."[93] The modern research university could hardly be more removed from disinterested science.

The new challenges posed by globalization and the increasing interconnectedness of our lives, our societies, do not call out for a return to disinterested scientists and universities—the old idea of the Ivory Tower. But these changes speak to the need to rethink, to reconsider who we are, what we value, and what kind of universities we desire. Now is also the time to reconsider the ways in which we allow capital to shape the university and its values. In essence, we raise questions about the kind of social institutions we want universities to be; this question inherently requires that we directly address the kind of society we desire and the forms of citizenship we hope to advance through our most vital social institutions. To do so, though, requires a thorough understanding of the ways in which academic capitalism and a corporate mentality have come to influence the modern university.

ACADEMIC CAPITALISM AND THE CORPORATE ACADEMY

In advancing the previous work of Sheila Slaughter and Larry Leslie,[94] Slaughter and Gary Rhoades developed a more theoretical understanding of academic capitalism in their book *Academic Capitalism and the New Economy: Markets, State and Higher Education*.[95] They developed clear connections between educational policy and the role of universities in serving the research and development needs of a postindustrial economy. In drawing heavily from Michel Foucault, theoretically speaking, Slaughter and Rhoades saw academic capitalism as the dominant regime of power, "displacing, but not replacing others, such as the public good knowledge regime or the liberal learning regime."[96] In utilizing Foucault's notion of "disciplinary regimes," Slaughter and Rhoades identified innumerable ways in which the logic of capital has come to dominate university operations and especially academic research.

Slaughter and Rhoades argued that, given the fact that the new economy is heavily indebted to knowledge and information, the role of the university in such an environment becomes pivotal. Consequently, they examined the ways in which the privatization of knowledge and profit taking, in which the claims of universities, academic scientists and inventors, and corporations come before those of the public, have become defining qualities of academe.[97] In essence, "Public interest in science goods are subsumed in the increased growth expected from a strong knowledge economy."[98] Furthermore, given the context of the neoliberal state, a variety of policy decisions were made over the past few decades to further advance capital over broader social concerns and propelled universities in the direction of an academic capitalist model. For example, Slaughter and Rhoades noted the importance of several policy initiatives, including the 1980 Bayh-Dole Act, the 1986 Uruguay Round of the General

Agreement on Tariffs and Trade (GATT), the 1986 Trade-Related Aspects of Intellectual Property Rights (TRIPs), and the General Agreement on Trade and Services (GATS) brokered by the WTO. "The neoliberal state redefined government, privatizing, commercializing, deregulating, and reregulating state functions to promote the new economy in global markets. While universities were not primary players in creating the neoliberal state, they often endorsed initiatives, directly or indirectly."[99] Of course, criticism of this model, deriving mostly from scholars operating in the social sciences and humanities, has become quite strong in recent years.

Stanley Aronowitz[100] argued that the role of the university in servicing the knowledge and information needs of government and industry was well laid out in Clark Kerr's influential work *The Uses of the University*.[101] Aronowitz maintained that Kerr not only found a rationale for protecting top-tier research universities but also helped to reorient the university's basic societal function: "If the highest mission of universities is to serve society, what greater achievement than to provide the knowledge required to assure general prosperity by advancing the scientific and technological revolution and 'freedom'— read America's world dominance—and the scientific and technical personnel required to produce it."[102] Kerr saw universities playing a most vital role in the emerging knowledge industry in terms of the contribution of their scientists but also in terms of the scientific and technical skills of graduates, who, educated within the context of the multiversity, would be better equipped to serve government and industry. Former Humboltian notions of the university as a center for history, culture, and literature—liberal learning in the classic sense of preparing a nation's citizens—were finally laid to rest. As Aronowitz explained, "For the Berkeley chancellor, there was no question that the humanities must recognize their secondary place in the new university order. They could uphold the values of Western civilization by teaching literature and history, but their role was clearly a subordinate one."[103]

Thus, following the changes of World War II—most notably the growing connections between government/industry and the university—Kerr's vision of the multiversity served to reinforce the role of university science in contributing to the technological, scientific, and economic development of an increasingly global society. The stage was firmly established then for a more complete emergence of academic capitalism, especially as the post-1960s political and ideological battles between the left and right increasingly were won by conservative and neoconservative forces, the result being a rapidly escalating erosion of the social progress associated with the decade of unrest throughout the final two decades of the twentieth century and the complete dominance of neoliberal economic policy making.[104] By the dawn of the twenty-first century, neoliberalism, and its emergence at universities in the form of academic capitalism, had assumed hegemony.

A notable critique of the influence of neoliberalism and corporate culture on the university was offered by Henry Giroux, who, in an article published in 2002 in the *Harvard Educational Review*,[105] maintained that "there is an increasing call for people either to surrender or narrow their capacities for engaged politics in exchange for market-based values, relationships, and identities."[106] Giroux went on to argue that market forces have dramatically changed the language employed in making sense of social life and civic engagement. Instead of speaking of the ways in which universities might foster critical citizens capable of engaging in meaningful social praxis, discussions are dominated by a discourse of personal gain, framed to a great extent by "market-driven notions of individualism, competition, and consumption."[107] For Giroux, as "the U.S. university reinvents itself by giving in to the demands of the marketplace," stature is gained by academic disciplines "almost exclusively through their exchange value on the market, and students now rush to take courses and receive professional credentials that provide them with the cachet they need to sell themselves to the highest bidder."[108] Still worse, not only do students sell themselves to the highest bidder, but many researchers do so as well. The consequence is a widespread compromise of academic science, as important social problems unlikely to generate sizable revenue streams essentially go ignored or are pursued by researchers who become peripheral academics given their lack of contribution to their university's bottom line. What we see then is the growing marginality of the social sciences and humanities and a "refusal on the part of universities to fund research in services such as public health that are largely used by people who can't pay for them."[109] Ultimately, we see a growing divide between revenue-generating faculty, centered primarily in the natural and applied sciences, and those existing on the margins of academic capitalism.

Jennifer Washburn, a journalist, echoed some of the concerns voiced by Giroux in her 2005 *University Inc.: The Corporate Corruption of Higher Education*. As captured in her book, Washburn found a somewhat reluctant ally in none other than the late Clark Kerr. Conversing at his home overlooking the Berkeley campus in the spring of 2001, Kerr indicated to Washburn that the current proliferation of university-industry ties "arises not just because we live in a highly competitive information-based economy, which has encouraged companies to want to get inside academia, but because they are, after all, being *invited* in. . . . [L]ots of faculty members and administrators see advantages in getting extra money from private industry, and they may be willing to make concessions which from their own point of view are quite all right, but which are bad for the university."[110] Kerr went on to note that serious problems may arise when a "money-seeking group on the inside" colludes with a "for-profit group on the outside." As he maintained, "The university ought to remain a neutral agency devoted to the public welfare, not to private welfare."[111] We can only imagine that Kerr had underestimated the power of capitalism to assume control of the university, once he had helped to open its doors to the flood of revenue that eventually followed. Perhaps he should have listened more intently to the critical voices in the humanities and social sciences that his vision of the multiversity had helped to marginalize.

Washburn described one of the most egregious cases of academic capitalism—the agreement between the Department of Plant and Microbial Biology (PMB) at the University of California, Berkeley and Novartis. In exchange for receiving $25 million in research support over five years, Novartis was to have "first right to negotiate licenses on roughly one-third of the department's discoveries, including the results of research funded by Novartis, as well as projects funded by state and federal sources. The agreement also granted the company unprecedented representation—two of the five seats—on the department's research committee, which determined how the money would be spent."[112] Although close relationships between academic scientists and industry obviously are nothing new, what marked the PMB-Novartis agreement as something different was the way in which an entire academic department's research products were sold to private interests. What of the public's investment in the University of California, Berkeley and the tax revenue used over the many years to develop the university and its reputation? Aren't the scientific outcomes of professors at a public university to benefit the broader public in some way? These concerns were echoed by Professor Ignacio Chapela, elected chair of the executive committee of the College of Natural Resources, in which PMB is located: "I'm not opposed to individual professors serving as consultants to industry. If something goes wrong, it's their reputation that's at stake. But this is different. This deal institutionalizes the university's relationship with one company, whose interest is profit. Our role should be to serve the public good."[113] Chapela felt that his communications with colleagues in PMB had become compromised, because any ideas that he might share could be turned over to Novartis and used for profit-making purposes. As he explained, "I just can't talk to them anymore. If I have a good idea, I'm not going to just give it away."[114]

Although our discussion of neoliberalism and the university more or less has focused on the emergence of academic capitalism in the United States, for explanation's sake, the trend is not limited to only the U.S. higher education landscape. Indeed, Slaughter and Leslie examined the growing strength of academic capitalism among universities within the context of not only the United States but also Australia, Canada, and the United Kingdom. Others also have documented the growing dominance of entrepreneurialism, marketization, and commercialization (all akin to academic capitalism in some manner or form) in Australian, Canadian, and European universities.[115]

Although universities in central countries clearly are leading the academic capitalist knowledge regime—primarily because these countries are also driving global capitalism—the impact is felt around the world. For example, in their book *The University, State, and Market: The Political Economy of Globalization in the Americas*, Robert Rhoads and Carlos Alberto Torres include a variety of chapters documenting the growing influence of Western models of university entrepreneurialism and academic capitalism throughout Latin America, and most notably in countries such as Argentina, Brazil, and Mexico.[116] Additionally, in separate studies of universities in southern China, Ka Ho Mok and Rui Yang documented the growing influence of marketization and commercialization as a consequence of the higher education reform movement in the People's Republic of China.[117] They tie these changes to the growing influence of Western models of the university, linked to a great extent to China's post-Mao Open Door policy and the subsequent influence of global capitalism.

The powerful influence of academic capitalism and corporate culture thus are changing the very fabric of academic life in the United States and around the world. Although the tide is clearly on the side of big money and the corporatization of academic life, resistance still exists and tensions between a public good vision and an economic-based neoliberal model are fairly evident, both in national and international contexts. In many ways, the battleground is only now coming into focus.

THE LAST BATTLEGROUND?

The contemporary university, in accepting its pivotal role in advancing global capitalism of the neoliberal variety, by implication becomes a participant in the new imperialism of central countries such as the United States. The new imperialism is advanced today primarily through the spread of unchecked capitalism, as absolutist free-market ideology paves the way for economic exploitation and cultural penetration. A world ruled by the market has no social conscience. The model of global capitalism is presented as the natural outcome of a Darwinian evolutionary schema of fair competition among world systems and not as the domination of the United States and its allies, contingent, of course, on their superior economic and military might. With U.S. hegemony moves the new imperialism across the global countryside painting an assortment of territories and landscapes in their own likeness, rejecting the colonialism of old, embracing instead a nationalistic zealotry framed by a manifest destiny to police the world and advance their own political, economic, and social interests. The model advanced by the United States is pointedly clear: Look out for the interests of your own corporate and political elites. This is the way of global capitalism. Consciousness of the perils of today's world matters not. Said recognized this problem quite clearly:

We live in one global environment with a huge number of ecological, economic, social, and political pressures tearing at its only dimly perceived, basically uninterrupted and uncomprehended fabric. Anyone with even a vague consciousness of this whole is alarmed at how such remorselessly selfish and narrow interests—patriotism,

chauvinism, ethnic, religious, and racial hatreds—can in fact lead to mass destruc-
tiveness. The world simply cannot afford this many more times.[118]

Nations are no longer in the business of empire building, at least not in
the old sense of dominating a distant territory, planting settlements, displacing indigenous populations, and subordinating them on the basis of racist
theories of inferiority—us-versus-them logic taken to the extreme. No, imperialism is advanced through different forms of domination today. Again, we
find Said's *Culture and Imperialism* helpful:

For reasons that are partly embedded in the imperial experience, the old divisions
between the colonizer and colonized have reemerged in what is often referred to as
the North-South relationship, which has entailed defensiveness, various kinds of
rhetorical and ideological combat, and a simmering hostility that is quite likely to
trigger devastating wars—in some cases it already has. Are there ways we can recon-
ceive the imperial experience in other than compartmentalized terms, so as to transform our understanding of both the past and the present and our attitude toward the
future?[119]

The latter question posed by Said is at the heart of our quest for a less imperial, more thoughtful, more caring, more transnationally connected form of
citizenship—what we call global citizenship. We see the university as one of
the last frontiers for hope of a more globally aware populace. But if conservative and neoconservative politics and ideology in conjunction with the unquenchable thirst of free-market liberalism (neoliberalism) have their way,
the university will soon become a complete manifestation of global capitalism, advancing corporate-directed science and preparing knowledge and
service workers with neither the ability nor inclination to see the larger
picture—to see the forest and not simply the trees.

Of course, the university still poses the possibility of fostering a deeper
consciousness of the perils of today's world. Indeed, conservatives and neoconservatives clearly recognize this fact and have responded mightily by attempting a far-reaching takeover of academe. Given the potential that universities might offer toward advancing the sort of public regimes advocated
by Bakan[120] in *The Corporation* or the kind of socially responsible national
project advanced by Santos[121] in his idea of democratic and emancipatory

university reform—both of which offer hope for developing the kind of counter-hegemonic civil society Antonio Gramsci[122] advanced in his work and in his vision of oppositional movements—it is hardly surprising that conservative heroes such as David Horowitz have charged onto the scene to save academe. Cofounder of the Center for the Study of Popular Culture, Horowitz helped to found Students for Academic Freedom, "a national watchdog group that helps college students document when professors introduce their politics in the classroom."[123] With the backing of large conservative foundations, including the Lynde and Harry Bradley Foundation ($2.2 million between 1998 and 2003), the Sarah Scaife Foundation ($1.3 million between 1998 and 2003), and the John M. Olin Foundation ($1.265 million between 1998 and 2003), among others, Horowitz and his center have waged an assault on what he described as the liberal bias of today's university (we can only assume that Horowitz is *not* offended by the fact that nearly every business school in the United States advocates a political and economic ideology almost entirely consistent with neoliberalism).[124] If Horowitz has his way, state legislatures around the country eventually will pass his academic bill of rights, potentially imposing a variety of restrictions on what professors can and cannot say in their classes. Given that conservative ideology and corporate capitalism have been effectively normalized, situated within the very heart of the academy, we can expect that the views most likely to be censored and silenced are those seeking to challenge the dominance of conservative/neoconservative ideology and neoliberal capitalism.

There are many other examples of the ways in which conservative and neoconservative forces have sought to gain greater control over academe, often presented in the name of protecting the academic freedom of marginalized conservative voices. Their position is clear—too many liberals and radicals populate the university, and so they must be controlled, limited, perhaps erased. The Ward Churchill episode is an excellent case in point. In using an analogy in which the victims of the World Trade Center attacks of September 11, 2001 were compared to "Little Eichmanns," Churchill became the center of a national controversy and his words brought about calls for his firing, despite his being a tenured professor at the University of Colorado, Boulder. When leaders at his university realized that he could not so easily be removed, they decided to build a case against his scholarship, raising questions about his academic integrity. Nationally speaking, Churchill's example was turned into a broader call to weaken (or erase) ethnic studies programs, as Churchill taught within the ethnic studies program at Colorado. Conservatives—and traditionalists, for that matter—have long recognized ethnic studies (as well as women's studies) as sites of resistance against the manifest-destiny of U.S.-led global capitalism. The Churchill incident was used then to bring to the public's consciousness ways in which ethnic studies programs propagate "antipatriotic" sentiment, because after all, what kind of person speaks harshly of the victims of the World Trade Center? The Churchill case thus was an example of how academic discourse must be controlled or even eliminated; as universities represent some of the few remaining sites to be fully colonized by the conservative-led march to the free market, left-leaning scholars as a source of resistance must be contained.

This brings us to an important question at the heart of this work: As one of the last frontiers to be entirely conquered by the conservative-led neoliberal assault, how are universities and within them, faculty and students, *as citizens* reinforcing and/or resisting the neoliberal imperative? What hope remains within the walls of academic institutions, in the form of teaching, research, and service revealed in the work and academic experiences of faculty and students? Do we witness forms of resistance, or are oppositional voices simply drowned out by the vim and vigor of global capitalism of the neoliberal variety? And if faculty and student resistance exists, how can we make sense of their agency in ways that may advance other oppositional acts and movements and at the same time inform our broader understanding of citizenship?

With the influence of global capitalism as well as academic capitalism spreading around the world, we find it necessary to examine from an international/comparative perspective the ways in which contemporary universities are advancing particular conceptions of citizenship. From our perspective, conceptions of citizenship are revealed in the ways that faculty go about their duties in relation to teaching, research, and service. And for students, conceptions of citizenship primarily are revealed through their studies and the forms of engagement they have during their undergraduate or graduate school years.

WHAT FOLLOWS

In this section we discuss the chapters to come and highlight four university cases forming the thrust of our inquiry into global citizenship and the university. The four universities were not selected because they are remarkable examples of the ways in which universities might advance global citizenship, but instead were chosen because they offer unique and thought-provoking challenges to how we might conceptualize citizenship in an age framed by the increasing influence of global capitalism. In essence, we use these cases to inform and challenge neoliberal conceptions of society and citizenship. The four universities—Guangdong University of Foreign Studies (GDUFS); the University of California, Los Angeles (UCLA); the University of Buenos Aires (UBA); and Central European University (CEU)—are important because of their geopolitical locations and the potential each has to advance our understanding of global issues and a global perspective on citizenship. Thus, in what follows we briefly discuss the uniqueness of each case and the ways in which the particular university context addresses issues relevant to global citizenship.

In Chapter 2, " 'One Coin Has Two Sides': The Globalization of University Life in Southern China," we focus on GDUFS in Guangzhou, China. In particular, we examine the ways in which global forces are refashioning university life in the post-Mao era and contributing to emerging notions of citizenship. We explore the ways in which faculty and students at GDUFS conceptualize globalization as a first step toward better understanding social changes taking place within the academic community. Four major changes are discussed: the growing importance of English, the influence of foreign professors, pedagogical changes and challenges, and the emergence of a "publish or perish" mentality in conjunction with increasing manifestations of academic capitalism. The preceding changes are indicative of the growing influence of the West on China, as a consequence of the nation's adoption of the Open Door policy of 1978 and the subsequent impact of more recent forms of globalization, including most notably China's increasing participation in global markets.

As Western influences and the strength of capitalism have steadily impacted campus life at GDUFS, collectivist traditions and values have come under attack. This is most obvious when one examines the academic community of workers (known as the *danwei*) and the ways in which the communal spirit so valued by many faculty at GDUFS appears to be fading in the face of growing emphasis on individualism and competition. However, although some global changes may seem inevitable, many faculty and students nonetheless envision opportunities for taking the best of such influences and blending them with highly valued aspects of Chinese social life and culture. In this regard, the case of GDUFS sheds light on the ways in which citizens in a global age may struggle to create more hybridized societies by combining values, norms, and practices heavily influenced by both local and global forces.

Changes in the academic community of workers at GDUFS reflect broad changes taking place across the Chinese landscape. These sweeping changes are refashioning conceptions of citizenship. In some instances, particularly among undergraduates at GDUFS, the economic challenges and opportunities prove to be quite enticing, as individualistic conceptions of citizenship centered on economic entrepreneurialism become common. In other instances, social changes evidence a growing international awareness and a concern for China's participation in global affairs, as students and faculty express a civic-minded commitment to China as "the motherland." Still other students and faculty proactively seek to balance "both sides of the coin," hoping to help fashion a bold, new, hybridized China, reflective of a combination of global and local influences and responsive to pressures deriving from both capitalism and socialism. Whether taking advantage of the economic individualism inspired by the rise of capitalism or seeking to advance the motherland's interests in a global age or working to refashion social life in light of global forces and local traditions, the academic lives of students and faculty at GDUFS reveal in great clarity a landscape in which global capitalism and socialism meet face-to-face on a scale the likes of which we have never before witnessed.

Chapter 3, "Pluriversity Knowledge in a Mobile World: International Graduate Students and Citizenship at UCLA," explores academic life at UCLA in the United States. Through examining the views and experiences of graduate students from the diverse countries of Brazil, China, and Italy, we present a portrait of the various ways in which international graduate students at a major, globally engaged, public research university conceptualize their citizen rights and responsibilities as long-term although temporary migrants in a highly industrialized nation. In doing so, we pay particular attention to students' conceptions of rights and responsibilities in the economic, social, and political dimensions of citizenship and emphasize their engagement in the creation of pluriversity knowledge, a form of knowledge driven by the goal of societal contextualization.[125]

Findings from this case study suggest that a major determinant of students' conceptualizations of citizenship centers on the various geographic locales that they feel connected to in their personal, educational, and professional lives, representing a set of locales ranging from their home countries and regions to the United States and a global sphere of existence. Importantly, the knowledge and skills that the students acquire and create during their sojourns in Los Angeles and at UCLA are often contextualized in connection to these various locales, playing a significant role in defining their views and actions as citizens. In some instances, this means direct engagement in political issues and civic action, while in other examples the primary focus falls on assuming the important role of cultural mediator in an effort to bridge borderlines between different cultures. Yet other examples focus on the economic and professional dimensions of citizenship, highlighting students' efforts to leave an imprint on their fields of study through their academic contributions and to impact a range of societal issues through the professional application of knowledge gained and created in graduate school. Besides such emancipatory applications of pluriversity knowledge, however, some students focus more on the mercantilistic dimensions of knowledge, emphasizing the importance of individualism in their citizen rights and responsibilities.

Our chapter on UCLA international graduate students also draws attention to the importance of responsibilities and rights in understanding the reach of citizenship. In the case of international graduate study, the question of rights in a foreign land highlights the implications of national and institutional support for international educational exchange, especially in light of immigration and transnational visitation challenges associated with the aftermath of the September 11, 2001 terrorist attacks.

Chapter 4, "Resistance to Neoliberalism: North-South Tensions in Argentina," centers on the case of UBA and forms of resistance following the economic collapse of December 2001. More specifically, we focus on how

North-South relations are shaping life in Argentina and how faculty and students at UBA engage in forms of protests in conjunction with community-based movements, as a means of opposing the hegemony of global capitalism and the dictates of intergovernmental organizations such as the IMF. The case of UBA focuses on the work of faculty and students and offers important insights into alternative conceptions of citizenship in an age shaped so powerfully by neoliberalism's rampant individualism. The examples of activism presented in this chapter offer evidence of the sort of counterhegemonic movements still possible in today's global environment.

The backdrop for this chapter is a society under economic siege. One consequence of the economic assault waged against Argentina is the rise of powerful grassroots movements aimed at derailing unchecked global capitalism. We reveal how the actions and risks taken by UBA's professors and students contributed to growing resistance throughout the country. Support for Argentina's oppositional movements during the early part of the twentieth century made possible former President Néstor Kirchner's resistance to structural adjustment policies advocated by the IMF and ultimately fueled an economic resurgence within Argentina. The case of the Argentine grassroots rebellion, as it came to be called by many, is significant in that the rebellion and its related movements offer insight into the limitations of neoliberalism and direct us toward alternative conceptions of a globally informed citizenship in which a collectivist, community-oriented spirit might thrive. Additionally, the ways in which faculty and students linked their academic work to the concerns of workers, the unemployed, and the dispossessed offer key insights into how we might conceptualize a more democratic and socially transformative university capable of counterbalancing neoliberalism and unchecked academic capitalism.

In Chapter 5, "Postcommunism, Globalization, and Citizenship: The Case of Central European University in Hungary," we highlight the academic lives of faculty members at Central European University (CEU), a young, private university with legal ties to the United States and Hungary. The chapter focuses on faculty work at a university that came into being to address the postcommunist context of Hungary and other countries of East Central Europe, as well as Central Asia. Founded by George Soros, the Hungarian-American financier and philanthropist, CEU was established in the early

1990s with the aim of helping along the transition of the region's countries from communism to a market-driven, capitalist economy. As CEU was driven by a strong mission oriented toward the development and strengthening of open societies in the region, one of the university's original goals was the education of a new generation of elite in the tradition of Western academic values.

At the beginning of the twenty-first century, as a more established university now located in a member nation of the European Union, CEU confronted a new era, one driven by a form of academic capitalism that increasingly emphasized revenue generation, entrepreneurialism, quality control, and competition while accompanied by significant support for faculty work, a continuing focus on societal engagement, and a democratic environment for citizenship. At the same time, the university transitioned its focus to the sphere of the global, expanding its reach from the postcommunist region to nations experiencing democratic transitions in any part of the world. Faculty members in this new institutional environment expressed a variety of views and actions, sometimes in line with CEU's original regional mission and later global emphasis, and at other times critiquing the university's focus on Western, capitalist development. Some faculty actively contributed to addressing globally relevant issues, while others stayed more local in their scholarly emphasis. In a similar vein, some professors defined their role as making significant links between their scholarly work and societal applications, while others focused more on theoretical contributions. Reflecting and supporting these various faculty views and actions, CEU gave rise to an academic climate that reflected the university's commitment to democratization and the active development of open societies. The efforts of CEU and the work of its faculty offer much to consider in weighing citizen obligations across local, regional, and global contexts.

We conclude our book in Chapter 6, "Global Citizenship and Changing Times for Universities," by first summarizing and then synthesizing our findings from the case studies. We do so mindful of the key theoretical points and assumptions established in Chapter 1. Based on a more integrated analysis of the cases (by this we mean looking at the cases in their totality), we delineate key points related to citizenship and the challenges confronting today's universities and the broader societies in which they exist. A key aspect of our discussion focuses on the typology presented in Chapter 1, as we offer rich examples drawn from the case study data. We pay particular attention to the four types of citizenship suggested by our model, with emphasis placed on globally informed, collectivist forms of citizenship (Type 2), or what we prefer to call global citizenship. We argue for the benefits of citizens being globally informed and adopting a collectivist orientation—qualities that we see as critical to an increasingly complex and globalized existence. We conclude Chapter 6 and the book by returning to the role of universities, and most specifically, the responsibilities and challenges they face in advancing forms of global citizenship. This final section of our discussion is organized by the three major knowledge domains of university work: knowledge production, knowledge management, and knowledge application.

CHAPTER 2

"ONE COIN HAS TWO SIDES":
The Globalization of University Life in Southern China

INTRODUCTION

Walking around the campus of Guangdong University of Foreign Studies (GDUFS), one cannot help but notice the gentle calm that seems to emanate from the countless trees lining the campus walkways. The serenity is captivating especially in the deep shade along the stone-walled stream cutting through the heart of Guangwai, as the campus is known to locals. It was along this stream that we first noticed a common practice. Frequently, students collect along the stream, often separating themselves by twenty feet or so, to practice their recitations, in English, Japanese, Indonesian, or one of the other languages offered at the university. When we first observed this practice we imagined that it represented a long-standing campus tradition of some sort. Perhaps the trickling, serpentine stream was believed to offer magical powers to strengthen recollection. Or maybe it was a mysterious source of good luck for one's studies. During one of our visits to GDUFS we asked students about this practice. Their explanation proved to be less mystical than anticipated. "My room is about four meters by three meters," explained one hard-working, male student. "I have five roommates. It's stressful. The stream is one place where I can practice my English without disturbing them or being disturbed."[1]

The preceding student's explanation suggests much more than simply a rationale for practicing one's recitations shrouded by the serenity of a shady campus stream. Indeed, his devotion to English in the face of great stress deriving from a massive population and China's increasing participation in global competition provides the backdrop for a case study of students and faculty at GDUFS. Their experiences are used to shed light on some of the major changes taking place in Chinese society and the ways in which such changes are recasting notions of citizenship as well as the very structure of universities.

We were not alone in observing the commitment of GDUFS students to learning English and preparing themselves for a global marketplace. A visiting U.S. professor[2] of international business at GDUFS, Hua Zhou,[3] was also fascinated by this phenomenon:

One thing that stands out in my mind is that so often I see many students studying on their own. It's not unusual to see students just standing up against a wall, looking at the wall and nothing else, and just reading aloud from some kind of English textbook or practicing some English phrases. When I first saw this I thought, if I saw this in America, if I saw students studying up against a wall, I would think, "This guy is crazy." But here it's very common.

Many students at GDUFS see mastering English as a vital element of an education aimed at preparing them for a changing world. For these students, English is the key to enhanced professional opportunities, either working in an international context within China or working abroad. Their attitudes and commitments reflect a growing openness to the West in particular and to globalization in general.

Citizens throughout China increasingly face pressures that come with the adoption of a free-market system and the onslaught of global capitalism. This is most apparent among the youth of China, where use of the Chinese word for anxiety has become an everyday term and some 66 percent describe themselves as being under heavy pressure.[4] A twenty-one-year-old junior studying computer science at GDUFS offered insight into the challenges that come with globalization and China's changing role: "For the younger generation, the global village, or globalization, raises a direct challenge to our personal capacities, as we are not only required to compete with elites in our own country, but also we have to face challenges from talented foreign competitors." Another twenty-one-year-old junior, a foreign language major, offered a similar point of view: "Globalization means more chances in life. . . . As I have come from a backward place [the countryside], I have only one route to success—that is to find the opportunity and seize it. With globalization, the opportunities are flowing into our country. Now there are far more opportunities for success. But at the same time I feel that I face greater pressure."

Throughout our conversations with students and faculty at GDUFS, the theme of globalization as both "opportunity and challenge" came across loud and clear. Global technologies such as the Internet have made it possible for Chinese citizens to communicate instantaneously around the world, and yet at the same time they find themselves inundated with information and choices. Qiang-Shao Yuan, a twenty-year-old sophomore, said it best: "It's getting easier to communicate with others. But sometimes a person gets depressed because of the excessive amount of information. Just imagine how down you may get when you open your mailbox and find 200 unread e-mails! So globalization, on the one hand, provides us with convenience. While on the other hand, it brings inconvenience, as people can find you wherever you are. There is no hiding anymore."

With the price of higher stress levels, Chinese citizens face economic opportunities hardly imaginable in previous times. Along these lines, a U.S. correspondent to China described the changing context for Chinese urbanites, especially the present generation:

Young urban Chinese enjoy a lifestyle their parents only dreamed of. Car and apartment ownership is at an all-time high, and conspicuous consumption is all the rage. Many people are earning huge sums through job skills that would have landed their parents in reeducation camps during the Cultural Revolution—such as a global mind-set, a command of foreign languages and an intuitive understanding of capitalism. The Communist Party's grip on their lives is weakening as Beijing increasingly supervises rather than controls the roaring economy, allowing those with talent to get ahead.[5]

Consequently, today's youth face fewer limitations than their parents and in turn have greater expectations. "We tend to seek our dreams, regardless of the potential risk," explained a junior majoring in accounting at GDUFS. The twenty-one-year-old continued, "Being rebellious is a distinguished trait of youth. It is a symbol of the energetic and dynamic spirit of our generation. And the push toward globalization only adds to our rebelliousness, since our vision becomes broader and broader."

Greater opportunities and increased stress are just a couple of the changes taking place in China, as the country elevates its participation in the global marketplace. And, of course, as the very nature of Chinese society changes, so does what it means to be a Chinese citizen. This is most apparent at universities, where the educational opportunities and challenges faced by faculty and students suggest new ways of thinking about and acting as citizens. In a country that has long isolated itself from the outside world, differences now abound within the context of a society and culture seemingly under global assault.

"ONE COIN HAS TWO SIDES"

In China, as in many other places, there is an old adage: "One coin has two sides." Another commonly used expression points out that China must "seek harmony out of the differences"—the presumption being that China must find a harmonious way to integrate international influences with the best of Chinese culture and tradition.[6] The relevance of the latter expression is also captured by President Hu Jintao's call for "A Harmonious Society," a pledge "to bring the ruling Communist Party back to its core values of discipline, virtue and collective effort; and to focus resources and political will on the have-nots"[7]—this in the face of out-of-control conspicuous consumption by many Chinese citizens benefiting the most from global capitalism.[8] Interestingly, calls for balancing both sides of the coin or seeking harmony were commonly made by faculty and students in discussions about global influences on their lives and their university. Huijian Hu, a forty-ish professor of

English language and culture, put it this way: "We're combining cultures, societies. We're integrating the outside world within China, and China into the outside world. We Chinese have a saying. We say, 'Seek harmony out of the differences.' If we can adopt some things from the outside world, and if we can retain some of the good things about our society, then this will be ideal, and good for China." And June Lai, a nineteen-year-old sophomore studying English, explained, "Every coin has two sides," when asked to comment on globalization and its impact on China. A first-year student majoring in Chinese offered a similar perspective: "Globalization offers something good and something bad. Just like a coin has two sides. If we can take advantage of global opportunities, then it will help us a lot. I have a positive opinion, mainly because I have seen some of the benefits brought by globalization in my daily life." As was typical of interviews conducted with students at GDUFS, they tended to focus on the positive side of the coin, especially with regard to the broader impact on Chinese society. Only on rare occasions did students point to potentially negative consequences associated with globalization, such as the possibility of China losing out economically or valued elements of the culture potentially being replaced by Western forms.

GDUFS faculty were far more likely than students to raise critical concerns about globalization, although most generally saw China's growing world engagement as quite positive. The biggest concern among several professors, especially more senior faculty, was a fear that key aspects of Chinese culture may be lost or displaced by Western influences. Some even used terms such as the "Americanization" or "Westernization" of China and hoped that the society could find ways of preserving long-standing traditions and practices while adopting only those external influences most beneficial for the society. In general, though, younger faculty members seemed far less concerned about negative influences and were more willing to fully embrace globalization.

Faculty and students recognized a variety of global forces acting upon China in general and higher education in particular, including the growing importance of English, the influence of the West, and the spread of market capitalism, but saw their university responding in its own unique way. Hence, a central concern of this chapter is to make sense of the influence of globalization on GDUFS and the lives of its key organizational actors—faculty and students. In essence, we seek to examine local responses to

global pressures (both challenges and opportunities) and better understand
the ways in which Chinese citizenship may be changing as a consequence
of such influences. As a first step in approaching these concerns, we find it
helpful to explore the complex changes taking place throughout the broader
society.

CHINA IN THE POST-MAO ERA

When Deng Xiaoping[9] announced China's new Open Door policy in December 1978, the proclamation in many respects marked the beginning of the
end for the Maoist utopian vision that had shaped China for some thirty years.
China's "Four Modernizations" were designed to generate excess revenue toward the goal of advancing agriculture, industry, national defense, and science
and technology. Revenue was to be garnered through the nation's increasing
embrace of a market-oriented economic vision. In *A Nation-State by Construction*, Suisheng Zhao noted, "After Mao's death, Deng Xiaoping launched a
campaign to 'reassess' (criticize) Maoism. His original intention was to eradi-
cate all ideological and psychological obstacles to market-oriented economic
reform."[10] In drawing on Jie Chen's work on political and ideological reform in
China, Zhao explained that the unexpected consequence of the campaign
was "the widespread demise of communist ideology" and the emergence of
three crises of faith: a crisis of faith in socialism, in Marxism, and in the official communist party.[11] Zhao added,

It was truly astonishing that after several decades of communist authoritarian rule,
the once presuppositional notion of a Chinese nation uniting behind and sacrificing
for a Communist state to maintain Chinese independence and prosperity was quickly
discredited among more and more Chinese. Communist ideology, now of interest to
hardly anyone in China outside the political elite, was seen as self-destructive and
guilty of miring the Chinese in socioeconomic wretchedness and as having kept China
poor and backward. Marxism-Leninism-Mao Zedong Thought as the official ideology
no longer provided convincing arguments of the need for the general public to preserve
communist one-party rule. Nor did it explain how the socialist market economy that
the party claimed to be building in China was different from, or superior to, the
capitalist market it once vehemently opposed.[12]

With a growing dissatisfaction with socialism, Marxism, and the official communist party, liberal movements began to gain strength, ultimately posing a challenge to the authoritarianism of the ruling Chinese Communist Party (CCP). The strengthening democratic pulse within China was observable to the world in the spring of 1989, when antigovernment protests by students took place at Tiananmen Square in Beijing.

Demonstrations at Tiananmen Square began as a gathering to commemorate the April 15 death of former Communist Party General Secretary Hu Yaobang, whom students saw as a source of support for democratic reform. Over the course of several days, expressions of grief over the loss of Hu Yaobang turned to growing protests rooted in political dissatisfaction with the ruling party and its more recent shift toward hard-line policies. As the size of the student-led protests steadily grew, so too did the unease within the Communist Party and among its principal leaders, Deng Xiaoping, Premier Li Peng, and a group of CCP veterans known as the Elders.[13] With many CCP hard-liners interpreting Tiananmen as a crisis of leadership, Deng Xiaoping called for a military intervention, first sending in lightly armed troops but later, when they failed to end the demonstrations, authorizing greater levels of force, although insisting that "no blood be spilled in the Square."[14] On June 4, 1989, the standoff reached its climax, this after Beijing had been under martial law since May 20.[15] Massive force in the form of tanks and automatic weapons was brought to bear on the student movement in what came to be known as the June 4th Massacre. When all was said and done, anywhere from 300 to more than 1,000 protesters and soldiers died (some estimates suggest deaths in the thousands, but a conclusive figure seems impossible to reach given a lack of factual information).[16]

The Tiananmen Square crisis may be understood as the outcome of a growing democratic movement within China throughout the 1980s, reflective of increasing levels of dissatisfaction among the youth (especially college students), and the growing influence of the outside world, including changes taking place in the former Soviet Union (captured by the ideals of glasnost and perestroika). Previous large-scale protests took place in several major cities in 1985 with outbreaks continuing up to Tiananmen. One of the largest protests occurred in Shanghai, when in December 1986 several thousand demonstrators, believed to be mostly college students, marched to the People's

Square, "demanding greater democracy and calling on the government to accelerate its economic and social reform programs."[17] When charges of police brutality surfaced, resistance grew even larger as "thousands of students marched in the streets of Shanghai in protest, and within days the number of students in Shanghai swelled into the tens of thousands."[18]

Paradoxically, although China's democratic movement of the 1980s sought to challenge restrictive governmental policies—a common cry was "Long live democracy!"[19]—it was actually a shift toward progressive reform by the CCP that made such protests possible. However, as a consequence of the escalating student movement, CCP hard-liners steadily gained greater control and used the demonstrations "to clean house and purge top offices of the party of liberals; the most notable target of the purging was progressive Hu Yaobang. . . . The party blamed General Secretary Hu for failing to control the student demonstrations effectively and expelled him in 1987."[20] With the CCP applying the brakes to progressive reform and purging the party of many liberal-minded politicians, students once again took to the streets in response. Driven by the growing influence of hard-liners, as well as the death of Hu Yaobang, the Tiananmen demonstrations became a symbol of student-led resistance against authoritarianism and the call for increased democracy worldwide.

The demonstrations at Tiananmen Square helped party leaders see that a more open and democratic China likely was inevitable. In a world increasingly marked by global communications and rapid cultural exchange, isolating a society from outside influences was difficult to imagine, let alone engineer. The CCP had to evolve in order to keep pace with changes already taking place within the consciousness of its people. Under Deng Xiaoping's leadership, the CCP turned away from its focus on ideology and instead wholeheartedly pursued national development. A common saying in China captured this pragmatic turn (paraphrased here): It doesn't matter whether the cat is black or white as long as it can catch a mouse. Nonetheless, a more pragmatic market-oriented turn resulted in a weakened commitment to the principles of communism and rendered the CCP in the awkward position of guiding a country away from what the party represented. And so as China increasingly became less committed to socialism and more committed to the free market, as well as modest democratic reform, the CCP was faced with the task of reconstructing itself as a legitimate political force. Thus, throughout the 1990s and up to the present, political leaders have turned to advancing Chinese nationalism with the goal of building a more unified China with the CCP at the center. As Thomas Christensen pointedly noted, "Since the Chinese Communist Party is no longer communist, it must be even more Chinese."[21] The strength of Chinese nationalism and the strong hand of the CCP were never more visible than during the 2008 Beijing Olympics, when the beauty, grandeur, and lavish complexity of the opening ceremonies sent chills up the spines of observers around the world.[22] One could not help but wonder about other monumental or even miraculous achievements that a coordinated China might be able to reach.

TWO STEPS FORWARD, ONE STEP BACK

In the years following Tiananmen Square and the pro-democracy movement, China has taken many additional steps to reform the society, although with every two steps forward the CCP often takes one step back.[23] This is evident in rising public demonstrations (in light of increased liberalization) aimed at challenging oppressive government practices, while at the same time such grassroots movements often are still met by high levels of violence enacted by government officials. A clear example of this took place in December 2005 in Dongzhou, a seaside village in Guangdong Province, when a police commander executed anywhere from ten to twenty disgruntled farmers protesting the seizure of their land by the government. Another several dozen were said to be injured or missing, while reports suggested that government officials had attempted to pay off locals willing to confess that protesters had been killed by their own explosives.[24]

Events at the 2008 Beijing Olympics also suggested that moving forward for China often involves taking a step back. As a condition to being awarded the summer Olympics, the Chinese government promised that basic human rights would be protected, including the right of citizens to organize in protest. But during the Olympic Games, Beijing officials practiced forms of authoritarianism that the government had agreed to avoid. Reports included arrests of Chinese citizens who followed strict procedures for submitting applications to engage in organized protest at one of a few government-selected sites (typically out of eyesight from Olympic events). As it turned out, the application process was used more as a vehicle for identifying and controlling (even arresting) potential protesters, including two women in their seventies who filed an application to protest based on a disagreement over compensation they received when their homes were seized for redevelopment, a common complaint among Chinese citizens during their nation's sustained economic growth.[25] More recently, the Chinese government permitted extended strikes by Honda factory workers, offering evidence once again that the government may be willing to consider greater democratization.[26]

The two steps forward, one step back approach is in part embedded in the tension between China's socialist foundation and its push toward the free market. As the CCP gradually opens the door to capitalism—with the goal of advancing a socialist market economy—the relevance of a socialist mindset and lifestyle increasingly is called into question. As a consequence, the CCP has felt the need to reassert its place within Chinese society. Most notably, in January 2005, the CCP launched a mass education campaign to reestablish the party's control and "shore up the organization's power base, stem abuses, improve the party's public image and contain dissent."[27] As part of the effort to instill discipline in its seventy million members, the education program was unlikely, however, to stem the tide of increased dissatisfaction and confusion over the role of the party. In fact, many CCP members did not appear to take the mass education program seriously. As one twenty-something participant attending a study session of her coworkers commented, "A few of our managers stood up and gave speeches. It was very boring. I only stayed an hour and mostly just chatted with friends. Some people used the time to catch up on their reading. I can't really remember what they said."[28]

As economic competition increases within the broader society and as more and more Chinese find their success linked to career and vocational ambitions—and not party membership and participation—interest in the pro-democracy movement has waned. Indeed, Dingxin Zhao noted that students and intellectuals were major beneficiaries of China's economic growth during the 1990s and consequently became somewhat depoliticized.[29] Dan Wang, who as a student at the age of twenty helped to lead the Tiananmen Square demonstrations, later moved to Los Angeles, where he served as a visiting scholar at the University of California, Los Angeles (UCLA) and worked to finish his dissertation at Harvard. He remained optimistic about democratic possibilities in China: "The dissident movement used to be very strong. People used to be very supportive, and now they've lost interest. It's natural. . . . I'm a history student; I know democratic movements come in waves. We're at the bottom of the wave right now, but I'm looking forward to the peak."[30] Dan Wang can only hope that the seeds of democratic struggle will grow in China. The fear is that neoliberal forms of globalization will become so dominant and intoxicating that individualism and the push for fame and fortune will be elevated over all else, including more communal visions of democratic life.

GLOBAL CAPITALISM AND A SOCIALIST MARKET ECONOMY

There is a paradoxical quality to contemporary China—the idea of a communist party running a country that increasingly is tied to global capitalism of the neoliberal variety. This paradox was evident throughout many of our conversations with faculty at GDUFS, although professors who are members of the CCP offered alternative interpretations. For example, Hua Zhou saw problems with the CCP's notion of a socialist market economy:

Of course, hardcore party members will insist that the country has not given itself over to capitalism. The CCP is still very strong and China is still a communist country. But there's a paradox, because capitalism is increasingly evident here. I think that the way the CCP handles this paradox is very traditionally Chinese. Namely, they argue that as long as the form is communist, who cares what the content is? And I think that is how they're addressing it.

Binglong Chen, a young and introspective business professor, described the phrase *socialist market economy* as a "very ambiguous phrase" and pointed out that in the beginning the phrase implied that the largest portion of the national economy would be state owned. Professor Chen went on to explain, "But nowadays this is changing, because more and more the private sector is playing such a dominant role. So, to some extent the state-owned part is losing out in that competition. . . . We used to have a lot of state-owned enterprises and they used to play a bigger role, but the problem is that they were not very good. So, a lot of state-owned enterprises were sold, or what we called 're-structured,' and they actually were privatized."

Other faculty, particularly those affiliated with the CCP, were less critical of the idea of a socialist market economy and instead saw value in such an approach. "My thinking is that we have to understand our own problems," explained Jia Wang, a dynamo of a scholar in her mid-fifties with the energy and verve seemingly to conquer any academic challenge—including explaining the complexities and contradictions of a socialist market economy. Professor Wang continued,

We have to find ways to solve our problems, and find ways to develop our own social and economic theories, because China, like every country, is different. Maybe you can learn from this foreign theory, or this foreign practice, but then it may not fit our situation. . . . I think of the example of Deng Xiaoping. In the beginning, nobody understood him when he said China should follow its own path, go its own way, to be a socialist market economy. Nobody fully understood him. Everybody said, "Oh, that's only another form of capitalism," or something like that. But now, more and more people realize that he's actually quite correct, because China is very different.

A July 2005 move by the Chinese government to raise the value of the nation's currency may shed some light on what is intended by the phrase *socialist market economy*. In lifting the value of the yuan by 2.1 percent against the U.S. dollar, the Chinese government brought to mind the role it plays in guiding the national economy in the interests of its own citizens. China's steps toward a more market-driven economy have been somewhat measured, as political leaders seek to cushion the society from a full-scale onslaught of global capitalism and retain some semblance of socialism. Nonetheless, even the measured steps of China's political and economic elites have produced striking changes, some of which are recasting China's place in the global economy. As Don Lee noted in the *Los Angeles Times*, "China's move . . . to reform its currency system set the nation on a path to greater financial independence and stronger integration with global markets. It also marked a milestone in China's dramatic rise from a poor communist state to a powerful force in the world economy."[31]

With its rising participation in the global economy, China increasingly must respond to pressures from countries such as the United States. For example, journalists Lee and Ching-Ching Ni pointed out that the revaluation of the yuan was implemented in the face of mounting pressure from Washington for China to "make meaningful change in its currency policy."[32] One can expect, however, that the appetite for increased marketization of the Chinese economy among U.S. political and economic leaders will not be satiated until the Chinese government more fully abandons its role in guiding the national economy, receding to the background and essentially eliminating the socialist elements of its present socialist market system. In the end, it is highly unlikely that the neoliberals steering the global economy will tolerate socialist interventions in the global marketplace. Thus, China faces a major choice: resist the domination of neoliberalism by maintaining various socialist ideals and elements (including some economic controls and regulating mechanisms), or succumb to unchecked global capitalism and allow those ideals advanced by socialism to whither on the vine.

Part of the problem with comprehending China's socialist market economy appears to be rooted in a bit of dualistic thinking, primarily deriving from Western logic. Professor Binglong Chen, for example, explained that many Westerners with whom he has spoken have a hard time understanding the idea of a socialist market economy: "They see capitalism and socialism as polar opposites and completely incompatible. Westerners do not see the possibility of wedding the two." He explained that it is as if the West must always prevail, and therefore, capitalism must annihilate socialism. "Certainly, it's confusing," noted Professor Chen, before adding, "The Chinese government continues to try to convince the rest of the world that the country is practicing a market economy, because the U.S. denies this and has not for the most part recognized China's market economy." He pointed out that his Western colleagues think the Chinese government should drop the term *socialist* from the phrase *socialist market economy,* so that it is easier for the rest of the world to recognize China's efforts in this arena. "Perhaps the real paradox," concluded Chen, "is rooted in the limitations of Western thought and the reality that objects and ideas, from a Western perspective, often are either this or that, black or white, and rarely are understood as a combination of differences or oppositionals—the *yin and yang,* so to speak."

In actuality, when one seriously analyzes national economies, it is quite evident that both market forces and society-driven needs—enacted through a variety of regulating mechanisms and socialist-like policies—are used to develop and advance national economic interests. Even in the United States one sees social security, welfare, public schooling, regulating mechanisms of the Federal Reserve and its chair, Ben Bernanke (and Alan Greenspan before him), as well as many tax incentives and subsidies for corporations and whole industries (e.g., agriculture and steel). More recently, federal intervention to support mortgage giants Fannie Mae and Freddie Mac as well as AIG (American International Group) in September 2008 certainly cannot be cast as allowing the free market "to work things out" as only the fittest companies survive in a highly competitive world.[33] Most dramatic, the bailout of the financial industry in 2008 through the Troubled Asset Relief Program (TARP) certainly did not reflect free-market idealism. Obviously, the U.S. government does not support a pure market-driven economy when it comes to its own interests, although many U.S. officials prefer not to admit this publicly. Of course, hard-core neoliberals prefer to see many social programs eliminated, especially those that take the commonweal to heart, such as public schooling and social security. Some obvious examples of neoliberals (and neoconservatives) seeking to wreak havoc with social programs include the former Bush (George W.) administration attempting to eliminate social security in favor of privatized retirement accounts and the Republicans leading the effort to privatize schools through the implementation of voucher programs. Oddly, one rarely hears much from neoliberals in the way of eliminating tax breaks for the corporate sector—a form of "corporate welfare," as Jesse Jackson has long described it.

Whatever phrase one ultimately selects in describing China's economic philosophy (and its present reality) seems to matter less than recognizing that serious changes are under way. Clearly, reform within China, including most notably the opening up of the Chinese economy to global markets, has had a dramatic effect on universities throughout the country and has set the stage for new forms of citizenship to emerge. This was quite evident in our discussions with students and faculty at GDUFS.

UNIVERSITY REFORM IN CHINA

Part of the backdrop for a discussion of academic life at GDUFS is the broader landscape of higher education reform in China and the growing influence of globalization on universities throughout the country. Thus, although some international influences have been ongoing (e.g., international trade in southern China and the Pearl River Delta region has a long tradition, in part given its proximity to Hong Kong's more market-driven economy), others are more recent and reflective of global processes involving enhanced communication (e.g., the Internet), improved transportation (e.g., more affordable air travel), and increasing cross-cultural ties (e.g., student and scholarly exchange since China adopted the Open Door policy in 1978).

A significant outcome of China's increased participation in the global marketplace is the growing commercialization and marketization of higher education. The commercialization of higher education is a global phenomenon that for the most part has been analyzed in the context of world regions other than China.[34] Many scholars see the rise of commercialization—including the commodification of academic work and the privatization of institutions and programs—as a consequence of the growing influence of neoliberalism on universities.[35] Neoliberalism understood in this context is seen as the quest for capital grounded in a belief that the logic of free markets ("market liberalization," hence "neoliberals") ought to dictate public policy. Translated to the realm of higher education, neoliberalism (or neoliberal globalization) is seen to have had a dramatic impact on higher education policy and the increasing marketization of colleges and universities and their services. In Western countries, including Australia, Canada, Great Britain, and the United States, globalization of this form contributes to what Sheila Slaughter and Larry Leslie[36] and then later Slaughter and Gary Rhoades[37] termed "academic capitalism"—understood as the engagement of universities and their actors in market and market-like behaviors with the goal of generating institutional and individual revenues. Others, including most notably Burton Clark,[38] have written about the growing influence of entrepreneurialism, arguing that universities face major economic challenges and therefore necessarily must be more innovative and revenue generating. Whether one speaks of academic capitalism or entrepreneurialism, what is clear is that universities, especially research-oriented universities, have shifted a good deal of their focus from undergraduate education to the growing commodification of a variety of university services, including most notably research (this has occurred over several decades but has intensified since the 1980s). The phenomenon of academic capitalism is also apparent in parts of Latin America, where

economic pressures associated with globalization, including structural adjustment policies mandated by the International Monetary Fund (IMF) and
World Bank, have sought to raise tuition, reduce public investment in higher
education, and advance what some criticize as a "mercantilist" view of the
university.[39]

Although it is hard to imagine the changes in Chinese higher education
yielding a culture of "academic capitalism," given the long-standing influence of socialism, nonetheless there are clear signs of the commercialization
of academic work. Given this important shift, a study of academic life in
China must in some way come to terms with changes linked to globalization
and the potential impact of market forces. And although one might argue
that increased commercialization in Latin America and the West has resulted
in some very negative consequences (e.g., decreased access, casualization of
the faculty workforce, increased levels of management, emergence of a corporate culture, and so forth), no assumptions about the nature of outcomes
have been made in this case, given the dramatic differences between other
regions of the world and China. Additionally, it seems conceivable that, given
the overwhelming size of the Chinese population (the need for higher education expansion is pressing) and a history of government-controlled, highly
centralized universities, increased competition as a consequence of the introduction of market forces could have quite positive effects on higher education
throughout the country. Perhaps increased commercialization and privatization are necessary steps in light of the challenging circumstances confronting
China. In any case, a key question for this chapter concerns the ways in
which these important shifts may be altering the nature and context of academic work. Furthermore, given its international focus, GDUFS offers an
excellent site to examine the potential impact of globalization on academic
culture in general and notions of citizenship in particular.

To better understand the impact of globalization on Chinese higher education and GDUFS, we find it necessary first to explore the term *globalization*, through conceptualizations commonly found in the literature, as well as
through the ways in which members of the academic community at GDUFS
chose to define it. A common view of globalization stresses increasing levels
of international integration such that individuals and institutions, including

nation-states, are increasingly interdependent.[40] For example, globalization theories recognize that actions in the United States have the potential to influence events in the People's Republic of China, and vice versa. Furthermore, given the increasing interaction and interdependence of societies, a natural consequence is greater cultural exchange and sharing, having the effect of the hybridization or creolization of social and cultural life.[41]

Common conceptions of globalization were evident in the way that students and faculty described the phenomenon. One student put it this way: "I think globalization means that the world is joining together and different countries will rely more on each other. Take the European Union for example. It is a successful case of how different countries enhance their overall power by relying on each other. The EU is just a beginning. More and more countries in the world will join together in order to make full use of their resources." And Tina Sun, a nineteen-year-old sophomore studying English and international finance, explained, "I think globalization means the distance between nations is getting smaller. All countries are more tightly linked with each other." Similarly, faculty used such phrases as "international integration," "transnationalism," and "cultural and political interdependence" to describe globalization and its impact. From perspectives such as these, globalization suggests that sophisticated analyses of higher education can no longer simply examine colleges and universities in terms of local and national trends and processes but also ought to include analyses of global factors,[42] including the influence of broad economic, technological, and scientific trends.[43]

Historically speaking, the context for this study is the post-Mao era of higher education reform in China and growing evidence that the state's retreat from "its monopolistic role" as a provider of educational services has opened the door for "local initiatives, individual efforts, and the private sector."[44] Such a shift is believed to be tied directly to China's efforts to participate in global markets, albeit on their own terms and defined within the context of a socialist system.[45] Accordingly, a variety of post-Mao policy initiatives have challenged the higher education system in China to increase decentralization, diversification, and marketization, as part of an effort to expand postsecondary educational opportunities and further develop a highly educated workforce suitable for global competition.[46] Such changes have resulted in closer ties between industry and education, greater emphasis on vocational education, and a flourishing private-sector higher education market.[47]

Although greater emphasis on income-generating activity has helped to produce additional revenue and expansion of the private sector, there also are problems associated with rapid growth and commercialization.[48] For one, China has a serious shortage of highly qualified academics. In part, Chinese universities face major challenges in competing for the top minds; this is especially true given the context of an increasingly competitive international market for scientists and researchers. For example, a professor at GDUFS by way of Canada noted that academics make virtually nothing by comparison to those working in industry. He pointed out that many professors' graduate students go on to make ten times the salary of an academic. This professor went on to conclude, "It's just one of those things in which China is kind of shooting itself in the foot, because the good ones leave as soon as possible or they just don't consider an academic career. Academe just doesn't offer the lifestyle that they think they deserve."

A second concern relates to the quality of new educational initiatives emerging in such a dynamic and high-growth environment. As the government increasingly pulls back its regulating mechanisms to further decentralization, the opportunity to exploit students through the development and implementation of weak or questionable academic programs grows. Although one might be tempted to think of these new initiatives as part of the "privatization" of higher education in China, the reality is that the public-private distinction so commonly employed in the United States is not so easily applied to the Chinese context. Writing about the growth of private colleges and universities in China, Qiang Zha, for example, noted,

[I]t is now difficult to draw a very clear public-private distinction in China's education sector, especially when public schools are becoming more "private" as ideas/principles and practices, which are popular in the market/private sector, are also employed by public schools. In this regard, a discussion on development of private higher education in China would be necessary to include not only institutions that call themselves private but also public ones that in many ways appear increasingly to be private, thus making the distinction between private and public problematic.[49]

Ka Ho Mok made a similar point when he explained, "It is extremely difficult to pinpoint exactly what a 'private school' means because views regarding
such a concept in mainland China are too diverse to adopt any one dictionary
definition."[50] Nonetheless, there are clear educational initiatives (far-ranging
in their quality) that are increasingly removed from government oversight and
are more and more accountable to "clients, namely, the students, parents and
donors."[51] From the government's perspective, the growth of the private sector
is somewhat disturbing, given what the CCP sees as the "aristocratic" and
"patrician" elements of privately owned institutions, as well as their overall
antiegalitarian ideals.[52]

Finally, there is a growing concern that the nature of academic work is
being altered by the increased emphasis on commercialism.[53] For example,
Mok noted that when competition is introduced within the Chinese higher
education sector, rewarding winners and embarrassing losers, faculty members experience intense pressure to increase their research productivity.[54]
Project 211, introduced by the CCP in 1995, as part of the country's ninth
Five-Year Plan, specifically sought to reward those institutions identified as
among the top 100 universities throughout the country; the central objective of Project 211 was to enhance the national effort to modernize through
scientific and technological advancement. Additionally, Project 985 targeted
roughly 40 universities for increased funding with the goal of elevating
them to world-class status. In fact, so much government money has poured
into China's best universities that some have successfully recruited top scientists from leading Western universities, as when Tsinghua University in
Beijing successfully recruited top computer scientist Andrew Chi-chih Yao
from Princeton.[55] As a consequence of increased pressure on universities
and academics to contribute to China's national challenge, Feng Wei argued that some Chinese academics may in fact be "floundering in a sea of
commercialism," feeling overwhelmed at times by the demands of the market.[56] Although Wei's point is well taken, what is clear from the limited
research on this topic is that more in-depth studies are needed to better
understand the changing context of academic work during a period of high
growth and global influence. A study of GDUFS thus seeks to add some
richness to a discussion of the changing context of university life and academic work in China.

THE CASE OF GUANGDONG UNIVERSITY
OF FOREIGN STUDIES

With the preceding in mind, in this chapter we specifically explore the degree to which academic life and citizenship in China are influenced by a variety of forces associated with globalization, including the push toward increased commercialization (and privatization, as difficult as it may be to define). More specifically, we examine the academic lives of professors and students at one university in southern China—GDUFS. In focusing on one university in southern China, we seek to make sense of how global forces are interpreted and in turn reconstituted within a particular geographic context by locals acting on the basis of their own culturally rooted experiences and understandings. Here, we follow an objective identified in the work of Allan Luke and Carmen Luke, whereby an effort is made to resist the dominant reading of globalization as "capitalocentrism"—a view that stresses "the effects of globalization in determinist, causal, and unidirectional terms; north to south, west to east."[57] This is not to suggest that we deny the globalizing effects of capitalism and the expansion of neoliberal, free-market ideology, as articulated in Chapter 1. Instead, we simply intend to stress that globalization produces different sorts of consequences depending on the particular cultural and economic context and that local settings around the world also may generate their own "effects." Given the importance of the local context, we find it helpful to discuss GDUFS in some detail.

GDUFS is a young university, having been officially founded in 1995 as a result of the merger between the Guangzhou Institute of Foreign Languages (founded in 1965 as one of three institutes of foreign languages under China's Ministry of Education) and the Guangzhou Institute of Foreign Trade (founded in 1980 as one of four institutes of foreign trade). Today, GDUFS is one of three major foreign-language universities in China, with the other two located in Beijing and Shanghai. Given that the roots of GDUFS are in language and culture as well as international business and trade, these areas of study continue to constitute the heart of the university's identity in the early years of the twenty-first century.

Central to the mission of GDUFS is its international focus and the preparation of students for a global environment (this is another key reason why the university was chosen for the study). The university's president, in his "Message from the President," contained in the university's handbook, makes the international focus of GDUFS clear: "By bringing the teachers' leadership role and the students' creative spirit into full play, we aim to turn out young talents who live up to our motto—'Moral integrity, outstanding performance and learning across cultures'—and are capable of competing and cooperating in the international arena. We shall do our utmost to become a trail-blazer in the internationalization of tertiary education and make our contributions . . . to the rejuvenation of our great nation." University materials also stress the relevance of international ties, pointing out that the university actively conducts academic and cultural exchanges with over eighty overseas institutions. The president's message was echoed by comments from GDUFS faculty. For example, Professor Huijiang Hu (English language and culture) explained, "Because this university is outward oriented, it emphasizes a combination of Eastern and Western ideas. In terms of curricular offerings, in addition to the different languages that the university offers, we also emphasize international perspectives and use original textbooks from Europe and America for teaching economics, management, as well as other subjects."

The university offers forty-six baccalaureate programs in nineteen faculties in seven basic disciplines: literature (including the study of cultures and languages), economics, management, law, science, engineering, and education. GDUFS also offers five doctorate programs in linguistics and applied linguistics, French language and literature, English language and literature, Japanese language and literature, and translation studies, and seventeen master's programs, including linguistics, economics, international trade, public administration, and various language and literature programs (e.g., English, French, Indonesian, Japanese, German, and Russian). The student population includes some 15,000 undergraduates and over 800 graduate students. Students are served by over 1,600 staff members, including nearly 400 full and associate professors and nearly as many lecturers (a lecturer is roughly equivalent to an assistant professor in the United States). Additionally, the university generally employs some fifty to sixty foreign experts or lecturers.

In terms of governance, the university answered to the national Ministry of Education in Beijing prior to 1995 (before the merger) and, with a jurisdictional shift from central to provincial governance, has since answered to the Guangdong Province Department of Education. As of 2006, the university operated on an annual budget of 400,000,000 yuan (roughly $57,000,000 U.S.), with 22 percent coming from Guangdong Province and 78 percent generated through student fees and other diverse revenue streams, including an attached English School and Middle School, as well as an International College administering franchised and articulation programs in partnership with a number of Australian, U.K., and U.S. universities. At one time the national government provided 100 percent of the university's funding, but this has changed as a consequence of the 1995 merger and as a result of a shift in higher education policy stressing diverse revenue sources, including a greater role by provincial governments.

Students' views of the university were variable. Some saw great opportunities at GDUFS, while others stressed its limitations. The following comments are typical of remarks students offered during interviews:

Guangwai is a university where you can pursue your dreams. It's a university where you can acquire all kinds of knowledge and prepare yourself in such a way that you can meet the challenges of the outside world.

                          Twenty-one-year-old junior majoring in Japanese

I think that *Guangwai* is a wonderful place for college students to acquire knowledge and develop the expertise for their future work. The teachers here are very good and the students are diligent. . . . And also the students are full of passion and creative in [extracurricular] activities. But I seldom participate in [extracurricular] activities because I spend most of the time studying and preparing for the TOEFL [Test of English as a Foreign Language] and GRE [Graduate Record Examination] exams. I don't feel that I've had ample time to enjoy the colorful life here. It is a pity, but I have to sacrifice something to pursue my goals.

                    Twenty-one-year-old junior majoring in computer science

This university is too young to take any controversial actions. It is heavily subjected to the government and the education bureau and so it dares not make any radical changes. On the one hand, it tries to maintain stability and achieve steady growth. On the other hand, it confines the students' thoughts and behaviors out of a desire for stability. I don't think this is good for the development of the students.

                          Nineteen-year-old sophomore majoring in
                              English and international finance

The remarks and descriptive data throughout this section speak to some of the strengths and weaknesses of GDUFS and offer basic insights into the organizational identity of a rather young teaching university. But the university is not an isolated academic community, geographically speaking, and thus it is important to discuss the city and region in which it is situated.

THE GEOGRAPHIC CONTEXT

The Pearl River Delta region is one of China's most successful economic centers and has for many years been open to international trade, even before China's Open Door policy was officially introduced in 1978. The city of Guangzhou is the heart of this vibrant southern economy, and along with Guangdong Province the region differs dramatically from other parts of the country, especially by comparison to the north. Mok noted, for example, that problems between the Pearl River Delta region (the Guangzhou area) and the Chinese government have in part been linked to a "fundamental ideological conflict, characterized by a tension between an 'outward-looking' value orientation commonly shared by the people in the south and an 'inward-looking' and exceedingly conservative tradition in the north."[58]

Guangzhou, known to many Westerners as Canton, is approximately 125 kilometers northwest of Hong Kong and is considered the center of Cantonese culture. As a key southern port for international trade, Guangzhou is home to one of the world's largest trade fairs, commonly known as the Canton Fair. The Chinese Export Commodities Fair, as it is officially called, has been host to millions of business people since 1957 and in present times can expect as many as 200,000 international traders. During this twice-a-year event (the city organizes spring and fall sessions), Guangzhou is abuzz with international visitors and economic activity to such an extent that the normally dense but manageable city traffic nearly comes to a standstill and thick clouds of exhaust smoke seem to shroud the entire city.

Many students from GDUFS find temporary employment as interpreters during the trade fair, when the sudden influx of internationals, many with limited knowledge of Chinese culture and the ability to communicate in Cantonese or Mandarin, necessitates the hiring of scores of students with multilingual abilities. Professor Jia Wang (English) noted, "Every year we send our students to the Trade Fair—the famous Guangzhou Trade Fair—and most of them find jobs. Our university is known for teaching foreign languages. So, our students are seen to be more fluent in speaking, listening, conversing."

Although many parts of China, especially the rural areas, remain underdeveloped and economically deprived, this is not true of Guangzhou and Guangdong Province, where, for example, owning a car is so common that air quality has become a serious problem for many residents. Several professors alluded to the economic vitality of Guangzhou and Guangdong Province and ties to international trade. A professor of international communications described the region as "the world's factory." She recalled reading that the region produces about one-third of the world's computers. She added, "It's one of the earliest cities to open up to the outside world. Guangzhou was open to international trade even in the ancient times of China. Guangzhou was a port even during the Chang Dynasty. It was the only port that was open to the outside world." A professor of journalism from the United Kingdom noted that Guangzhou has always been a key trade port in China: "This has always been the biggest gateway to China—the southern gateway to China. Guangzhou has always been a trade center. The people here have always known how to make money, more than anywhere else in China. My impression is that few people in this region see Chinese economic reform as a threat. They're not monks here. They've been engaged in economic competition for many years, for many centuries."

Guangzhou's distance from Beijing has served the region well, in part fueling the city's economic success and its international contacts. As Andrew Becker, a professor of English, pointed out, "I think if you study Chinese history you'll recognize that when somebody in Beijing shouted, many people in Guangzhou replied, 'So what? We're 2000 miles away. Why do we have to pay any attention to what they say in Beijing?' Southern China has always been kind of a different world and many students here feel that if somebody publishes a law in Beijing, then they don't have to follow it." A professor of legal studies in her early thirties sought to explain some of Guangzhou's international character:

Because Guangzhou is close to Hong Kong, it has benefited from international trade as well as immigration. The city and the region—mainly Guangdong Province—have strong international ties. I don't know the exact statistics, but there used to be a saying that every household in Guangdong has a relative either in Hong Kong, Macao, the Philippines, Malaysia, or Singapore, and now maybe even the United States, Canada, or Europe. Guangdong Province along with other coastal provinces [has] throughout China's history been very open to the outside world. The people have more contact with the outside. They understand the outside world better when compared to people in other parts of China.

ACADEMIC LIFE AT GUANGDONG UNIVERSITY OF FOREIGN STUDIES

With the increased openness of China to the outside world, universities such as GDUFS are confronted with major changes, including new ways of thinking about life and work in China and at their own university. A beginning point for understanding these changes is to explore the ways in which faculty and students talk about globalization.

Broad Views about Globalization. Consistent with the expression "One coin has two sides," students and faculty described globalization as having both positive and negative implications for China. Some spoke of various global forces acting upon China and their lives at the university, while others addressed a host of new opportunities accessible through increasing global ties and networks. For example, a twenty-year-old sophomore studying English noted, "I think globalization means sooner or later the Chinese people will face a knowledge, technology, and information explosion. The borders between nations no longer impede interaction. Obviously, we will have more chances and better jobs in the future. But the pressure we face also will be greater, because we will have to compete against foreigners as well as against other Chinese. It's a give-and-take dilemma for us. Both success and failure are possible." Similarly, a second student described globalization as a "double-edge sword," offering both advantages and disadvantages, including the possibility of her country's losing "the most valued thing—independence."

Professors also spoke of the advantages and disadvantages of China's growing global participation. Some noted that along with the economic opportunities globalization has produced for China, there also is evidence of increasing environmental degradation—as a consequence of China's becoming the "world's factory." At least one professor worried about the price (in terms of health) future generations of Chinese will have to pay. Another professor spoke of the long-term economic costs the country pays for allowing the rest of the world to "plunder China" for its cheap labor and natural resources.

Several professors expressed concern about preserving the best elements of Chinese society and culture. For example, a professor of language and culture noted how his students increasingly are preoccupied with the integration of Western norms and values. This left him to ponder: "Will we lose our own culture? Globalization, does it mean that we must lose our traditions?" This professor described working with students who face many choices—so many that he described their current situation as one of "cultural chaos." Others spoke of the increased "standardization," "homogenization," and "Westernization" of Chinese norms and values, as the society is forced to adjust to global markets and worldwide expectations. This was seen to be potentially devastating, culturally speaking.

A central point of discussions about globalization focused on relationships between China and the United States. More than one professor expressed a refrain commonly heard throughout the developing world: that globalization essentially amounts to "Americanization." For example, a soft-spoken professor of legal studies in his early forties discussed the views of his students and their resentment toward the "American" way of doing things:

Many students regard globalization as Americanization. They see the power of America, the ideology of America, the force of America, and how much impact America has on the world, especially on the students, the university students. So, they hate that aspect of globalization. . . . They hate the politics of the United States. Many students see American politics as the central influence of globalization and this is what many describe as "Americanization." But maybe some of them like other aspects of globalization, because it brings advanced technology and various cultural changes to China.

This professor was careful to make an important distinction: that Chinese students and faculty distinguish the U.S. political machinery from the broader society and its people. He noted, for example, that although many people in China resent U.S. political dealings, nearly as many indicate that they would visit the United States "without hesitation" if they had the chance. "They hate it, and at the same time they love it," he remarked.[59]

In contrast to criticism of U.S. politics, many students described with enthusiasm, bordering on preoccupation, their view of U.S. influence on cultural life in China (this was seen by students as a positive side to so-called Americanization). This was most obvious in their seemingly unquenchable fascination with Hollywood and the film industry, television sit-coms commonly shown in China, and celebrities from sports and entertainment. In our visits to GDUFS classrooms, for example, we were invariably hit with numerous Hollywood-related questions—some rather sophisticated ones at that—as well as other questions related to popular media figures. The following is a sampling of such questions:

Professor, do you think the popularity of action-figure movies such as *Spiderman* is a reflection of America's attempt to regain its sense of international superiority in the face of 9/11?

Professor, what do you make of your country's fixation with violence in films and music videos? Do you think this is a healthy situation for the youth of the society?

Other questions were more innocent in nature, but interesting just the same:

Professor, who is your favorite character on *Friends* and what episode do you think is the funniest?

Professor, do you prefer *Friends* or *Sex and the City*, and how many hours a week do American college students typically spend watching television?

Professor, do you think Kobe Bryant is guilty or not [in reference to rape allegations at the time]? And do you think he is as good as Michael Jordan?

The preceding sort of questions and their responses generated countless laughs as well as some provocative exchanges during classroom visits. We were left with the very clear feeling that many Chinese students' conceptions of the United States and its citizens are profoundly linked to the media and in particular television and film.

Several professors were highly critical of students' unending interest in U.S. popular culture, noting that Chinese students more and more resemble American students in terms of their style and dress. For example, Bo Li, a professor of language and culture, referred to the "spiritual pollution" and the negative cultural messages conveyed by Hollywood movies. A professor of English and a Westerner at that was quite sanguine about the impact of American culture: "Globalization and the whole dominance of English on the Internet is I guess one more example of the Americanization of the universe. And American popular culture plays a huge role. The whole idea of romance and love and teenage heartbreak and all that stuff that comes out of American movies and music . . . is somewhat contrary to traditional Chinese culture." Ni-Man Jiang, a young professor of international communications, discussed such concerns by referencing "cultural globalization" and "cultural imperialism," expressing fear that today's youth may be turning away from Chinese tradition. She explained, "They watch Hollywood movies and they go to the Internet and get news about things going on in America. They know quite a lot about Western fashion, the fashion trends. I think they know quite a lot about the Western lifestyle. Maybe more than they know about their fellow people in western China." And a senior professor of English noted with some remorse that today's youth seem to have little interest in "traditional Chinese culture, traditional Chinese writers, and classic Chinese novels. . . . The loss of cultural identity is terrible."

In contrast to the criticism aimed at outside forces acting negatively upon China and Chinese culture, several faculty noted advantages linked to globalization. For example, faculty spoke of improvements in products sold in local stores and a general increase in consumer choice. Several discussed increased political freedom as a by-product of economic liberalization. As one professor explained, "The window is wide open. China cannot turn back. So, as the economy liberalizes, and that's exactly what it's doing, the government has to weigh that against political freedom. I say this because as the economy liberalizes, people also will enjoy economic freedom, but along with that they'll want more political freedom." Professor Ni-Man Jiang noted, for example, that women's rights have been enhanced throughout China, in part, as a consequence of the ways in which prejudice against women and patriarchy have been challenged in Western societies. "It's true," remarked Professor Jiang, "that the introduction of some Western ideas refresh the old Chinese ways and bring something beneficial to women, to children, to lots of people." A nineteen-year-old sophomore explained, "The outside world has changed China tremendously and it will continue changing China in the future. One of the most impressive points for me is the change in ideology. A lot of new ideas, which were forbidden 20 years ago, are now widely accepted by the public. People now show more understanding of different ideologies. The transparency of the entire society is far greater today."

Faculty also discussed globalization in terms of China's influence on the outside world, particularly its influence on the United States. Several noted how the United States paid greater attention to China as both a potential partner and an adversary. Although most expressed dismay over some of the critical proclamations about China, primarily deriving from U.S. political leaders, they nonetheless relished the fact that China increasingly mattered as a player on the global stage. This element of Chinese nationalism was also voiced in anticipation of China's hosting the Olympics in Beijing. Faculty and students discussed the impending Olympics as a crowning event in China's emergence as a world leader and its increasing ability to influence other nations.

The fact that Guangwai faculty noted the growing power of China to shape world events was reinforced by various media reports. This was evident by U.S. political announcements coming out of Washington during the summer of 2005, when the U.S. government seemed particularly concerned about developments in China. For example, former U.S. Defense Secretary Donald Rumsfeld criticized China's rapid development of missile capability. As one *Los Angeles Times* article noted, "In his most blunt assessment to date of the global implications of China's efforts to build a state-of-the-art arsenal, Rumsfeld warned that the expansion threatened not only the delicate balance between China and Taiwan, but the overall strategic equilibrium in a region increasingly vital to U.S. interests."[60] Similarly, a China-Russia joint military operation conducted on the Shandong peninsula, titled "Peace Mission 2005," only served to heighten Washington's concern about China's increased militarization and contributed to criticism from former U.S. Secretary of State Condoleezza Rice, this despite the reality that "U.S. military spending is 17 times that of China and 77 times that of China on a per capita basis," according to a senior Chinese official.[61]

The U.S. media were particularly mindful of China's official stance on the Taiwan matter, noting the passage of an antisecession law and an elevated measure of rhetoric by President Hu Jintao, who was quoted as saying, "We shall step up preparations for possible military struggle and enhance our capabilities to cope with crises, safeguard peace, prevent wars and win the wars if any."[62] Several years earlier, in April 2001, Thomas Friedman warned in a *New York Times* Op-Ed piece that the two primary barriers to the stabilization of U.S.-Chinese relations were the authoritarian stance of the Chinese government and rising popular nationalism, including the desire to reintegrate Taiwan.[63]

Newspaper stories throughout 2005, the busiest year of our data collection at Guangwai, repeatedly highlighted the growing impact of the Chinese economy on the United States, and relatedly, Washington's increasing concern. This was particularly relevant when the Chinese government raised the value of the yuan against that of the U.S. dollar[64] and when the Chinese oil company Cnooc sought to buy Unocal[65] but faced stiff congressional resistance ("a host of Congressmen" who had received "political money" from Chevron—Cnooc's primary competitor for Unocal—argued against the Cnooc deal, "saying it could threaten America's long-term energy interests").[66] Ultimately, Cnooc ended its takeover bid, and in a statement explained, "Cnooc has given active consideration to further improving the terms of its offer, and would have done so but for the political environment in the U.S. . . . Accordingly, we are reluctantly abandoning our higher offer to the clear disadvantage of Unocal shareholders and employees."[67] This, of course, paved the way for the U.S.-based Chevron Corporation to acquire Unocal at a much lower price than that offered by the Chinese. So much for the global free market advocated by U.S. political and economic elites. One *Los Angeles Times* headline seemed to capture the general sentiment coming out of both Washington and Beijing—"More U.S.-China Battles Are Likely." Indeed, in reacting to the Cnooc-Unocal debacle, correspondent Paul Richter warned of battles to come: "A Chinese oil company's fight to buy Unocal Corp ended Tuesday in an angry retreat, but not without leaving clear signs that other political battles loom in Washington over how much more of America the cash-rich Chinese can acquire."[68]

Clearly, the political and economic context in China faces significant transformation as a response to the country's increasing participation in global affairs. Just as certain is the fact that social life also is changing throughout many parts of China, including major cities such as Guangzhou, and at universities such as GDUFS. The discussion to this point has focused on globalization broadly conceived and its impact on Chinese society at large. In what follows, we direct attention to specific matters relating to university life in general and issues at GDUFS in particular. We organize the discussion around four central themes uncovered at GDUFS: the growing importance of English, the influence of foreign experts, pedagogical changes and challenges, and the emergence of a "publish or perish" and academic capitalist orientation. In turn, we use a discussion of local responses to globalization to develop a more nuanced understanding of the changing context for citizenship within Chinese society and culture. A central feature of our discussion of citizenship is a concern for the fading relevance of the tradition of the *danwei*—the socialist ideal of a community of people living and working together as a collective unit.

The Growing Importance of English. One of the most obvious manifestations of a changing China is the growing importance of English.[69] GDUFS certainly is one Chinese university where this trend is readily observable; nearly every student and faculty member with whom we spoke stressed the growing relevance of English as part of their analysis and discussion of globalization and increased international integration. For example, a twenty-year-old, first-year student commented, "Globalization means more frequent communications and exchanges between China and other nations. Thus, as a communication tool, English will certainly become more important. And there surely will be greater opportunities for those Chinese who can master English."

Many students discussed learning English as a matter of competition on the road to professional success. For example, Eva Peng, a twenty-year-old junior, noted, "English is becoming more and more important for people's everyday life and their work. I think that no matter how well you know English, you can always do better—the smarter, the better. There's an old Chinese saying, '[I]f you know yourself well and your enemy well, then you can win.' So, if you know yourself well and know the other's language well, then you can always get ahead of the competition." And a twenty-year-old junior in business administration said, "In order to get better jobs and have greater opportunities, one must learn English. If my English is good enough, then I'll have the opportunity to study abroad. In that case, my future choices will be greatly enhanced. When I hunt for a job I will have more choices."

Faculty also noted the increasing relevance of English, and indeed, many had received their advanced degrees—both at the master's and doctoral levels—in Western, English-speaking countries. In describing the growing influence of English, faculty noted such things as the increasing ease with which English-speaking tourists and business people are able to negotiate cities such as Guangzhou, mainly because of the prevalence of English signage, as well as the number of residents capable of speaking and understanding English. Others discussed the acquisition of English-language skills as an "absolute necessity" in today's global economic context, so much so that the Chinese government places great emphasis on its citizens' learning English. Younger professors in particular were likely to be quite fluent in English, while some of the more senior faculty seemed more resistant (or even opposed) to learning English, with the exception being those senior faculty teaching in English or English-related areas (e.g., business English) or in fields in which English was deemed a necessity (e.g., international trade).

The Influence of Foreign Experts. One of the most visible signs of China's Open Door policy and the increasing influence of globalization is the growing participation of foreign professors at GDUFS. As was noted earlier, there are likely to be some fifty to sixty foreign professors working at the university at any one time. These "foreign experts," as they are commonly called, primarily come from Western countries such as Australia, Canada, the United Kingdom, and the United States. A large number teach in one of the various English faculties (e.g., English for Business, English Language and Culture, Institute for English Language Education), although many also work in academic units such as European Languages and Cultures, International Communication, Management, or International Trade and Economics.

The foreign experts appear to have a significant influence on the campus, especially in terms of their daily interactions with students. Comments from students reinforce the validity of the preceding statement. For example, a nineteen-year-old sophomore suggested that her confidence in speaking and using English improved dramatically as a consequence of her interactions with foreign professors: "They've helped me to see that learning English is not so difficult. They've injected confidence in me." Other students noted that their interactions with foreign professors had helped them to understand cultural differences between China and the West. And a twenty-year-old sophomore studying English explained, "Foreign teachers not only help me to learn English, but they also expose me to their value system. Because we have a totally different background, I have acquired knowledge of cultural differences and how to solve problems that may arise as a result of those differences."

Faculty talked about the advantages of having foreign professors on campus and the opportunities to converse about issues relating to international politics and cultural change. Chinese faculty spoke of the foreign professors as providing an opportunity to create closer ties with Western countries and the importance of such scholarly exchanges to both China and the countries from which the foreign professors came. Indeed, both groups—Chinese faculty and foreign professors—saw the participation of internationals at the university as a key component of China's foreign policy aimed at building stronger transnational ties. Faculty also discussed the contributions of foreign professors in the area of teaching, specifically noting a growing challenge to more traditional views of classroom instruction, a key point of discussion in the following section.

Pedagogical Changes/Challenges. Comments from professors—both foreign and Chinese—consistently spoke to the growing influence of Western notions of classroom instruction and the complex relationships among teachers, students, and knowledge. Indeed, there is some tension at the university related to two different conceptions of teaching and learning. One style may be seen as more authoritative—based on Confucianism (according to some professors)—and the other more constructivist, participatory, and democratic. The more authoritarian style tends to promote passive forms of learning among students as well as higher levels of respect for teachers as knowledge brokers. The more constructivist style tends to encourage greater student participation in the classroom and active forms of knowledge acquisition in which the teacher is less of a knowledge expert and more of a facilitator.

Students' comments also spoke to the pedagogical changes taking place. For example, several students reinforced the reality that Western instructors tended to stress more open and conversational classrooms. For instance, a twenty-year-old junior noted, "I had a foreign teacher during my first year. From her, I observed that foreign teachers have a more open way of teaching. They teach students that learning needs to be more active than passive. In her class much time was under the control of students. I think that this helped to better motivate us and generate more enthusiasm for learning."

Professors also addressed pedagogical changes taking place at the university. "Well, these changes are slow," noted Andrew Becker, a foreign professor of language and culture. "But I hope they're inevitable. Slavish memorization has always been the rule. How many facts can you memorize and spit back and write down on a test?" Professor Becker went on to describe elements of the pedagogical challenge, from his perspective:

Passivity is encouraged. Reform must begin with the overall education system in the schools, and the ways of learning that are fostered. Of course, like in Germany a hundred years ago, this means authority with fixed rules, fixed contents, and fixed methods. All of the students must accept what the teachers say. The system must not encourage creative thinking. What this means is that when students get here, when they arrive at *Guangwai*, they already have learned to memorize and copy things. But they really struggle to do anything using the scientific method or doing research on their own. This is really the essence of the problem.

Ming Liu, a professor of language and culture, echoed the preceding view to a certain extent, highlighting, however, the fact that students' expectations also play a role:

I think there are some cultural elements of the West that the university would like to embrace, but from an educational point of view, from an instructional point of view, the students are still quite passive. They still want the teachers to give them everything they need to know and they don't want to do anything on their own. Very few seem to want to take initiative, to be very active in the classroom.

Along these lines, several students noted differences in the way Chinese and international students from Western countries interact in classroom situations, alluding to active versus passive forms of knowledge acquisition. These students noted that Chinese students often prefer to remain silent, out of fear of "embarrassment and feeling shameful." The preceding comment, in part, speaks to the notion of "face" and how it influences classroom interaction among many students and teachers at GDUFS. A twenty-two-year-old senior studying computer science approached this issue directly:

I've had contact with international students [mostly referencing international students from Western countries]. Their character is quite different from Chinese people. It seems that they're more active, extroverted, and never afraid to speak out about their ideas. I think this is worth learning, because you can make people understand you more clearly. The Chinese are afraid of losing face. Thus, on most occasions, we will keep silent. But opportunities escape you when you're silent.

The issue of face becomes even more relevant when one considers that at Chinese universities such as GDUFS there is an emphasis on a cohort or group-oriented approach to education; in essence, cohorts of students with the same class standing take many of the same courses together throughout their undergraduate years. Professor Becker discussed the importance of face and its relevance to the cohort-oriented form of education so common in China: "Face is very important. My students just finished an essay in which many of them wrote about how important it is not to lose face to this group [their cohort of classmates]. The group that you have is the group that you will have for all four years and that's very different from a U.S. university." Becker went on to note that his students often ask questions after class that they could have asked in class but did not do so because of fear of losing face: "They don't like the other students to hear about their own problems—what they know or they don't know."

Interestingly, students did not always respond positively to foreign instructors, or Chinese instructors for that matter, who tried to create a more interactive and participatory classroom. Given concerns about face and years of socialization suggesting a different type of relationship between youth and knowledge (or wisdom), change does not come easily. One foreign professor addressed some of these issues:

Sometimes it's difficult to carry on a conversation [in class] for any length of time. The students are used to very different teaching styles. There's no question about that. My expectation is that we have invested very heavily in foreign teachers from all sorts of countries, not just because they're native speakers and know the language, but because they also have different teaching styles, different perspectives on learning. That can cause a bit of a clash and a culture shock in the classroom, both for the students and for the teachers. The modes of asking and answering questions are quite different in a Chinese context.

More than a few professors pointed out that sometimes the students write negative evaluations of the teachers who seek to create more participatory classrooms. A common criticism from the students, explained a professor of language and culture, is that they "wish the teacher would provide more teaching rather than conversation." Clearly, many students do not expect important insights and relevant knowledge to come from more dialogical encounters in which students are key participants. Just as clear is the fact that some faculty at GDUFS have mixed feelings about giving up the authority associated with more traditional views of being a teacher or professor. Again, as it was with views on the growing importance of English, there appears to be a divide between a new generation of Chinese professors with close ties to the West and an older, more traditional generation deeply steeped in authoritarianism and respect for tradition.

Publish or Perish and the Emergence of Academic Capitalism. As part of the broader shift within Chinese higher education and in conjunction with local endeavors by the GDUFS administration to elevate the university's status, efforts are under way to increase research productivity. The degree to which the university is succeeding in its push to attain status as a teaching *and research* university—as opposed to simply being a teaching university—remains unclear. Historically speaking, Professor Jia Wang located the origins of a nationwide research emphasis to a period near the end of the Cultural Revolution, in combination with later influences deriving from Western countries: "After the Cultural Revolution, there emerged a growing trend to pay more attention to academic research. Of course, during the Cultural Revolution nothing was really allowed. But after the Cultural Revolution, many people went to study abroad and so they brought back to China university traditions of the West, especially doing research and doing things in a very academic or scientific manner. Much more emphasis was placed on data and engaging in more research, more scholarly work."

The research push is most obvious in discussions about the changing context of academic work and a general perception among faculty that greater pressure is being brought to bear on scholarly productivity. Interestingly, several faculty even used the phrase "publish or perish." Hai Chan, a professor of journalism and communications, explained it this way: "Publish or perish. I think it's happening now in China." She went on to describe the growing influence of an academic market for professors, grounded primarily in one's scholarly productivity:

A lot of benefits are connected to your professional title, your status. If you're a professor, you're entitled to a larger apartment. If you're a lecturer, you're only given a small place to live or you may have to share your room with others. Nowadays, the competition between universities is also very keen and academics are freer to change jobs—you know, there is brain drain from other provinces to Guangdong, or to other more developed places. And once you move, then your professional title and your research record are the key things that likely go with you.

Professor Bo Li reinforced this view, while also raising a key concern: "Increasingly, we are shifting to an American model of evaluating people by their publications. However, because many professors here do not produce serious work, it's very difficult to expect them to suddenly shift gears." Professor Li went on to comment, "When the decision-makers pressure too much, people tend to respond by manipulating the system so that they can meet the minimum standard, and in doing so they tend to evidence very poor quality work."

Some see the push to increase research productivity as part of a broader trend to tap into external revenues, following the academic capitalism model delineated in the work of Slaughter and Leslie[70] and Slaughter and Rhoades.[71] Relatedly, Professor Hai Chan pointed out that the university's president often talks about the university becoming a research university, perhaps in ten to fifteen years. All teachers are supposed to adapt themselves to this goal. "You should no longer regard yourself as simply a teacher or a teaching fellow," Professor Chan explained.

Nowadays, the funding system in China is also changing. In the past, it seemed that you just wrote articles and you got published. That was enough. Now, they talk a lot about funding. It seems that a lot of funding opportunities are now available, are there for serious scholars. Now, how can you apply for that? To me, it seems more and more related to the kinds of practices you find at foreign universities. It's related to an international standard, an international expectation of academic work.

GDUFS's goal of elevating its status as a university, by placing greater emphasis on research, reflects a common phenomenon found in the United States, as well as in other Western countries. Here, we refer to the idea of "institutional drift" (also discussed as isomorphism) whereby colleges and universities seek to alter their status by becoming more like the elite research universities (e.g., Harvard, Princeton, Stanford, etc.). In China, similar pressure exists, but it is more likely translated into wanting to break into the top 100, joining universities such as Peking, Fudan, Tsinghua, or Zhejiang—and thus benefiting from revenue streams tied to educational policies such as Project 211. If indeed the university's vision is to shift to a teaching *and research* university (nearly every faculty member with whom we spoke reiterated this goal), then perhaps a structural problem exists—to a great extent the reward structure remains tied to the amount of teaching one does. The easiest way to boost your salary at GDUFS is to teach more, as Professor Ming Liu explained: "If you don't teach, you don't have money. You don't get some of the bonus money, some of the extra allowances that come from your teaching hours." Professor Liu went on to contrast the salary structure of the university with that of a British or U.S. university, pointing out that one's salary in the United Kingdom or the United States is not so much dictated by the number of class hours one teaches. Research on faculty work in the United States, of course, supports the preceding comments, as such research consistently has revealed that a professor's salary and status are less tied to the amount or quality of teaching and more tied to research productivity.[72]

There are, however, structures in place to encourage research at Guangwai, but the rewards deriving from these structures do not appear to outweigh the rewards for teaching. For example, a number of professors pointed out that a policy exists whereby faculty who meet various publication targets may receive bonuses: For each faculty title—Lecturer, Associate Professor, Professor—there are different publication targets. At the end of each academic year, faculty are expected to complete a form summarizing their scholarly contributions. The amount of an individual's contributions generates a specific point total, which is then used to determine incentive pay. Additionally, within some faculties and departments, academic deans and department chairs have sought to implement a more localized reward structure for those faculty who publish exceptional work, typically evaluated on the basis of where a piece appears. For example, the financial reward will be greater for an article published in a top research journal. But again, it is not clear that the incentives to produce quality scholarship outweigh incentives to teach.

In discussing the university's quest to become a teaching and research university, and ultimately a research university, Professor Huijian Hu (English language and culture) offered some insight into the tough road ahead for GDUFS: "If we want to be considered a real university, then we have to become a research university. But, I think it's going to take a long time for us to achieve that goal. First, we have to shift from a teaching university to a teaching and research university, with the final destination of course being a legitimate research university." Professor Hu went on to point out that Guangdong's provincial government presently places greater emphasis on serving the economic needs of the region and providing higher education to as many students as possible. Consequently, he concluded that, for "the next five or ten years, our major work will still be focused on teaching, even though we would like to make the shift from teaching to teaching and research."

CHANGES IN COMMUNAL LIFE

As Chinese society faces new challenges in a global age, its citizens respond in innovative ways. This befits a long-standing characteristic of life in China: to make the best of the situation in which one finds oneself. An analysis of the changing context of academic life at GDUFS reveals many of the challenges and opportunities the nation's universities are likely to face as well as the unique responses of key organizational actors—students and professors. With changes in social life, most specifically life at a university, new conceptions of citizenship are needed to address the evolving complexities related to globalization. Given the long-standing ideological influence of socialism, a most obvious concern at the university is the nature of the *danwei* (the community of workers) and its place in a society increasingly operating on the basis of the market.

The Changing Danwei. Social reform in essence involves the remaking of social organizations, as within the historical context of modernity, or even postmodernity, organizations provide the defining structures to human interaction and identity. From William Whyte's[73] classic *Organizational Man* to Michel Foucault's[74] treatment of the role of discipline and punishment enacted through a variety of organizations (most notably, schools, universities, prisons, hospitals, and factories) or to more contemporary works challenging traditional notions of organizations and their transformative power, as in the work of Manuel Castells[75] and Alain Touraine,[76] it is hard to escape the reality that to transform society is to transform its fundamental organizations. Furthermore, universities, as key sites for socializing a society's future leaders as well as bastions of a society's culture, are vital to a nation and its reformist objectives. Thus, in a very real sense, university life at an institution such as GDUFS may be interpreted as a microcosm of the broader social context, revealing many of the challenges and opportunities confronting the society. This clearly is the case at GDUFS, where the changes sweeping across China's landscape are front and center, seemingly on the mind of everyone, and certainly attracting the attention of the university's many students and faculty.

The changes under way at GDUFS connect in one form or another to the broader global pulse that now beats throughout much of China, especially in the highly populated and more urbanized coastal regions such as Guangzhou and Guangdong Province. These changes are producing new forms of living and working together, and in their totality are refashioning the nature of the community of workers at the university. Here, the socialist concept of the *danwei* moves front and center, given its relevance to Chinese society since the Mao-led communist movement came to power. Like other socialist ideals, ranging in their measure of adaptability to global capitalism from open to reform to steadfastly resistant, the *danwei* faces pressures intent on a serious refashioning, much as the former Chinese socialist economy has had to be reconfigured along the lines of a socialist market economy.

In a provocative work, Professor Ouyang Huhua,[77] a faculty member at GDUFS, conducted a rich ethnographic study of his university and its efforts to reform English-language teaching. Carried out as part of his doctoral thesis at the City University of Hong Kong, Huhua's study represents more than simply an examination of teaching reform, but in fact, it reveals deep layers of cultural challenges confronting GDUFS and the wider society, as Western influences steadily reshape social life. As Professor Huhua noted in the introduction to his book, *Remaking of Face and Community of Practices*, "What is seemingly a pedagogy-only and beneficial-to-all reform entails in fact a remaking of ideologies, power relations, and the remaking of the community of practices from a *danwei*-type to a civil-society type."[78] Huhua characterized the civil-society model as a social form involving "contractual relationships, individualism, egalitarianism, and mobility."[79] Later, he offered greater clarity about the strains of reform at GDUFS and tensions between foreign experts (and their Chinese supporters) and more traditional-minded Chinese faculty (described as "old-timers" by Huhua):

Guangwai's old-timers' perceptions and reactions towards the foreign experts' endeavors in reform are fully "justified" and "grounded" in [their] reality. The old-timers are simply behaving in accordance with norms of a *danwei* community of practices while the foreign experts are behaving with norms and values that are taken for granted in a different community of practices, namely a civil society. Individual freedom, contractual relationships, and egalitarian competition are among the central messages brought by the foreign reformers to the Chinese *danwei* society.[80]

Huhua's thesis reinforces a central argument of this chapter: that reform at GDUFS is not simply about changes at one academic institution, but in fact is indicative of broader changes within Chinese society linked to the growing importance of global capitalism. This is most obvious in challenges posed to the spirit of the community of workers at the university. However, whereas Huhua focused mostly on pedagogical reform (and its social and cultural implications), we see the global challenges and opportunities confronting the university extending to other areas of academic life, including most notably growing pressure to elevate individual scholarly productivity and enhance the institution's status.

Several professors in this study addressed the changing social context of the university and the larger society, attributing such changes to the influence of globalization and the related phenomenon of international integration. One professor theorized, for example, that Chinese in poorer, more rural regions of the country actually care about one another in deeper ways than those living along the coast or in urban areas, where technology is more accessible and modernity more prominent. He believed the forms of communication and technology advanced by an increasingly global society are eroding the intimate face-to-face encounters encouraged by the more communal, socialist tradition. Such views call to mind writings in the 1950s in the West that began to explore the phenomenon of urban loneliness. We are particularly reminded of the book *The Lonely Crowd* by David Riesman, Nathan Glazer, and Reuel Denney,[81] in which emerging forms of social life were believed to produce new kinds of psychological problems and social concerns. Discussions of social change in China also may be informed by the long-standing sociological work of Ferdinand Tönnies,[82] in which he outlined shifts in the nature of community (as a consequence of industrialization and modernity), as societies moved from being organized on the basis of personal and familial ties (*gemienschaft*) to those organized more around impersonal and labor-related relationships (*gesellschaft*). Of course, socialism, in some sense, is a rejection of the socially imposed separation between the personal/familial and the impersonal/work-related and ideally seeks to create a personal *and* work-based social unit—the essence of the *danwei*. However, it is increasingly clear that the growing influence of global capitalism, and the concomitant emphasis on individualism, poses a serious challenge to any social unit stressing communal ties and social cooperation.

Several faculty were struck by what they described as a decline in the sense of community among today's college students as well as among more recent faculty hires. More times than not they attributed these changes to the sort of competition generated by China's growing participation in the global marketplace. Notions of community were also seen to be negatively influenced by increasing reliance on advanced technology, including the widespread use of the Internet for information, and the growing impact of Western popular culture, as evidenced by the influence of music, film, and television. These faculty increasingly saw a culture of individualism replacing long-standing, group-oriented values and norms. They pointed to higher levels of academic competitiveness among students and the trend for faculty to leave one university for another as competition for top professors increases and as the influence of the academic job market grows. This trend, in their mind, represents an example of faculty acting more on the basis of self-interest than on the basis of community needs or a commitment to the broader social good.

Findings suggest that the growing importance of English, the influence of foreign professors ("foreign experts"), changes in pedagogical practice (and correspondingly, conceptions of knowledge and its construction), and the emergence of academic capitalism and a more competitive publish-or-perish environment all reflect broader changes taking place at GDUFS that may undermine to some extent a traditional culture rooted in communalism and the ideals of the *danwei*. However, there are complexities and contradictions here. For example, on the one hand, the growing acceptance of a more dialogical pedagogy may in fact reinforce a sense of cooperation as well as advance a more community-based view of knowledge (as in a social constructivist view). This element of pedagogical change hardly seems threatening to the ideal of the *danwei*. On the other hand, the democratic view of knowledge suggested by more dialogical classroom encounters may also encourage a critical questioning of the university's traditions and norms, potentially contributing to increased scrutiny of various socialist traditions.

The changing *danwei* reflects the growing influence of international forces acting on China, and in particular, the growing strength of a market-driven society. Many students indicated great excitement over such a turn of events and seemed to welcome all aspects of globalization with open arms, especially those elements altering the Chinese economic structure. Many students were uncritical in their acceptance of globalization and its potential for refashioning Chinese life and citizenship. Comments such as the following by twenty-year-old Ping Liang were quite common: "Today, the Chinese people recognize fairly well that only through cooperation can we achieve greater success in the political and economic spheres. Decades or even centuries ago, we didn't realize this—each country depended on its own. Now, by realizing the importance of globalization, and working within its limitations and benefits, people are better off. Thus, I consider globalization as a positive development for human beings."

THREE VIEWS OF CITIZENSHIP

Three themes coinciding with particular dimensions of citizenship tended to resonate throughout our interviews with students and faculty at GDUFS; these themes are fairly consistent with the way in which citizenship is conceptualized in Chapter 1. The first view of citizenship tended to focus on the economic dimension (with entrepreneurial elements) to Chinese life under the growing influence of capitalism. This view was quite dominant among the students and stressed the possible economic and occupational benefits available to those individuals prepared to take advantage of the new global environment. A second commonly held view stressed the civic or political aspects of a changing China and the role of its citizens. Students and faculty embracing this view tended to adopt a more nationalistic tone, not only expressing concerns about globalization in terms of what benefits them but also discussing benefits for the "homeland" or "motherland." A third and final view of citizenship centered more on social and cultural changes in China. These students and faculty tended to discuss the social consequences of globalization, focusing on how Chinese citizens might preserve valued norms and traditions while also embracing emergent social forms seen to be beneficial to the broader society. Most of the viewpoints represented by the students and faculty in our study were fairly globally informed, although some of the more senior faculty seemed relatively disinterested in events taking place outside China. There were also some differences in terms of commitments to individualism versus collectivism, with students more likely to discuss using their knowledge of globalization for personal gain, while faculty were more likely to be concerned about the broader academic community and issues facing China.

Economic/Occupational Conceptions of Citizenship. Several students stressed a more individualistic view of citizenship and focused on economic challenges and opportunities, while preparing themselves for the occupational journey that lies ahead. Jenny Zhao, a twenty-two-year-old senior, captured this sentiment: "Well, the challenge is apparent when I'm hunting for jobs. In order to be recruited by a multinational company, I have to compete not only with native Chinese, but also foreigners. . . . I know that the future will be mixed with challenges and opportunities." And nineteen-year-old Tina Sun added, "I want to work for a foreign bank and have a fairly high salary. I think foreign banks offer better salaries because they usually are more profitable than local banks. I want to earn as much money as possible in order to realize my dream of traveling around the world." Other students spoke in entrepreneurial terms befitting the character of a global free-market economy. Twenty-year-old Eva Peng reflected this line of thinking: "My career goal is to own my own website and listed company. It's a wild dream, but I think with globalization anything is possible. The global environment is very favorable for us to have our own companies, especially if we possess skills in the area of advanced technology."

Several faculty pointed to increased mobility and professional choices among professors at GDUFS as a benefit of China's growing openness and participation in the global marketplace. For example, Professor Bo Li specifically addressed how Chinese universities increasingly participate in a global academic marketplace, and as a consequence, faculty have greater mobility. Professor Li even used the term *global citizenship* to describe a group of transnational professors increasingly populating Chinese universities:

We see more and more the idea of global citizenship. For instance, we can see very clearly the expatriate teachers working as our staff members here at *Guangwai*. They are very much global. They have been working in Southeast Asia, Africa, the Middle East, Europe, East Europe, the United States, and South America. They have been traveling a lot. Many have dozens of years of teaching experience in those places. They have mobility, freedom to choose where they want to work. They are free to move to wherever they can get jobs and their teaching takes on a global quality. And China increasingly is becoming part of such a global working community.

Here, Professor Li's use of the term *global citizenship*, as applied to an analysis of foreign experts, seems more focused on rights and less concerned about responsibilities. Elsewhere, we have discussed this version of citizenship as the "global free marketeer" (or "global free marketer"), because of the emphasis on individual opportunity.[83] From our perspective, this form of citizenship lacks the collectivist quality that we see as critical to notions of global citizenship.

The examples of citizenship expressed here are those most adaptable to the advance of capitalism in China and the entrepreneurial spirit so valued by capitalists. This economically oriented view of citizenship tends to fit in quite nicely with the individualism advanced by neoliberalism. At the same time, such a view rubs up against the strong socialist traditions within China and many of the group-oriented, more communal aspects of the culture. In a very real sense, the entrepreneurialism of many Chinese, especially as it was expressed by the students at GDUFS, poses a serious challenge to the communist programs and ideals that so defined China prior to the Open Door policy of 1978 and before China launched its present-day economic reform programs. Only time will tell the degree to which neoliberalism takes hold of the Chinese people and culture, but those who embrace a vision of citizen as economic entrepreneur seem quite supportive of such a shift.

Political/Civic Conceptions of Citizenship. A second conception of citizenship commonly expressed by students and faculty at GDUFS essentially spoke to the political/civic dimensions of social life and reflected a deep concern for China as the "motherland" in an age increasingly defined by globalization. Comments such as the following student's were typical of this line of thinking:

Threats and opportunities go hand in hand. Globalization is an unstoppable trend. Globalization offers greater opportunity for people to tap into larger markets around the world. It means that they can have access to more capital flows, technology, cheaper imports, and larger export markets. But markets do not necessarily ensure that the benefits are shared by all. Countries must be prepared to embrace the policies needed, and in the case of the poorest countries, they may need the support of the international community to do so. China must become more competitive and be prepared to handle threats and take advantage of the opportunities. I intend to help in whatever way I can. I want China to compete successfully.

Several students emphasized the political and international challenges facing China in an age of global relations. Huiling Li, a twenty-one-year-old studying public policy, saw the global possibilities for China, as well as the importance of Chinese-Japanese relations: "My studies have helped me to realize the importance of China to the world market, and the important relationship between China and Japan. The relationship is not only one of economic cooperation, but also depends on building strong political ties, and a recognition of the relevance of historic and geographic disputes between the two countries, and even resentment or hatred among the people. Globalization makes me care more about these issues." Twenty-one-year-old, international studies major Kan Zheng also expressed a desire to enhance Chinese-Japanese relations. She saw advantages in studying foreign languages beyond English and wanted to use such knowledge to benefit China: "I study Japanese because I want to master another foreign language in addition to English. This is a challenge for me but I love language learning. It is a challenge in developing myself. I want to contribute to the friendship between China and Japan." Several students stressed the importance of China-U.S. relations as well as their interest in building stronger ties between the two countries. Once again, Kan Zheng explained, "As America is the most powerful nation and China has the world's largest population, I believe every subtle change in the relationship between the two has the potential to create a global impact. I pursue studies in this area because I care about the Sino-U.S. relationship and want to contribute."

Many students spoke directly to the relevance of developing more advanced understandings of the world and using such knowledge to inform their role as citizens of China. A first-year student spoke in nationalistic terms of her desire to study abroad but then return and give back to her "motherland": "As China is regarded as one of the fastest developing countries of the twenty-first century, I have every reason to come back to build my motherland and realize my dream to be employed in a public service–oriented company." Another student expressed her desire to better understand international law and the relationships between governments and societies. She plans to study abroad for the purpose of exploring how people develop "a better understanding of the law and their legal rights." This student saw advantages in developing a more internationally based knowledge of government and society: "It helps me to understand problems from multiple perspectives, from multiple sides, and then better serve the needs of my country."

Most professors with whom we spoke noted the key relationship between China and the West in general and the United States in particular and sought to enhance China's global role through their academic and professional activity. A few professors noted the importance of scholarly exchange and collaboration between China and the United States, but feared that U.S. travel restrictions in the post-9/11 era somewhat curtailed such interaction. One professor openly wondered why it was more difficult for Chinese scholars to travel to the United States than it was for U.S. scholars to travel to China. It seemed to him that China valued the relationship between the two countries more than U.S. officials did, although he clearly separated his views about the U.S. government from his discussion of U.S. citizens, noting that he "had nothing but positive interactions with American citizens." This professor, along with several others, sought to strengthen ties with the United States by personally seeking collaborative opportunities with U.S. universities and their professors. This was a way for this group of professors to strengthen China's position within the global academic community.

A handful of professors also noted an important change within the broader Chinese society: They described a trend in which average citizens increasingly demonstrate an interest in global political affairs and China's role around the world. For example, Professor Xiaoan Zhang (legal studies) observed, "A few decades ago, few citizens cared about what happened around the world, in Iraq, in Russia, in Korea, or even in Japan, or in Northeast Asia. But now, many people talk about world problems. Common citizens talk about the issues now. I see this as a consequence of globalization. The people care more about world affairs than ever before." Another professor attributed the rise in global political interest to the emergence of the Internet as a source of information as well as to greater freedom within the press corps in China, although she also pointed out that the government still had a long way to go: "Our leaders still regulate public information to some extent."

Social/Cultural Conceptions of Citizenship. A third commonly expressed view of citizenship tended to stress the importance of the social and cultural elements of Chinese society and a desire to protect and preserve aspects of traditional culture in the face of a global assault. This view was more pragmatic than nativistic, in that many saw value in integrating elements of the West, but without completely annihilating Chinese culture and tradition. This was a view more commonly expressed among the faculty than on the part of the students. For example, faculty expressed the need to preserve Chinese culture in the face of a host of Western influences linked to increased communication and trade. They either aspired to contribute in their own way or wondered why the government was not taking a more proactive stance in preserving the best of what China represents. Along these lines, Professor Jun Qiang (international communications) stated,

In terms of culture, especially the relationship between the introduction of foreign cultural products and the protection of local cultural products, I think that's something that we have to address, especially our leaders. We have to consider the effects of globalization carefully. In some countries, especially in the poor or less developed countries, they import a lot of foreign cultural products and these cultural products are cheap . . . are cheaper than what they can produce, and perhaps better. The local cultural products are likely to disappear because of increased global competition. This could lead to a loss of jobs as well as a loss of some significant cultural traditions. I'm not saying that we should completely resist foreign culture or popular culture, but at the same time, measures must be taken to protect those traditional things. It's not easy, but the government should do something.

In discussing the "Americanization of the world," a second professor expressed his desire to work to preserve the values and traditions of Chinese society, lest they be lost for good: "If we get too much Americanization there won't be any Chinese culture left. It'll be a small part of the society, a very small part. And since Chinese culture and traditions have survived all these centuries, it would be nice if they could survive in their own little niche a little longer."

Other faculty expressed a more integrationist stance, supporting the hybridization of Chinese culture, as they argued for combining the best of the West with the best of what China has to offer, socially and culturally speaking. Professor Ming Liu (specializing in language and culture) explained his position: "Well, I think that today's Chinese society should catch up with most of the things happening in the rest of the world—the cultural changes. But, I also think that we should keep some of the qualities of Chinese culture. For example, I still value the ideals of Confucianism, like diligence, effort, hard-working spirit. I want to retain some of these qualities and also integrate some of the qualities of the global world." Other faculty also noted improvements in women's rights and career opportunities as well as greater government attention to ethnic inequalities and the importance of cultural diversity throughout China; they discussed such issues in the context of global influences linked to the women's movement and multiculturalism, originating primarily in the West. A notable example here includes the offering of the first undergraduate course on gay studies at a Chinese university, at Fudan University in Shanghai, in the fall of 2005.[84] The example of the gay studies course at Fudan, as well as other broader changes linked to enhanced human rights and the protection of minorities, represent the kind of social/cultural changes that several professors (mostly younger professors) saw as beneficial to a more hybridized China. But again, they stressed that the integration of Western values should not come at the expense of key values and traditions long rooted in Chinese cultural life. In a very real sense, they sought a delicate balance in terms of social and cultural change and used their work as academics to elevate the consciousness of their students—with whom they believed the future of China rested. These faculty were quick to admit, though, that they faced a serious challenge, given the tendency for college students in particular and China's youth in general to become enamored with Western culture, most notably American popular culture.

CONCLUSION

In a very real sense, China finds itself in a kind of middle world, trying to hold on to long-standing ideals rooted in collectivism and at the same time facing the growing influence of global capitalism and the rampant individualism that capitalism inspires. Clearly, there are both external and internal forces at work that have as their aim China's increasing participation in global capitalism. At the same time, such forces run up against a society still under the powerful influence of socialism. The paradoxical condition of contemporary life in China is quite apparent at GDUFS, where students and faculty operate within an institution that values traditional elements of a communal life and at the same time pushes for individualistic and competitive processes befitting the emergence of an academic capitalist model of the university. Although a thoughtful read of the history of conflict between competing world views (i.e., socialism and capitalism) may lead one to adopt an either/or position—that is, a society must be *fully* committed to one ideological project or the other—such a read is increasingly inadequate for today's global age. Perhaps the time has come to recognize that hybridism is the defining quality of the world's present state. It should be more and more clear that "cultural experience or indeed every cultural form," as Edward Said argued, "is radically, quintessentially hybrid."[85] Hence, hybridism demands a more complete understanding of "intersecting histories," and not simply the sort of capitalocentrism in which much of the world is defined as passive recipients of "Euro-American authored" influences.[86]

Given the present-day context of a rapidly changing China, it should come as no surprise that new challenges and opportunities may also be recasting notions of citizenship. Of course, globalization serves as the primary source of these changes and was quite evident in our discussions with students and faculty at GDUFS. The vast majority of the students were very much caught up in the rise of capitalism and the exciting and challenging professional opportunities they perceived on the horizon. Many of the faculty too expressed positive feelings about the emergence of an academic job market, offering them the potential for greater mobility and increased professional rewards. However, nearly as many faculty looked at the rising influence of capitalism (and academic capitalism) as a threat to some of the more positive qualities of Chinese social life and citizenship—namely, the spirit of collectivism.

Among many of the students and faculty with whom we spoke there was a strong sense that citizens throughout the country were becoming more internationally aware and that such awareness was the consequence of Chinese society being more open to the outside world. But with such openness the country and its citizens face difficult social and cultural choices in which emerging trends, primarily deriving from but not limited to the West, must be weighed against values and norms rooted in a more traditional China. Students and younger faculty generally were comfortable with these choices and seem well-prepared to step into a bold new world. Not too surprisingly, more senior faculty at GDUFS were more likely to adopt the role of tribal elder, seeking to protect and preserve important elements of Chinese social life while looking upon Western influences with greater degrees of skepticism.

Broadly speaking, though, our discussions with faculty and students at GDUFS suggest a rather exciting and perhaps optimistic possibility: that China may take the lead in forging a society that adopts the best of both sides of the coin as it seeks to blend preferred cultural elements and traditions with emerging global influences. However, the challenge seems monumental at times, as the foreboding force of capitalism, which, if we take the U.S. higher education system as an example (here, we particularly refer to academic capitalism), appears to have an unquenchable thirst for power and influence.[87] Nonetheless, and given the tremendous need for revenue to support its massive postsecondary education needs, China pushes forward, and proclamations about the need to seek harmony and return to some of the basic values of socialism reveal an interest on the part of the nation's leaders to control to some extent the impact of globalization and particularly global capitalism.

Indeed, many faculty at GDUFS spoke quite enthusiastically about building and maintaining a socialist market economy (others were skeptical of such a possibility, fearing the Americanization of China), as well as the broader effort to advance a more harmonious society based on the integration of global/local differences. In this sense, GDUFS is a microcosm of the broader society, embodying the localization of global influences and the general challenges and opportunities confronting China.

Whether institutions such as GDUFS and its academic citizens will find ways to seek harmony out of the differences or take advantage of both sides of the same coin remains to be seen. One thing that is certain, though, is that two world systems are meeting on a global stage the likes of which we have never before witnessed. Clearly, such dramatic changes are refashioning the very notion of citizen as well as challenging any definitive sense of what it means to exist in a global age. As past notions of social life increasingly fade from view, only time will tell if Chinese citizens and their institutions, including universities, will find creative ways to blend multiple and at times competing world views, cultures, and systems. But if we are to learn anything from the rich history of China, it is recognition that we should not underestimate the spirit of its people and the nation's ability to forge its own identity in the face of overwhelming world influences. In this regard, perhaps China represents an important cultural battleground leading to an ideological hybridization that ultimately puts to rest the endless capitalism-versus-socialism either/or debate and in the end produces the kinds of citizens and cultural complexity necessary for meaningful survival in a global age.

CHAPTER 3

PLURIVERSITY KNOWLEDGE IN A MOBILE WORLD:

International Graduate Students and Citizenship at UCLA

"GLOBALIZATION HITS UCLA"

"Globalization Hits UCLA," proclaimed a headline in the February 8, 2005 issue of the *Daily Bruin*, the University of California, Los Angeles, student newspaper. "Globalization is a big word. But a new major in global studies aims to give UCLA students the tools to understand it," the author of the article went on to state in his introduction of a recent major added to the university's many curricular offerings.[1] Part of the Global Studies Interdepartmental Program, the major engages UCLA undergraduates in a critical interdisciplinary examination of globalization around three specific themes: culture and society, governance and conflict, and markets.[2] Explorations of globalization in the major are not geographically bound to the campus in Los Angeles; global studies students also participate in a study-abroad experience through the summer Global Learning Institute.

Although the global studies major is an important development in UCLA's engagement in global issues, the reader of the *Daily Bruin* article must wonder whether 2005 was truly one of the first major instances that the university was "hit" by globalization. After all, UCLA's location makes the presence of strong globalizing forces far from surprising. Nestled in an affluent suburb of West Los Angeles, the university is a major academic presence at the confluence of peoples, cultures, and languages; regional, national, and transnational trade; international media and pop culture; and political forces transcending national boundaries. The city of Los Angeles is often identified as a foremost representative of global-ness, at times even described as a trendsetter in what is to transpire in other major urban centers.[3] This latter idea is reflected in the L.A.-as-prefigurative thesis in urban geography, portraying Los Angeles as "the window of the future, the place where actually existing practices and social processes prefigure those that will appear later in other parts of North America and beyond."[4] Norman Klein's fast-moving, eclectic images also provide a powerful glimpse of global influence:

Global LA does not exist physically in Southern California. It is a portable—or exportable—"place." It "speaks" English, but not "American;" and speaks to businesses too vast to be merely American: Daimler-Chrysler; German publishing giants owning Random House or St. Martins Press; Rupert Murdock's empire; German and French cinema filmed in English. It is a designer language for consumer glitterati, reflected in the British fashion magazine *Wallpaper*, or in special effects blockbuster movies by directors who are as likely to be European or Asian as American.[5]

And although Los Angeles may be a magnet for foreign-born movie directors, more important to note is the high percentage of the city's population born in other countries of the world. In the 2000 U.S. Census, a whopping 40.9 percent of the city's population were foreign-born.[6]

UCLA has also attracted large numbers of international students. In 2008–9, the university placed eighth in the number of foreign students it hosted among all institutions of higher education in the United States. In that academic year, international students at the university numbered 5,590.[7] The international roots of the student body are reflected in the high percentage of second-generation immigrants as well. In 2008, only 32 percent of

UCLA undergraduates indicated that both of their parents were born in the United States.[8]

Other signs of globalization and the university's engagement in issues of global significance abound. At the center of its efforts with a global emphasis stands the UCLA International Institute, providing leadership for eighteen research centers and programs and defining its overall mission as helping to "meet a national need for increased knowledge and expertise about our complex world, the U.S. role within it, and to promote global citizenship and life-long learning."[9] In its primary role, the UCLA International Institute brings together the university's efforts in teaching and research with an international emphasis.

UCLA's global reach also includes endeavors in science and medicine and human rights. In just one example, the UCLA AIDS Institute engages in cutting-edge research at locations in Los Angeles, Brazil, China, India, and Sub-Saharan Africa, overcoming national boundaries in its efforts to combat HIV and AIDS around the world. And when it comes to human rights reaching beyond the borders of the United States, one case in point is the crisis in Sudan, drawing major activism from UCLA students under the auspices of the Darfur Action Committee. The committee makes information about the violence in Sudan available to students, faculty, and staff through special events such as lectures, vigils, and demonstrations. In one of its most publicized achievements, the committee was successful in its effort to end the University of California's investment in companies conducting business in Sudan, a first for a major public university system in the United States.[10]

The fight for human rights, scientific discovery to solve global health problems, and efforts to understand the impact of globalization on various world regions, however, are not the only activities adopted by UCLA in light of an increasingly global environment. Other aspects of the university's functioning reveal an institution very much aware of—and oftentimes enthusiastic about—the place it occupies in the world system, conforming to the demands of the global economy. Perhaps most importantly, UCLA has fervently embraced its role in furthering economic development. As stated in the *UCLA Magazine*: "UCLA accounts for almost $10 billion in economic activity in California, and the number rises every year. The latest statistics prove it: The university is one of the Golden State's most potent growth engines."[11]

At the beginning of the twenty-first century, separating the regional economy from the global, especially when the region in question is California, is an arduous task. In fact, UCLA's self-proclaimed role in economic development is clearly linked to the global sphere. One important activity promoting UCLA's global reach is technology transfer, the process of commercializing scientific discoveries. As the university's Web site explains in describing UCLA's impact:

New inventions and advances in technology are absolute necessities for a healthy global economy. As one of the world's leading research universities . . . UCLA is uniquely situated to make the most of California's innovative drive. Through technology transfer, the process of developing applications for the results of scientific research, UCLA plays a vital role in bringing new innovation into the marketplace. In fact, new startups based on UCLA discoveries are launched every year.[12]

The numbers reflecting the extent of commercialization speak for themselves. According to a report, "UCLA Invents," the university's portfolio under the auspices of the Office of Intellectual Property recently included 1,560 inventions, 535 active U.S. patents, 537 active foreign patents, and 227 active licensing agreements. The financial implications of these commercialization efforts are considerable: In fiscal year 2008, gross sales from UCLA licenses amounted to $156,146,062.[13]

Major fundraising campaigns are another key undertaking in revenue generation. During a recent ten-and-a-half-year campaign, UCLA raised $3 billion from 225,000 donors, making it the most successful academic endeavor to raise funds in the nation.[14] Efforts to encourage potential revenue from trademarks and logos are also at the forefront. The UCLA Trademarks and Licensing Office coordinates programs to protect the UCLA brand name at home and abroad. Through its appearance on products from toothbrushes to sandals to kites, the UCLA logo signifies an important source of revenue. Perhaps even more importantly, the logo is a crucial element in UCLA's institutional identity as a world-class public research university with increasing emphasis on privatization, international competitiveness, entrepreneurialism, and self-sustainability, key manifestations of the impact of neoliberal forms of globalization on university life.[15]

PLURIVERSITY KNOWLEDGE AT UCLA

UCLA thus represents a prime example of a variety of global forces present in U.S. higher education, from practicing medicine with a global reach to commercialization. Indeed, UCLA is both a human rights activist and an avid entrepreneur, a public university concerned about the impact of neoliberalism on the world and a globalizing force accepting and promoting its role in the commercialization of higher education. Although these forces are seemingly contradictory, they are key examples of the production of pluriversity—as opposed to university—knowledge, a form of knowledge that is profoundly linked to recent university transformations.[16] Pluriversity knowledge is readily recognizable by its focus on application and societal contextualization, re-creating the relationship between knowledge and society. The circumstances of application, however, can vary greatly. As Boaventura de Sousa Santos explained:

Pluriversity knowledge has had its most consistent realization in university-industry partnerships in the form of mercantile knowledge. But, especially in the central and semiperipheral countries, the context of application has been nonmercantile as well—cooperative and dependent on the solidarity created by partnerships between researchers on the one hand and labor unions, nongovernmental organizations (NGOs), social movements, particularly vulnerable social groups (women, illegal immigrants, the unemployed, people with chronic illnesses, senior citizens, those afflicted with HIV/AIDS, etc.), working class communities, and groups of critical and active citizens on the other.[17]

By contrast, university knowledge is a remnant of previous eras of higher education, indicating knowledge that is disciplinary in nature and decontextualized from society and application. In short, university knowledge is produced without much concern for its use by society: "It is a knowledge based on the distinction between scientific research and technological development, and the autonomy of the researcher is translated as a kind of social irresponsibility as far as the results of the application of knowledge are concerned. . . . The university produces knowledge that the society does or does not apply, an alternative that, although socially relevant, is indifferent or irrelevant to the knowledge produced."[18]

Santos's understanding of twenty-first-century knowledge production should leave no question in one's mind about the possibility of opposing ideals coexisting at UCLA. After all, pluriversity knowledge can be applied in a variety of ways, be that for humanitarian or mercantile purposes. Equally important, university knowledge has not disappeared; the shift to pluriversity knowledge is ongoing at best, the process far from completed. In this context, contemporary universities are situated as breeding grounds for a variety of goals and influences that create vastly different—and in many ways, contradictory—environments across campuses. In fact, it would be more than feasible at UCLA, on the very same day, to attend a class session decrying the commercialization of public universities and to participate in a workshop providing expert advice to young academic entrepreneurs wanting to bring their scientific discoveries to the marketplace.[19]

PLURIVERSITY KNOWLEDGE AND INTERNATIONAL GRADUATE STUDENTS

Against the backdrop of globalization, an important question we intend to explore relates to the ways in which the experiences of international graduate students are shaped at the intersection of knowledge systems, in the context of knowledge creation and application that characterizes higher education at the beginning of the twenty-first century. Specifically, the research study discussed in this chapter focuses on findings from in-depth interviews concerning the views and experiences of thirty students from Brazil, China, and Italy enrolled in graduate programs at UCLA. A central goal of these interviews was to gain an understanding of international graduate students' conceptions of the geographic reach of their citizenship, including their home countries and regions, the United States, and a global sphere of existence.[20] As such, this study is driven by the recognition that international graduate students face critical choices about their own role in the world: As future leaders in their professions, as political actors, voters, taxpayers, and activists and as key players in local, national, and global economies, they must determine the types of work they will undertake and the kinds of social changes they will seek to effect, if any. As Fazal Rizvi noted in his study of international students in Australia: "As mobile groups, it is they who are able to imagine the nation and its links to the outside world in radically new ways. With formative international experiences, they are able to look at the world as dynamic and multicultural. This is so because they operate within a hybridized space and are equally comfortable in more than one cultural site. Their identity is intercultural with multiple cultural defining points. They typify the new global generation."[21]

International students play an important role in shaping a university's reputation and focus on creating an internationalized environment. In fact, foreign student recruitment is a central component of institution-level program strategies adopted to increase internationalization, an umbrella term for efforts defined as "the process of integrating an international, intercultural or global dimension into the purpose, functions or delivery of postsecondary education."[22] International students, especially at the graduate level, are also key actors in the population movements facilitated by globalization. In the migratory process, international graduate students often bring with them knowledge and skills highly coveted by the global economy. The purpose of their stay abroad commonly augments their knowledge and skills in the interest of achieving goals that may become relevant on both the personal and societal levels. At the very core of international graduate students' experiences is thus knowledge production itself. Importantly, international graduate students are not only recipients of knowledge as students but also engaged in intense academic inquiry, participating in its creation and application as researchers-in-training and as teaching assistants. The experiences of foreign graduate students, then, raise important questions of whether and how they incorporate knowledge and skills into their notions of personal and professional citizenship. How do international graduate students fit the rubric of knowledge in the global era? What is their relationship to the production of knowledge, and do they come to apply the knowledge they gain in the United States—both as graduate students at UCLA and as participants in U.S. society—to larger societal contexts? If so, are their home countries and regions, the United States, or a global sphere of existence the geographic context of their knowledge application and their conceptualizations of citizenship?

PLURIVERSITY KNOWLEDGE, GLOBAL CITIZENSHIP,
AND INTERNATIONAL GRADUATE STUDENTS

The utility of Santos's description of knowledge systems in higher education is reflected not only in its emphasis on the changing relationship between knowledge and society [23] but also with regard to the implications pluriversity knowledge holds for understanding the role of citizenship assumed by universities and actors within them, including international graduate students, in the context of globalization. Before discussing the views and experiences of the Brazilian, Chinese, and Italian graduate students participating in this study, however, we find it useful to describe a framework situating Santos's notion of pluriversity knowledge within the context of the key debates over citizenship outlined in Chapter 1.

In recent years, citizenship has been at the center of debates on globalization and immigration. Although conceptualizing citizenship by looking beyond state borders has a long history, these two forces have left their distinct mark by bringing renewed emphasis to the expanded geographic scope of belonging, allegiance, and civic participation in an increasingly global space. Indeed, "global," "cosmopolitan," "fluid," "postnational," and "flexible" are frequent attributes of citizenship, stressing the need to go beyond the nation-state in describing the rights and duties of citizens.[24]

In attempts to understand the viability of citizenship practiced in the global sphere, some political theorists have argued that global citizenship, in fact, is difficult—or even impossible—to attain beyond the expression—as opposed to the practice—of global obligations.[25] David Miller, a key proponent of this argument, posited that citizenship is possible only in the presence of a shared public culture and clear, committed participation in a political community. According to Miller, citizenship becomes impracticable in the absence of active commitment to the common good and participation in political life through specific political institutions, both of which can be seen as impossibilities in a global sphere. For example, in what global political institutions do individuals participate, especially in the absence of world government? And how is a commitment to the common good possible across national borders without a shared public culture existing across those borderlines?

Others have stated that global citizenship is not only desirable but also highly possible. Nigel Dower has argued against the seeming opposition between global citizenship being just a moral obligation and a series of actions enacted through political institutions, such as world government.[26] Instead, Dower depicted citizenship as a combination of moral obligations that will, in essence, drive individuals to use existing institutions and to create additional institutions necessary for its practice. Global citizenship thus becomes more than a transient and difficult-to-enact moral obligation. Instead, citizenship on the global plane might be practiced in a number of ways. Dower suggested a few examples:

First, a citizen may seek to influence the policies of her own government *vis-à-vis* the good of others outside the state by seeking to influence government, such as writing to MPs [Members of Parliament] or seeking to influence the political party she joins. Second, people may join NGOs and thus either support or engage in actions seeking to influence governments, individually or collectively, for instance at conferences developing international law. In both cases they may be seeking to influence a nation-state's policy, but they are pursuing global remits.[27]

Miller's and Dower's focus rests on the possibility—or impossibility—of recognizing and enacting responsibilities and duties in global citizenship. However, equally important to consider is people's access to rights and privileges, with an emphasis on the attainment of these rights outside the borders of one's country of citizenship. On one side of this discourse stand those arguing that the existence of international human rights has made it possible for individuals to meaningfully participate in a country of immigration—for example, having civil and social rights—without becoming citizens.[28]

Others have insisted that the role of the nation-state remains critical today. Rogers Brubaker, in his groundbreaking work, *Citizenship and Nationhood in France and Germany,* highlighted the nation-state as the "architect and guarantor of a number of distinctively modern forms of closure" that continue to define an individual's rights.[29] Territorial closure, the control a nation-state exercises over entry into its territory, is one of the most important forms of closure, essentially determining who may or may not have the rights to participation. Domestic closure is another form, "excluding noncitizens, viewed as politically unreliable, from the suffrage, from military service, or from positions in public administration."[30] In the presence of such exclusion, the nation-state continues to be the sole entity able to provide full protection for individuals.

Christian Joppke has also directly critiqued proponents of postnational membership.[31] Referring to the United States, Joppke described U.S. citizenship as particularly amenable to granting a wide array of rights and privileges to noncitizens, with actual citizenship only conferring few rights not already enjoyed by individuals holding the immigrant designation of "permanent resident." Joppke traced the availability of these rights to the historical context of the country's development, rather than the system of international human rights, stating that "in a society cherishing markets over the state and the open border over bounded community, entry and residence have always been more meaningful than citizenship. Accordingly, the American Constitution and legal order make personhood and residence, rather than citizenship, protected categories."[32] In Joppke's view, then, the rights enjoyed by noncitizens in some, mainly Western, countries remain to a large extent attributable to national policies.

Citizenship has also been an important concern in higher education circles. When calling for the active citizenship role of colleges and universities, the emphasis most often falls on responsibilities and participation, on providing opportunities for disadvantaged populations, on enfranchising the disenfranchised, on promoting the public good.[33] Using Santos's terms,[34] this treatment of citizenship is reflective of the emancipatory aspects of pluriversity knowledge, where knowledge produced at an institution of higher education is applied with the purpose of promoting equality and fighting injustice.

Although the connection to the global nature of citizenship, as practiced by U.S. colleges and universities, is rarely discussed in the higher education literature,[35] it only takes a cursory glance at the diverse activities at UCLA (some of which are described at the beginning of this chapter) to notice the enormous relevance of the global in defining the role of citizenship in higher education. The Darfur Action Committee and UCLA's fight against the global spread of HIV and AIDS are clear manifestations of emancipatory knowledge production or active citizenship in the interest of creating a more equitable world. The relevance of the global becomes even clearer when discussing citizenship from the perspective of individuals who undertake graduate education in one country while being citizens in another. What is the reach of international graduate students' civic, professional, and political engagement?

International students' notions of citizenship are far from negligible given our present time of political instability, the growing role of the United States in global relations, and the challenges to international education following the tragic events of September 11, 2001. Coming into intense contact with the U.S. geopolitical and cultural context, while maintaining connections with their home countries, international students in the United States face the possibility of an expanded consciousness about important political, cultural, and economic issues, many of which cut across boundaries of nation-states. As such, they become well-positioned to develop a globally rooted civic mindedness, or a sense of responsibility linked to membership in an increasingly interconnected global community. And if students opt to actively engage in the enactment of this responsibility, the university itself may become the type of institution that Dower references as crucial in facilitating the enactment of moral obligations.[36]

Alternatively, educational opportunities in the United States may be viewed in a more instrumental fashion. Aihwa Ong argued that international students studying at U.S. colleges and universities focus more on "global acceptance based on amassing individual knowledge capital, rather than on sharing basic values (e.g., democracy, equality, pluralism) of democratic citizenship. In this instrumental approach, professional education is a means to a career trajectory that will take them through the upper reaches of global markets."[37] Ong thus identified international education as a space for the development of a form of "flexible citizenship," referring to the "cultural logics of capitalist accumulation, travel, and displacement that induce subjects to respond fluidly and opportunistically to changing political-economic conditions."[38] If one is to adopt Santos's terminology,[39] Ong's argument rings with the tone of mercantilistic knowledge application, whereby the skills and knowledge attained at an institution of higher education further individual advancement in the interest of wealth creation, with little concern for emancipation. An important concern explored in this study, therefore, relates to the tension between mercantilistic and emancipatory applications of knowledge by international graduate students in the United States.

However, although the application of knowledge is a key consideration in examining the citizenship views and experiences of international graduate students, restricting the study to knowledge application reveals only part of the story. In considering citizenship in any educational setting, it is necessary that the emphasis fall on both responsibilities and rights, accompanied by a discussion of the practice of those rights and responsibilities. After all, an individual's ability to recognize and act upon his or her responsibilities requires that a person be in possession of certain rights enabling responsible action. To illustrate this point with an example, U.S. undergraduates' work with disadvantaged schoolchildren is possible only if those students have the right to pursue their own education and have access to other basic rights that allow for the expression of civic duties.

When it comes to graduate education in a foreign land, students' rights become especially important to consider because of students' relocation outside the borders of their home countries for a prolonged period, leaving behind many of the immediate rights of citizenship that they enjoyed there. Using Brubaker's terminology, international graduate students, when moving to the United States, may come into contact with a number of forms of closure that prevent them from full participation in U.S. society.[40] The question then becomes whether in the presence of these forms of closure, international students have access to and enjoy the kinds of rights that enable them not only to live in U.S. society in a way that is acceptable to them but also to express and practice a range of responsibilities and duties. In other words, is emancipatory knowledge production among international graduate students made possible by a set of rights existing beyond the borders of their countries of origin, whether those rights are attributable to the internationalization of human rights, as proposed by Soysal or to the particularities of the policy climate of the United States as outlined by Joppke?[41]

What are, for example, the rights that make it possible for a foreign graduate student to engage in research that aims to promote the public good in a specific country, a set of countries, or even a transnational setting? Does access to graduate education in the United States bestow certain professional rights and privileges on international students that allow them to more fully contribute to a certain geographic sphere? And what are the possibilities for political participation among foreign graduate students who have chosen to undertake their graduate studies at UCLA? Questions such as these form the center of the discussion in this chapter.

INTERNATIONAL GRADUATE STUDENTS IN THE UNITED STATES: THE NATIONAL CONTEXT

In the 2008–9 academic year, 671,616 international students attended colleges and universities in the United States, representing an 8 percent increase from the previous year and a continuing rebound from significant drops in the number of international students immediately following the terrorist attacks of September 11, 2001. Close to 47 percent of these students were pursuing a graduate degree. India, China, and South Korea were the leading places of origin, followed by Canada and Japan. During the same academic year, California hosted the largest number of international students in the country, with an enrollment of 93,124, a number that approached 14 percent of the entire foreign student population of the United States. The University of Southern California and UCLA were among the top destinations for foreign students in the nation.[42] As the most recent evidence suggests, the number of international students on U.S. college and university campuses is heading upward. However, the rhetoric surrounding the role of the United States in hosting foreign students is best characterized as volatile, underscoring the vulnerability associated with spending time outside the confines of one's home country on student visas.

Reflecting this volatility, a recent *Open Doors* press release spoke of a highly supportive climate,[43] citing Under Secretary of State for Public Diplomacy and Public Affairs Judith A. McHale as stating:

The all-time high number of international students who studied here in the 2008/09 academic year testifies to the quality and diversity for which American higher education is known around the world. The Department of State actively promotes the benefits of an American education. Our large network of more than 400 EducationUSA advising centers plays a key role in matching international students with a U.S. academic institution that's just right for them. We strongly encourage international students to study in the United States, and are committed to helping them choose the American college or university that best meets their needs.[44]

Although this comment depicts the United States as providing an open, hospitable atmosphere, it must be remembered that just a few years earlier, the U.S. government instituted a requirement that colleges and universities "track" international scholars and students in the United States through SEVIS (Student and Exchange Visitor Information System). In addition to the many bugs that have plagued SEVIS,[45] the idea of institutions of higher learning participating in tracking international scholars and students presents an unwelcoming posture. This role of U.S. colleges and universities is especially troubling when one considers that international scholars and students are members of the very academic communities that must conduct a form of surveillance of them.

Fluctuations in the representation of international students are driven by a varied array of circumstances. There is no disputing, however, that international student applications and enrollments experienced decreases in the years immediately following the terrorist attacks of September 11, 2001. At the graduate level, for example, the Council of Graduate Schools reported that admission of foreign graduate students declined by 18 percent from 2003 to 2004,[46] and more than 90 percent of colleges and universities experienced a drop in applications from non-U.S. applicants for the same period.[47] The decline in foreign applications for graduate study was even more severe than the decline in admissions: Colleges and universities saw a 28 percent decrease for the academic year 2003–4 and a 5 percent drop for 2004–5.[48]

Changes in approaches to hosting international students in the United States can thus be traced to variations in public perceptions of this student population. The war on terrorism represents a major force in shifting the generally positive attitude that has traditionally characterized the presence of international students at U.S. institutions of higher education. Perhaps the most important argument, raised again and again in support of foreign students, refers to the significant financial contributions these students make to the economy and their host institutions. Although critical voices have also emerged, positing that the recruitment of international students for their monetary contributions amounts to treating them merely as cash cows,[49] mainstream arguments continue to underscore the positive financial benefits of foreign students. In fact, a recent *Open Doors* report proclaimed that the substantial contributions of foreign students to the national economy—$17.8 billion annually—are some of the most significant factors in support of the continual recruitment of students from around the world.[50]

The financial advantages of hosting international students have, in fact, been taken so much for granted that only a few critics have addressed potential flaws in the calculation of benefits. One such critic is George Borjas, who has argued that taxpayer subsidies for the education of foreign students to offset the costs of education not covered by tuition dollars are larger than the economic gains the country makes from the presence of these students.[51]

Although the actual extent of monetary gains or losses most likely requires more complex analysis, the existence of substantial financial contributions continues to dominate when it comes to discussions of foreign students. In fact, some have situated colleges' and universities' efforts to recruit international students as part of an academic capitalist knowledge/learning regime,[52] whereby students from other countries are viewed as key in higher education institutions' revenue-generating activities. As Jenny Lee, Gary Rhoades, and Alma Maldonado-Maldonado noted,

higher education institutions can be seen as pursuing international students as a new circuit of knowledge that promises to generate increased organizational revenues. They can also be seen to be developing the internal managerial capacity to undertake and coordinate the pursuit and service of international students, in the form of an infrastructure of personnel and offices designed to work with such students. These professionals build and expand organizational capacity in the realm of international activities, and become another internal driver to pursue international students.[53]

International student recruitment is thus powerfully linked to the financial well-being of institutions of higher education and the development of managerial offices and staff undertaking the coordination of international activities.

Other prominent arguments calling for the presence of international students on campuses have pointed to the cultural aspects of international educational exchange, referring to the benefits of exposing U.S.-born students to the different ways of life and thinking that students from foreign countries bring with them. International students in the United States are thus often purported to promote cultural diversity and, through their interactions with U.S.-born students, to thereby contribute to intercultural understanding and global relations. [54] Emphasizing the importance of higher education some three decades ago, a United Nations Educational, Scientific, and Cultural Organization (UNESCO) report stressed, "In order to develop the study and practice of international co-operation, post-secondary educational establishments should systematically take advantage of the forms of international action inherent in their role, such as visits from foreign professors and students and professional co-operation between professors and research teams in different countries."[55] A more recent report from NAFSA: Association of International Educators echoed the concern for increased cross-cultural understanding: "The effective management of global unrest in the twenty-first century will require more, not less, ability on the part of Americans to understand the world in terms other than their own."[56]

Obviously, U.S. undergraduates, graduate students, and scholars studying and working abroad also are important in promoting cross-cultural understanding and international relations. Study abroad programs provide a critical tool for college students to come into contact with values and practices different from those they are accustomed to in their home country. Arguing for "a national effort to promote study abroad" among undergraduates, a report from NAFSA: Association of International Educators stated, "The challenges of the new millennium are unquestionably global in nature. This reality imposes a new and urgent demand on Americans, one this country has been all too quick to ignore: international knowledge and skills are imperative for the future security and competitiveness of the United States."[57] Related to this point, Nadine Dolby suggested that study abroad experiences may help U.S. students develop a more critical understanding of their identities as "Americans" and that such understandings are key to "future practices of citizenship."[58] Given these arguments concerning the relevance of citizenship in international educational exchange, we now turn to a discussion of international graduate students' citizenship views and experiences at UCLA.

BRAZILIAN, CHINESE, AND ITALIAN GRADUATE STUDENTS AT UCLA

In studying the citizenship experiences of international graduate students, it is important to recognize points of both convergence and differentiation. In the case of UCLA, as the host institution, the most important unifying force is presented by the central geopolitical place occupied by the United States and Los Angeles in the world order. One important point of similarity thus relates to the study abroad experience taking place in a wealthy and powerful country and, within that country, in one of the most globalized urban centers of the world. Also essential to note is the experience of being foreign-born in Los Angeles, presenting a form of identity that paradoxically is both common and unusual, and fraught with personal and professional opportunities and challenges. Equally important to consider is the fact that international graduate students arrive in the United States with the goal of engaging in the highest levels of education, planning to obtain master's or Ph.D. degrees. These educational aspirations place foreign graduate students at the highest echelons of professional training, with many of them having the potential to emerge as leaders in their fields and in the societies where they settle upon graduation. Alongside these similarities, however, points of differentiation are also crucial to consider, related most significantly to students' home countries. It is immediately apparent that Brazil, China, and Italy present vastly different environments related to the historical, political, economic, and cultural evolution of the three countries. These diverse country-specific backgrounds, no doubt, have an enormous impact on students' experiences of living and studying in the United States.

The sample of international graduate students was limited to the People's Republic of China, Italy, and Brazil for two reasons. First, one goal was to select students from diverse world regions—in this case, Asia, Europe, South/ Central America (graduate students from Africa, the Middle East, and the South Pacific region are few in number at UCLA). Second, the selection of students from countries that were well represented at UCLA assured a greater degree of anonymity to individual research participants. The focus on three specific sending countries allowed for a more in-depth examination of how national contexts shape citizens' views and experiences both within and outside their home countries.

In Brazil, the country's relatively recent emergence from a military dictatorship and current efforts at economic liberalization, political democratization, and both regional and global integration are some of the key aspects of the sending country's perspective. Economic globalization has had an immense impact on Brazil, and although instability, poverty, violence, and inequality remain persistent challenges, in recent years, economic growth has been evident.[59] With an annual average growth rate of around 5 percent, the Brazilian economy has been identified as a "major emerging economy." As noted by Reuters in 2008, "Brazil is finally punching its weight with a booming economy and stronger global leadership but it remains burdened by a bloated state and daunting social problems."[60] Among 177 countries, Brazil's per capita Gross Domestic Product (GDP) ranked sixty-seventh in 2005, and the Human Development Index (HDI)—encompassing such categories as living a long and healthy life, being educated, and having a decent standard of living—placed the country at seventy.[61]

Italian students arrive in the United States from a very different background. As an advanced capitalist economy with a population of around fifty-eight million, Italy is among the top twenty-five countries in the world in terms of per capita GDP (number twenty-one) and HDI (number twenty).[62] Membership in the European Union (EU) contributed to the massive internationalization of Italy's economy. As Grant Amyot noted, "The internationalization of the economy has strengthened the domestic forces that favour further internationalization and the removal of barriers that restrict it—forces such as multinational companies, exporters, and financial institutions with international interests."[63] Italian identity is strongly shaped by the country's membership in the EU, a supranational alliance of nation-states, signifying the institution of European citizenship and close economic and political integration. Italians in general hold positive attitudes toward Europe (according to the Eurobarometer survey, 67 percent expressed positive attitudes, while only 3 percent noted negative and 30 percent reported ambivalent attitudes). In terms of negotiating Italian and European identity, 69 percent of the population indicated that the two forms of identity were compatible, 26 percent identified exclusively as Italian, and just 5 percent noted that European was their only form of identity.[64]

The People's Republic of China presents yet another perspective, marked by major societal, political, and economic transitions in recent years. Driven by the Chinese Communist Party's Open Door policy, the last quarter of the twentieth century saw the beginnings of a new China, characterized most significantly by integration into the global economy. In one key outcome of this ongoing process, China joined the World Trade Organization in 2001, leaving many to fear the potential of Chinese economic domination, given the world's largest population and enormous GDP.[65] In essence, China fully recognized the global marketplace and the role of capitalist systems in shaping international trade. Consequently, Chinese social, political, and economic life today is marked by a paradoxical condition: The nation and its leaders seek to retain some semblance of a socialist tradition, accompanied by strong Chinese nationalism, while complying with the expectations of a global marketplace framed by capitalism of the neoliberal variety. Chinese officials' references to developing a "socialist market economy" represent an attempt to capture the contemporary complexities of a society in transition.

These considerations of similarities and differences in the experiences of Brazilian, Chinese, and Italian graduate students lend a helping hand in understanding the ways in which international students' notions of citizenship are constructed at the intersection of the cultural, economic, and political contexts of the United States and their home countries and regions. At the beginning of the twenty-first century, however, the primary underlying theme in both receiving and sending country contexts relates to the processes of globalization, commonly defined as "the intensification of worldwide social relations which link distant localities in such a way that local happenings are shaped by events occurring many miles away and vice versa."[66] A framework of globalization is also key in understanding the functioning of the contemporary university,[67] a major source of influence in the lives of international graduate students. Our explorations of the experiences of Brazilian, Chinese, and Italian graduate students at UCLA are thus grounded in a framework of globalization, with specific emphasis on implications for citizenship in a global context. The research questions addressed in this study are: (1) In what ways (if at all) do the experiences of international graduate students studying in the United States challenge and strengthen their notions of citizenship? (2) In what ways do international graduate students participate in the production and application of knowledge, and what are the implications of such knowledge production and application from the perspective of citizenship? (3) How (if at all) does graduate study in the United States contribute to more globalized notions of citizenship?

CITIZENSHIP: CONCEPTIONS AND LOCALES

A sense of belonging and emotional attachment to a locale or a set of locales—seeing oneself as Brazilian, Chinese, Italian, Latin American, Asian, European, or a person who "can choose to live in whatever country more or less freely"—was a central determinant of students' notions of citizenship.[68] In the words of Alessandra,[69] an Italian student in applied linguistics: "I would say that citizenship is a contract that you set within the society. It will give you a sense of belonging, a sense that you are part of an entity that you want to call society, community, nation . . . but you have also to pay homage to this contract and you have some duties to meet and respect and carry out."

Moreover, especially Brazilian and Chinese students described reconnecting with their national identities through their graduate experiences in the United States. Several Chinese students, across a variety of fields, described the duty they felt in defending China against criticism. As Ting, a student in social work, conceded: "There is a very strong sense from the government that they want to instill the idea of nationalism in you, that you have to be very proud of your country. . . . I think in my generation, we started to question this a lot. . . . But I think it's a common psychology . . . that in a foreign environment, like here in the United States, I would feel particularly defensive about my national origin." Gilberto, a Brazilian student in economics, noted: "To be a Brazilian citizen today, for me, maybe is more important than before. Because when you are far away from your country, you start to pay more attention to some aspects, you start to be proud of some aspects, and then you feel more responsible for some things. It's as if you have more obligations."

Perhaps most importantly, the majority of students' conceptions of the locales they occupied reached beyond their respective home countries. The interviews revealed a process of decentering, where the local and the national were by no means the sole focus of citizenship. Rather, students' views were broadened to encompass a larger whole that included the local or national context, to which were added—to differing extents—a sense of regional attachment, an increased identification with the United States, or a strengthened understanding of citizenship in a global sphere.

The expression of a strong regional identity was evident in the case of Fabio, a Brazilian student in political science, who noted that since leaving Brazil, he has been "feeling more Latin American than before." Natalia, an Italian film student, discussed an alternative perspective, with a focus on her attachment to the society that she happened to inhabit at a particular time:

I've been in an in-between state. I haven't been a citizen of the United States, but I also feel like I haven't really been responsible toward my country. So I think I live with a certain sense of guilt and at the same time, I have a pretty clear idea of what it means for me to be a citizen, but it's not necessarily about being an Italian citizen. It's more about a sense of responsibility toward the society we live in, whatever the society is.

Gemma, an Italian linguistics student, also characterized her conception of citizenship as indeterminate: "I feel like in a way I'm not sure anymore who should take care of my rights and I'm not sure anymore where I should put my effort in order to be sure that I will do my part." Gemma also drew upon her experiences in the United States to explain her shifting views of citizenship: "So you feel like you're sort of losing this part of your attachment to issues and problems in Italy. . . . I'm not transferring my responsibility to here [the United States]. My ideal would be an interest in the more general [global] picture."

Alessandra also put strong emphasis on the global elements of citizenship, explaining that "the idea of citizenship is more universal in the sense . . . [of] being a citizen of the world. But it is in fact, to me, a sense of really trying to understand what human beings have in common and could rely upon in order to have peaceful and tolerant relationships throughout the world." Huiling, a Chinese student in environmental science, related her own conceptions of the importance of being a global citizen: "I'm an individual in the world and the things that I do, I need to do them for the good of the world, you know, the benefit of the world. . . . I think it's very important because anything that does harm to the world will harm the next generations."

Not all students shared Alessandra's and Huiling's optimism about the possibility of a form of citizenship that is able to connect people from around the world. Gian Marco, an Italian student in materials science, for example, pointed to the absence of strong cultural links among nations, links that he thought were indispensable in making globally relevant citizenship possible. In explaining his point, Gian Marco referred to the Italian experience: "When they unified Italy, a politician said, 'We have made Italy, now we have to make Italians.' And Italy is a small country. I can tell you, people in the North don't like to deal with people in the South, not 100 percent, but many people. We don't have the same culture, the same tradition, so you cannot make [unity] happen, you know."

Expanding this argument beyond the borders of Italy, Gian Marco thought that the idea of global citizenship is even more far-fetched. He related, "We need to understand that there is diversity in the world and we live with this diversity. But don't push for something like, 'we're all united!' We don't come from the same place. We have differences. And it doesn't mean we need to go to war, but we just need to respect each other, but also we don't have to push the forced union."

As reflected in a number of the preceding quotations, the development of international students' conceptions of citizenship is often a hard-fought, evolving process at the intersection of national, regional, and global attachments. To be sure, all of the students lived their lives intensely connected to U.S. culture and society in their everyday interactions at UCLA, in Los Angeles, and beyond. At the same time, many emphasized the importance of maintaining strong ties with their home countries, reflected in weekly, sometimes daily, phone conversations with their families, following news reports from their home countries on the Internet, visiting home during vacations, keeping in touch with undergraduate professors and other professional contacts, and often selecting friendship groups based on national or regional origins, a preference that was especially prominent among Brazilian and Chinese students. It should thus be no surprise that students' ongoing experiences with their home countries and the United States were at a constant interplay in the further development of their notions of citizenship.

Although some students, for example, Natalia and Gemma, were conflicted about what citizenship meant to them, others gave a more secure impression in our conversations. Gilberto, the student who related his growing attachment to Brazil, exemplified this latter stance:

It's good to learn another culture, it's good to learn another language, it's good to know the way different people live. But at the same time, I think it's important to preserve your own view and own identity. Maybe sometimes it's hard to reconcile. In a practical situation, maybe it's hard to reconcile these two sides, but I think it's possible to manage them. It's possible to have your own identity and at the same time, to be a global citizen.

What is clear from these views is that ideas of what it means to be a citizen as an international graduate student studying in the United States were often pondered by the Brazilian, Chinese, and Italian students. Living as long-term, nonimmigrant sojourners in a foreign land, in the midst of one of the most globalized, diverse urban centers in the world undoubtedly precipitated a reevaluation of what citizenship entails and of what geographic spheres should be the focus of one's rights, obligations, and actions as citizens.

In what ways did the international graduate students conceive of their rights and responsibilities? In discussing this question, we place special emphasis on the social/cultural, political/civic, and economic/occupational dimensions of citizenship outlined in Chapter 1. When exploring the students' citizenship views and experiences, we further delineate the ways in which the three dimensions were present in terms of rights and responsibilities, and the enactment of those rights and responsibilities. The discussion reflects the ways in which the students discussed citizenship both within and across national borders, consisting primarily of the responsibilities they held in particular geographic contexts and the rights—or lack thereof—that supported or hindered the various aspects of their lives in the United States.

In setting the context to the discussion of the social/cultural, political/civic, and economic/occupational aspects of international students' citizenship experiences, it is important to highlight students' perceptions of their right to cross-national movement. Given the overwhelming significance of the ability to spend extended amounts of time in the United States for purposes of undertaking graduate education, the right to international movement took center stage in the students' discussions. The fundamental focus on this right was not surprising. After all, engagement in graduate education abroad is the key pathway to knowledge production and application in the United States. The ability to exercise the right to take up temporary residence as graduate students outside the borders of their home countries thus holds significant implications for all dimensions of citizenship in the context of international graduate education.

Many students spoke of a strong concern about the difficulties of obtaining a visa and passing through immigration when entering the United States, discussed in the context of the visa restrictions following the events of September 11, 2001. Binglong, a Chinese student in business, explained: "I don't know why the U.S. government is so excluding to foreigners. It just hurts its image and I'm pretty disgusted with this policy." Juliana, a Brazilian student in anthropology, related her recent experiences of returning to the United States:

And last time I came, I was in Mexico, before I went to Brazil, I went to Mexico, and then to Cuba for two weeks, and then when I came back, I almost didn't get in because the immigration officer said: "What is the purpose of your entering the U.S.?" I was going to get in to leave for Brazil the following day. I had an F1 visa. And I said, "Well, I'm here to sleep here tonight . . ." "No, you cannot get in with a student visa for other purposes, but to study. So if you're not studying, that constitutes fraud against the government."

Many of the students perceived the process of obtaining and maintaining a student visa in the United States as arduous, creating unnecessary fear in them and their family members, sometimes even altering their views of the country. Sandro, a Brazilian MBA student, spoke of the strong perceptions he and his wife had about coming to the United States, even before embarking on their journey:

What you do to get a visa and what kinds of things you pass through when you arrive at the airport. . . . You have people inspecting your baggage, people asking all sorts of questions. My wife, before coming here, was completely scared of this whole process. She was really scared that she would be treated badly. It made things more difficult and it somehow influences the way you think about the country and how the country treats foreigners.

Reflecting this caution and fear, even some of the students who never experienced problems in visa applications or while crossing the border were nervous about the idea of leaving and reentering the United States. The news stories and personal narratives of friends and relatives were enough to make them especially sensitive to what might happen to them in similar situations. As a Chinese student related: "I haven't been home in the past three years. It's because Chinese people always have visa problems. It's difficult to get a visa, so I'm afraid that if I go home, I won't be able to come back."

Although most students expressed at least some frustration over their limited rights in connection with studying and living in the United States in the post-9/11 climate, it is important to note that an Italian participant accepted the visa restrictions as necessary to make the country safer: "The government is trying to protect the country because before they let everybody in relatively easily and, after 9/11, they want that to not happen anymore and they put in more restrictions. So that makes my life more difficult because, unfortunately, I undergo those restrictions. If it's right or wrong, I don't know. I mean, I don't argue much about it just because there is not much to argue." Three others noted that despite the problems they experienced, being a foreigner did not make their lives in the United States too much more difficult than if they were citizens.

It is important to underscore that the students in this study were able to obtain student visas and those who visited their home countries for vacations were permitted to return to the United States. They did not experience the kind of territorial closure that, in Brubaker's terms,[70] would have prohibited their efforts to undertake or continue their graduate studies in the United States. However, the existence of negative experiences and fears highlight territorial closure as a perceived threat by the majority of the students, especially those arriving from Brazil and China. Against this backdrop grounded in the right to cross-national movement, the ensuing two sections discuss the social/cultural, political/civic, and economic/occupational dimensions of international students' citizenship experiences in terms of rights and then responsibilities.

RIGHTS

Economic/Occupational Opportunities and Rights. To put the discussion of economic/occupational rights in the larger context of individuals' access to education and professional opportunities,[71] it is useful to first examine the sources of funding that helped along the graduate students' paths to UCLA. In the case of graduate education abroad, questions of finances become especially important and complicated given the costs associated with the generally higher prices charged by U.S. colleges and universities to foreign students, the potential for higher living expenses than in the country of origin, and even the costs of traveling between home and the United States. The difference between students paying for their own education and those being supported by an outside entity can be significant, delineating a distinction between the truly financially privileged who can afford to study abroad using their own resources and those who are taking advantage of external support structures. Considering the funding situation of the Brazilian, Chinese, and Italian students is thus key in understanding their attitudes about the educational opportunities available to them at UCLA.

The majority of students gained access to graduate education in the United States through funding by sources other than their own. These sources of financial assistance included those from UCLA in the form of fellowships, research assistantships, and teaching assistantships and sponsorship from students' universities and employers in their home countries. In some cases, Brazilian students received funding from the Brazilian government. Others noted that they had to rely on a combination of funding from UCLA and their own resources to support their studies. Only two students indicated that they covered the full amount of their expenses on their own.

Despite the preponderance of outside sources of funding for their graduate studies, for some students, living and studying in the United States presented difficulties mainly in the realms of fellowships and employment, areas that relate to the economic/occupational rights of international students. One student explained that summer job opportunities were especially hard to find for international students: "So many potentials are open for Americans, but not for you." Juliana stated: "I am constantly reminded that I'm not a citizen, that I don't belong. You know, I'm a foreigner; things are made harder for me. I don't have access to a lot of things." Another Brazilian student noted that out of a large pool of scholarships available at the graduate level, only a portion is open for internationals. An Italian student complained about his inability to work over twenty hours per week as an international student, explaining that he would be interested in assuming job responsibilities similar to those of U.S. citizens.

Several students pointed to their perceptions of unequal rights in long-term employment opportunities as well. Two students in particular, both of whom were strongly contemplating staying in the United States to work after graduating with their Ph.D.s, lamented that they found fewer employment options for themselves because of their temporary visa status. Carla, a Brazilian economics student, who received significant funding for her studies from the Brazilian government, was applying for a variety of positions in both the United States and Brazil, "just to see what happens." Importantly, the governmental fellowship held that Carla return to Brazil upon graduation, a restriction that, if violated, would require her to pay back the amount of the grant. The decision to explore the U.S. labor market, then, was an undertaking for Carla with considerable financial consequences. Even so, she ventured ahead, only to find "several restrictions that companies impose when it comes to hiring non-Americans, non-U.S. citizens." Enzo, an Italian student, expressed similar sentiments with regard to his plan to seek employment in the United States with his soon-to-be-earned Ph.D. in chemistry. Interestingly, Enzo perceived his difficulties as closely related to the heightened security measures following the terrorist attacks of September 11, 2001. He was particularly discouraged when he found that, in Los Angeles, job opportunities in his field were most often available in the aerospace industry and defense, areas that emphasized hiring U.S. citizens. Still a few months away from actively seeking a position, Enzo was unsure of how this might affect his chances of finding a job and staying in the United States with his long-time partner, who was also living in Los Angeles.

Beyond the issues of cross-national movement and job opportunities upon graduation, international student rights and privileges were the subject of discussions in a variety of other contexts. Perhaps most importantly, the students recognized and strongly appreciated the opportunities they received by being members of the academic community represented by UCLA and their fields, thereby receiving economic/occupational rights. Many of these opportunities would not have been available to them had they remained in their home countries. What the students gained access to by way of this membership was knowledge production at a "world-class university," representing the attainment and practice of a right to some of the highest levels of schooling obtainable in the worldwide educational system.

The majority of the Brazilian, Chinese, and Italian graduate students spoke of their studies at UCLA as a privilege and an immense opportunity to gain an invaluable set of knowledge and skills. Even Carla and Enzo, the students who expressed concern regarding their chances of finding a job in the United States, realized that their UCLA graduate degrees would present them with a variety of privileges in their professional endeavors. These privileges were reflected in access to equipment and facilities, state-of-the-art research, leading professors in students' fields, a comprehensive knowledge base, and at times an environment of graduate student life perceived to be especially conducive to learning about their fields. Perhaps most significantly, all these aspects of graduate training at UCLA came together as representations of prestige that would contribute to the students' success in their professional endeavors. A student from China put it succinctly: "I and many other Chinese students think that we can go abroad and get covered by the 'golden surface.' It means that you are worth much more money and you will have better career opportunities in the future."

The students' explanations of the invaluable experiences and resources transferred to them by way of obtaining a U.S. graduate degree offered remarkable agreement, as exemplified in the following quotations:

It is common knowledge that if you come to the universities in the U.S., you will be exposed to cutting-edge research and you will be able to learn the most recent techniques. Carla

My main goal is to be a professor, a college professor. We don't have good Ph.D. programs in Brazil. The best are here. So I finished my Master's degree there and I decided to come here. I applied and they accepted me. Because the best schools are here and I like the methods they use here.

João, Brazilian student in economics

Advanced technology is the most important factor that attracted me here. Because here they have world-class professionals, professors are world-class scientists and they are at the front of the scientific field. Huiling

As a senior or even junior, I began to read literature and also studied textbooks and most of them are written in English. And most of the research, most of the advanced research is done here in the United States, you know. If you read a paper in a journal, it is mostly written and developed by some American university. So it was very natural for me to pursue graduate study at a better school in that sense.

Liang, Chinese student in electrical engineering

Inherent in students' accounts of the opportunities associated with the pursuit of a U.S. graduate degree was a comparison between the graduate educational systems of their home countries and those of the United States. Not all students elaborated on this comparison, and some acknowledged the importance of a number of other factors influencing their decision to come to UCLA, including their desire for intercultural explorations or the impact of information networks maintained with both family and friends.[72] One student had even obtained a Ph.D. at a university in her native Italy, and others simply saw their educational experiences in the United States as better fitting their future plans. Natalia, for example, noted that coming to the United States allowed her to focus more on the practical aspects of filmmaking as opposed to the more theoretical emphasis of Italian film schools. However, some of the student participants were quite open about their perceptions of the superior nature of a UCLA graduate degree, with negative notions of graduate training at home.

Two students, one in economics and one in business, also commented on the importance of their graduate education taking place in the highly international environments present in their academic departments at UCLA. Interestingly, as explained by the students, this international climate was created by the student population, since foreign students made up around 70 percent of the economics department and approximately 30 percent of the business school. The student in economics, who was engaged in a research project with an international scope, saw immense academic opportunity in his ability to gain information from his classmates about data specific to a variety of countries. And the MBA student's decision to pursue his degree at UCLA was strongly influenced by his prospects of interacting with students from a diversity of national backgrounds: "Just because in Brazil, the [MBA] program has mostly Brazilian students and [at UCLA] we have students from totally different countries. So just knowing these people and having contact with different business practices is valuable. . . . Because you are used to seeing business all in one way and when you're exposed to different ways of doing business, sometimes you learn things that you can apply to your own environment."

Although all students—by virtue of their decision to attend graduate school in the United States—recognized the opportunities offered by their choice, two Brazilian economics students faced an interesting dilemma regarding the perception of a U.S. doctoral degree in Brazil. Carla and Fabio related similar accounts of the sometimes unfavorable perception of going to the United States for graduate education. They both spoke of a debate in the field of economics, with one side in favor of training abroad and the other side opposing it as an education that leads to knowledge and skills that are irrelevant for understanding the functioning of the Brazilian economy. As to what reasons fueled the opposition, Carla noted: "I think that there is an objective part of it that is true. . . . The topics that people are interested in here are different than the research topics that Brazilian students have in mind. There's a potential for a mismatch. But I also think that part of this criticism is ideological and has to do with nationalism in the sense that we don't need to learn from these guys what we should do in our country." Both Carla and Fabio, however, were mentored by supporters of foreign graduate degrees. Fabio's professor, for example, held a U.S. Ph.D. and encouraged Fabio to study abroad as a way to fulfill his own intention to "create cohorts of people who can actually speak the same language." The professor's support was thus partly rooted in his own situation, wanting to expand the circle of economists who shared his educational background.

International graduate student rights in the economic/occupational dimension of citizenship were thus presented as a set of challenges and opportunities. In discussing challenges, the students indicated areas where they felt their rights were curtailed, especially with regard to their eligibility to various types of employment and fellowships. The students, however, also recognized and appreciated the opportunities made available to them through their graduate studies at UCLA. Opportunities and challenges were also at the center of students' discussions of their perceptions of the social/cultural rights they possessed in the United States.

Social/Cultural Rights. The students' perceptions of social and cultural rights were best reflected in their ability to practice home country traditions in the United States and their various degrees of participation in U.S. society. Many, for example, spoke of their ability to maintain and practice their home country traditions and habits:

Everyone in the department laughs because I'm so used to taking a siesta. . . . I definitely try to conserve some of my Italian culture and yes, I still have all the Italian clichés and how I dress. But something more in-depth . . . I think the most important thing besides food is trying to maintain close relationships with people. I think that's the most important part of my culture that I try to keep here and not lose.

Gemma

I think 80 percent of students go to Chinatown every week because we can buy authentic Chinese food and it's cheaper. And in Chinatown, everybody speaks Chinese, so you don't really need to know English to survive. The people there all speak Chinese and being there is like being in China.

Ning, Chinese student in information studies

We speak Portuguese, we speak our language at home and with our friends the few times that we go out with them. So we speak Portuguese. We decorate our home in more or less the Brazilian way, the way we set up our furniture. And we are more or less informal in personal relationships.

Luis, Brazilian student in chemistry

Los Angeles was a tremendous resource for the students in their sojourns in the United States, providing access to a variety of cultural practices and, perhaps most importantly, a level of international diversity that accommodated the needs and interests of students from all three countries. The relative ease that they encountered in finding country-specific products, foods, and events, however, did not mean that the transition process was without problems for everyone. Some spoke of a longing for their countries of origin as explained, for example, by a Brazilian student: "Sometimes I just miss Portuguese, Brazilian traditions. I mean, I just miss being home." Nevertheless, the students showed flexibility in making a comfortable life for themselves in the United States, facilitated by technology, the Internet, and the diverse communities of both UCLA and Los Angeles. This ease was perhaps best reflected in Juliana's comments: "A guy I met said to me: 'Wow, you're so Brazilian. You can just go abroad and bring Brazil with you.' I feel that way.

I feel like I carry Brazil with me wherever I go, but it's my own Brazil, my own version of it."

The students spoke considerably less of their participation in U.S. culture and social groups. And although many—although not all—opted to maintain friendship groups with people from their own national or regional origins, it was not clear from the interviews whether their choice to do so was a result of a mere personal preference or the difficulty they might have experienced in reaching out to U.S. citizens. A combination of these factors was reflected in comments offered by Huiling, who noted: "It's hard for a foreigner here to get involved in the local society. I mean, I have American friends, but all my very close friends are Chinese. This is because you can talk so freely with those friends and you have similar cultural backgrounds that you talk about, you all understand." A clear variety also existed in the social and cultural choices of students from the three nationalities: Italians indicated the highest propensity to actively participate in U.S. society, followed by Brazilians, with Chinese students noting the least amount of interactions.

Enzo, for example, had developed very strong ties to the United States, even noting, "It just seems to me that if you are here, you might as well associate yourself with the people who are here and the people who can teach you more about this place, i.e., Americans. When people have asked me about this in the past, I have said, 'Well, if I wanted to hang out with Italians, I would have stayed at home.'" On the other end of the spectrum, Ning's friendship groups were mostly limited to people from China. She and her husband were even members of various Web-based Chinese organizations designed to facilitate the lives of Chinese students and scholars in the United States.

An additional area for consideration in terms of cultural and social rights relates to the opportunities for intercultural interactions afforded by graduate education abroad. Many of the students mentioned these interactions as some of the foremost advantages of their experiences at UCLA, accompanying advantages they attained in the professional realm. Having the opportunity to live in a multicultural and international environment in itself proved to be a valuable learning experience for many of the students. Luis, a student from Brazil, was particularly forthcoming about the social/cultural benefits he gained from his experience at UCLA: "I got to know American culture from the inside and some habits, some festivities and the way it goes here. So it was personally a good experience, just in terms of personal growth, to personally know the culture and to know the people and the place. I also got to know people from different countries, so I liked meeting people from Arab countries and from Israel, from South America and Latin America and Europe and so on."

Students' rights in the social/cultural dimension of citizenship were thus centered on both the maintenance of home country culture and engagement in multiculturalism, with particular emphasis on the cultural contexts provided by UCLA and the global urban center of Los Angeles. Students' personal backgrounds, preferences, and national origins were some of the most important characteristics determining the role of both the home culture and the multicultural environment in their daily lives. These characteristics were also highly relevant in discussions of the political/civic spheres of citizenship.

Political/Civic Rights. Participation in the U.S. political process was not a significant issue among the students, reflected either in their lack of attention to the topic and/or acceptance of their status as individuals without related rights. This, however, did not point to a lack of carefully formed opinions about political life in the United States. Carla, for example, spoke of her feelings of being a "neutral observer," despite her disagreement with U.S. governmental policies. However, having spent four years abroad had not altered the strength of her interest in Brazilian politics, noting that "there's this big part of my life and a big part of the things that I'm interested in, for example politics, where I'm totally and completely connected and linked to Brazil." Reflecting this dedication to politics in her home country, Carla registered to vote in the Brazilian election through the consulate in Los Angeles.

Although none of the Italian students indicated that they had made arrangements to be able to exercise their voting rights in Italy's national election from the United States, several expressed disappointment at the difficulty of doing so. Natalia, for example, related that she ran into several obstacles in trying to exercise her right to vote from abroad, causing her considerable frustration: "I feel like I've lost part of my political identity simply because I haven't been able to vote [in Italy], and yet here there's only so much I can do in terms of expressing my own views because I can't vote in the United States and . . . I mean, I've been participating at forums, like Internet forums about political decisions, but there's a very limited amount of what I can do." Her inability to exercise her identity as a political citizen, then, did not prevent Natalia from expressing her views through other political channels, although undoubtedly these channels did not fully meet Natalia's expectations for political action.

Political rights were also relevant in our discussions with Chinese students, although with a flavor that was not present in interviews with students from the other two nationalities. Specifically, two participants compared the political systems of China and the United States, particularly emphasizing their views of democracy in the latter country. Ting, for example, who had an especially favorable opinion of the U.S. political system, explained: "The way that [Americans] know they can make a difference, an individual can make a difference, because in China you don't make a difference. You don't really have the power to vote someone out or someone in. Here, you have real power in the individual and I'm surprised . . . like sometimes you are only deciding one vote, it doesn't really count. But for them . . . I have my own right and I need to participate and the people will get in line waiting to vote."

Living in the United States and studying at UCLA thus presented the Brazilian, Chinese, and Italian graduate students with significant opportunities in the form of rights they gained to an educational experience that was not available in a similar form in their home countries. Their access to state-of-the-art teaching and research facilities and equipment, their cooperation with professors at the front of their fields, and their interactions with diverse, knowledgeable graduate student peers formed the bulk of the benefits they received from their graduate studies at UCLA. The students were also participants in a global, intercultural, and technologically advanced environment that allowed them to learn about and interact with other cultures while, at the same time, maintaining aspects of their own cultural heritage that facilitated their stay in the United States.

On the flip side of the coin, graduate education abroad also presented the students with a number of challenges, where they saw their rights curtailed in comparison to the privileges they had grown accustomed to in their home countries and regions. Strict and sometimes uncomfortable rules about cross-national movement, limited rights to fellowships and work opportunities, and constrained participation in the political sphere were some of the most salient areas highlighted by the students as significant challenges. Above all, these positive and negative experiences contributed to expanding the students' knowledge base that gave rise to or supported certain responsibilities in the social/cultural, economic/occupational, and political/civic realms. The following sections are thus devoted to the ways in which the students thought of and applied the knowledge they gained through their graduate studies and their societal experiences as international graduate students living and studying in the United States.

RESPONSIBILITIES

Economic/Occupational Responsibilities. In speaking of their economic and occupational contributions, based on the knowledge gained from their graduate studies at UCLA, the majority of the students made clear references to the geographic areas where they hoped their professional activities would have an impact. Some discussed their continued duties toward their home countries and regions, while others maintained hopes for a broader geographic reach, mainly in the transnational/global sphere. Many of the students in the latter category noted the responsibilities stemming from the training they received in graduate school, emphasizing a globalized economic dimension of citizenship. Using Santos's terminology, these student comments were important indications of the global reach of pluriversity knowledge, with significant implications for the societal contextualization of knowledge production and application. In the realm of research, Enzo, an Italian student in chemistry, explained: "Another contribution to the global community . . . I think of my work as being that. The scientific advances that come out of my publications are just a small, little piece in a huge sea of knowledge, but you know, it's still something that I did and nobody else did and may turn out to be very important. Everybody needs to try in order for that one key piece of technological advancement to benefit millions of people." Or in the words of Natalia: "I don't know if my goal is to cause change in the world, but I think that what I'm trying to do is based on my wanting to impact the world and to leave a trace."

Two students, one from Brazil and one from China, spoke of their occupational or professional responsibilities as intertwined with their civic duties, connecting both to the global sphere. Luis's academic specialization concerned the storage and generation of energy. In his professional life, his goals included teaching people to do responsible research and making scientific contributions to energy generation or alternative fuels. When it came to his civic responsibilities, the conservation of resources remained in the foreground: "I'm almost sick in terms of trying to print everything double-sided. I would find myself trying to make double-sided copies of printouts and I think we all have the duty of saving water, saving fuel, saving non-renewable resources."

Huiling, from China, referred to her field of environmental science in explaining the reasons driving her research and civic actions: "In my professional field, I want to do good to people, to our next generations. I want to use my knowledge to control and improve air quality and prevent people from exposure to toxics." Underscoring the importance of being a world citizen, Huiling went on to explain: "You have to think of the world as your family. It's like you won't do things bad to your family members and now your family members are all the people in the world and then you should think carefully before you do some things."

Undoubtedly, Enzo, Natalia, Luis, and Huiling might have arrived at globally minded conceptions of their professional responsibilities had they remained in their home countries to obtain their graduate degrees. It is also likely that they arrived at UCLA with strong preconceptions of their professional roles in the world. However, the students clearly linked their professional goals and activities to their learning experiences in the United States through better access to facilities, cutting-edge research, learning opportunities, and an international environment of scholarship. As Enzo explained: "Living abroad and having the opportunity to see things from a different viewpoint allows you to come into contact with people from a different culture and a whole new set of priorities, ways of doing things, organizing their time."

A number of students saw international graduate education as a site where they acquired knowledge, skills, and resources to take back to their home countries. In these instances, the context of students' engagement in pluriversity knowledge production was linked to the geographic sphere of the United States, where they acquired knowledge, and to students' home countries, where they hoped to apply the fruits of their knowledge acquisition. In the words of Gilberto: "I love the country. I love the people. I love Brazil. Actually, I came here because maybe I would be helpful to my people, to help them in things like economic problems. . . . I'm not here only with a personal goal in my mind, but also I have this idea to be helpful to my country." Or as Juliana explained: "I came to the U.S. to sort of accomplish projects that I had thought about and developed in Brazil and that I couldn't do there. . . . It's almost like being here is a means to achieve the ends that I had already foreseen before." Jia, a Chinese student in epidemiology, noted: "In my professional work, because I'm Chinese, I pay more attention to the Chinese population." For these students, although the ultimate goal of knowledge application was oriented to their home countries (a local sphere of existence from their perspective), their knowledge and skills were globally informed, based on their education in the United States.

Yet other students emphasized their aspirations to engage in professional activities that embrace the geographic region of the world where their home countries were situated. This was especially prominent among Brazilian students. Although Sandro recognized the unfair nature of income distribution in Brazil, he noted that it is likely that his professional endeavors will reach beyond Brazil: "Brazil is getting more and more integrated with other countries and other regions, so it's very likely that if I work with a company that has operations all over Latin America, I would take a position for the whole of Latin America."

The economic and occupational dimension of citizenship was emphasized by three students in one additional way. These students—one each from Brazil, China, and Italy—were driven considerably by their desire to attain certain privileges for themselves and their families (present or prospective) through pursuit of career interests. In a model of the mercantilistic application of pluriversity knowledge, with a special emphasis on individual gains, they looked upon their experiences in the United States primarily as a means to attain enhanced professional opportunities and saw their participation in a transnational sphere of existence, in both a personal and professional sense, as the road to financial success. Most importantly, these students did not consider responsibilities to others as an integral element of citizenship, but they conceived of their experience at UCLA as helping them along in their responsibility for their own well-being. For example, Binglong, a Chinese student in business, rejected the viability of individual responsibility in the world, deferring such duties to national governments and transnational organizations. Speaking of his career options and possible countries of settlement, he explained that whether he remained in the United States or returned to China depended on his perceptions of the professional and financial advantages that each country held for him.

Gian Marco also highlighted the importance of personal advancement: "I'm trying to get the best for myself and build a happy life for myself and for the people that are around me. But I don't feel like I have any specific duty to change the world, change how people think about something, because it's not possible." Gian Marco viewed citizenship as meaning that "you have a lot of rights to be [in a country]. Rights to work and vote . . . just to improve your life." João expressed a similar perspective, also noting his stance on antinationalism and the role of nation-states in serving their citizens:

The only good role that countries have . . . is to have . . . World Cup [soccer competition]. Because the other things just lead to war. Why not open the borders? You have terrorism because people feel they belong to a country and they have to kill their enemy. If people didn't feel that they belonged to a country, we wouldn't have that. I feel like you should be focused on individuals, not on countries. The only role of the countries is to serve individuals. It is not the individuals who have to serve the country.

Although the experiences of these three students were overwhelmingly individualistic, other study participants also discussed attaining occupational and economic opportunities. This was best reflected in their explanations for coming to study in the United States. As Huiling related, "If you have a U.S. degree, your career will develop a lot easier. No matter where you decide to stay, you have a lot better chance to get a good job and, you know, get ahead in your professional field." Such views were also prevalent among other students. For instance, Gustavo, a student in economics, explained: "The main factor that characterized my decision of coming here is that my expected income would be much higher."

However, in contrast to Binglong, Gian Marco, and João, the aspirations for individual advancement of the majority of the students were accompanied by a sense of responsibility directed toward global or local/national issues in a collectivistic fashion. As an example, Gustavo also related: "I see Brazil as one of the places where you have more problems and differences that . . . we should work on. So right now, I'm much more concerned about the Brazilian population than others." Individual advancement was thus just one goal, albeit an important one, complemented strongly by broader responsibilities.

Social/Cultural Responsibilities. The geographic scope of citizenship was also important in students' discussions of their cultural and social responsibilities. As previously discussed, participation in graduate education at UCLA brought with it an exposure to a diverse and international climate where students learned about other cultural forms and practices to varying extents. Italians were at the forefront of these experiences, followed by Brazilian and then Chinese students. Although Italians showed the strongest propensity to engage with diversity in the United States, several Brazilian and Chinese students also discussed their duties related to living in a multicultural environment.

The foremost expression of students' responsibilities in this realm was rooted in their efforts to become cultural mediators, recognizing their role as transmitters of their cultures in a foreign land. For example, Jia expressed her concern "to help other people to understand the Chinese, and also help the Chinese understand other people." Referring specifically to the people he met in the United States, Luis discussed his newly embraced duty to share his experiences with U.S. citizens: "Now I can contribute by telling my students or telling other people that some notions are just wrong about the United States and some things are better than they seem and some things are worse than they seem. . . . So, I think now I have a much more realistic, and even more optimistic, view of the United States." Ting, when discussing her intentions to work for an international organization that would allow her to maintain connections with both her native China and the United States, noted, "Basically, I feel comfortable culturally in different places and I would facilitate the communication between different countries, because I know both."

In a more general sense, some students felt strongly about the importance of showing respect for diverse peoples and cultures, with a strong collectivist undertone. Gilberto spoke at length about respect as one of the building blocks in the obligations of world citizens, relating his commitment specifically to his experiences at UCLA:

Here at UCLA, we have different people from around the world and you have a lot of different cultures, languages. In the very beginning, I was shocked because I was never exposed to a situation like that. . . . Here, you have different people, a lot of different people surround you and you have to be very careful, you have to learn their culture. . . . So you have to learn, you have to understand, you have to tolerate. But at the same time, you have to keep yourself as Brazilian or . . . Italian, such that they could respect you as well. And I think this is very important. In doing that, you are in a sense taking part in their culture. In a sense, you are taking part in globalization.

The application of knowledge—pluriversity knowledge—thus played a prominent role from the perspective of enacting responsibilities in the cultural and social dimensions of citizenship as well. Students' ongoing relationship with their home countries was especially important in this regard. Several students regularly discussed their experiences in the United States with friends and family at home; some maintained daily phone contact with people in their home countries and even those with the least amount of contact engaged in at least weekly phone conversations. The students understood the social dimension of citizenship as a system of give and take, composed of their duty to respect other cultures, while expecting respect for their own cultural practices in return. Thus, their appreciation for their home culture was informed by a more sophisticated conception of culture shaped by their experiences in a global sphere.

Political/Civic Responsibilities. Given their limited participation in the U.S. political process and their distance from political events in their home countries, the students found it most difficult to embrace responsibilities enacted in the civic and political realms. Political boundaries thus proved onerous to overcome. Still, as noted previously, some students did opt to cast their votes in their home countries' elections by transferring their voting registration to Los Angeles. These students found it important to actively maintain their political ties, in the form of living up to their citizen duties, to their nations of origin. Others mentioned hard feelings at the difficulties they encountered in either trying to transfer their voting rights or deciding to abstain from participating in their home countries' elections.

Not surprisingly, because of differences in the political system, Chinese students spoke of political/civic issues in different ways. Concern about the political well-being of their homeland, however, was not absent in our conversations with Chinese students. Wen-Hui, a student in education, explained:

I thought I was very open-minded. . . . But after I came here, I met people from other countries and I found that I actually am quite narrow-minded. . . . My country is rooted in me. And from a political point of view, I'm not very satisfied with the political system there and the bureaucracy, but after I came to the United States, I found that a lot of things are similar in politics. Here you also have bureaucracy and corruption. But still, I think that China could be more democratic. I'm very concerned about my country.

Wen Hui's views of the Chinese political system were thus significantly shaped by her perceptions of the political values and practices of the United States.

Discussions of the political situation in their home countries were also prominent among some Italian and Brazilian students. Italians expressed concerns about corruption and Italy's support for the Iraq war, and Brazilians spoke primarily of problems related to political instability and corruption. However, in a way similar to Wen-Hui, most students did not embrace these issues as problems that they could solve. Instead, they expressed frustration and sometimes even anger, prompting one Italian student to state: "When you get closer and closer, you really see how politics works over there and I think that's one of the reasons I would never go [back to Italy;] I would never live in a country where there's so much corruption and so much injustice about political decisions. It's not fair." Others expressed hope for the situation to improve but did not indicate intentions to take an active part in this process.

Some students emphasized global responsibilities, stressing the importance of protecting the environment, participating in demonstrations and Internet groups with a political agenda, volunteering for various organizations with an international focus, and boycotting the products of companies whose policies they found disagreeable and harmful to developing countries. This last concern was expressed by Alessandra, whose critical ideas developed when she was an Amnesty International activist while still in Italy and who, as a reaction to her experiences in the United States, presented a strong critique of the capitalist free-market economy:

Well, if you know of companies, like Nestlé, who carry out quite bad, unfair, and immoral actions and policies in Africa, and I know that, I mean I believe that I have a moral duty to make the life of that company as hard as possible within my possibilities and also maintaining my legal status, in the sense that I wouldn't go all over campus and just put on fire the vending machines by Nestlé. But I don't buy any Nestlé products. . . . So, I like to think that my little struggles in my daily life could help ameliorate the condition of the entire world.

Underscoring the global dimension of his responsibilities, Luis described the importance of contributing to the world community in a civic model of citizenship: "In a sense, we are all responsible for the world community, so we should do our share to preserve the world and pollute less and damage the environment less, or contribute to a nation in Africa that's suffering. So we have this world community and it also probably comes with globalization and awareness of the situation in different countries."

The international graduate students from Brazil, China, and Italy discussed a range of responsibilities arising from or strengthened by their experiences at UCLA. Some of these responsibilities defined their endeavors in the economic/occupational dimensions of their lives, while others were related to their social/cultural and political/civic views and activities. Above all, many of the responsibilities identified by the students reflected a strong focus on the application of knowledge, underscoring their recognition of the importance of pluriversity knowledge, with a strong potential for societal contextualization.

CONCLUSION

In 2007, more than 2.8 million students in the world were enrolled in post-secondary institutions outside the borders of their home countries. This number represents a 53 percent increase from the year 1999.[73] Postsecondary students engaged in educational endeavors in a foreign country are thus by no means a negligible population. Perhaps reflecting the significance of international educational exchange, international student mobility has not escaped controversy. In fact, public messages about foreign students have varied significantly in recent years, reflecting the importance of societal contexts and political events in the value placed on international student exchange. In the United States, international students have been described as ambassadors of international understanding, as contributors to U.S. economic and scientific development, and in the aftermath of the September 11, 2001 terrorist attacks, as threats to national security and even as financial burdens on the nation's economy.[74] Despite these contradictory perspectives, international students are rarely discussed within a comprehensive framework of citizenship, with most accounts of their experiences focusing on issues of language development, adjustment, psychological well-being, and educational engagement.[75] The research presented in this chapter offers the beginnings of such a framework, considering the implications of international graduate education for citizenship.

The focus on Brazilian, Chinese, and Italian students at UCLA provides only a glimpse at the lives of international students by focusing on specific subpopulations. However, this glimpse is powerful in highlighting the variety of ways in which a group of foreign graduate students at a major public research university in a highly globalized U.S. urban center confronted critical questions about citizenship. Many of these questions concerned students' contributions in the economic/occupational, social/cultural, and political/civic dimensions of citizenship.

Santos's notion of the emancipatory production and application of pluriversity knowledge was often at the center of these contributions.[76] The students drew upon their educational experiences at UCLA in defining their professional contributions and responsibilities. Many spoke of their intentions to use the knowledge and skills they acquired during their graduate studies in collectivist ways, to address issues of major societal significance in their professional endeavors. Some hoped to do work with the goal of improving the economies of developing countries, while others focused on environmental and energy problems. Although these plans may not readily set international graduate students apart from their counterparts studying in their home countries, several students perceived the educational climate of UCLA as contributing to their experiences over and above what they would have been exposed to at home. State-of-the-art facilities and equipment, professors with highly respected expertise, an international educational environment, and a novel understanding of issues in students' professional fields were all noted as key in redefining their contributions.

Another crucial aspect of many students' experiences was the support they received at UCLA for work on a variety of topics that involved locales from students' home countries and regions, specific groups of countries, or issues with a global geographic reach. Accordingly, some of the students continued to focus on their home countries and regions; some even came to UCLA with the goal of obtaining skills and knowledge that would enable them to become more helpful to their countries of origin. And some spoke of an expanded sense of responsibility encompassing a transnational sphere of existence, with hopes that their research and work would address questions in a variety of countries of the world. Perhaps most importantly, many of these students were highly intent on participating in the creation and application of pluriversity knowledge, with a strong focus on emancipatory knowledge production.

However, mercantilistic uses of pluriversity knowledge were also present in the students' commentaries. These forms of knowledge application were most apparent in the examples of three students who expressed a strong intention to use their knowledge and skills acquired at UCLA for their own professional and financial advancement, with little mention of how their present and future activities might lead to societal contributions. These students embodied Ong's notion of "flexible citizenship,"[77] a form of identity focusing on individual benefits to be gained through international educational exchange, representing a highly individualistic notion of citizenship. In essence, these students directed their sense of responsibility toward their own—rather than the public—good, stressing individual mercantilistic goals as some of the most important aspects of their learning and knowledge creation.

The disciplinary affiliations of these three students (business, economics, and materials science) also raise a question about the relationship between students' fields of study and their understandings of citizenship in a global context. Clearly, the three fields hold the potential to place their graduates at the center of the global economy. However, it is important to note that not all students in these fields placed such a strong emphasis on their individual advancement at the expense of societal contributions. It is thus difficult to draw definitive conclusions about the implications of a graduate field of study for one's conceptions of citizenship. Nevertheless, this study's emphasis on a variety of academic fields with a strong focus on societal contributions, from political science, education, and applied linguistics to chemistry, epidemiology, and information studies, might play a key role in explaining many of the students' insistence on making a positive difference in the world through their work.

The students' experiences at UCLA, and more broadly the United States, also played a significant role in shaping their understanding of responsibilities in the social/cultural and political/civic dimensions of citizenship. Building on their interactions with a diversity of people while at the same time also representing—to various extents—their home country traditions and values, many of the students portrayed themselves as cultural ambassadors and cultural mediators. An important goal for these students was to bring a heightened level of intercultural understanding to their relationships both in the United States and at home. These views and actions often reflected the students' involvement in the creation and application of the cultural aspects of pluriversity knowledge. In the political/civic realms, international graduate education challenged some students to rethink their political identities and belonging, while others were driven to express concern over the political climate in their home countries. In both of these instances, knowledge gained through their experiences in the United States was important in shaping the students' sense of responsibility toward their home countries and regions or toward a global sphere of existence. Although several of the students chose to apply their knowledge for emancipatory purposes, as reflected, for example, in their participation in volunteer activities or political activism, the political/civic dimensions of citizenship were perhaps the least likely to involve students in the application of pluriversity knowledge. This was especially visible in the students' often-voiced lack of political and civic participation both in the United States and in their home countries.

Undoubtedly, the students in this study arrived in the United States with certain predispositions toward citizenship. Questions of personality and the

cultural, political, and economic facets of home country contexts were especially important in this regard. Although it is impossible to decipher the impact of these factors from the influence of engaging in graduate studies
abroad, in many ways international graduate education provides a terrain for
challenging prior notions of citizenship by expanding, and arguably at times
limiting, citizen rights and responsibilities in a global context. Most importantly, the students spoke extensively of their experiences in the United States
as offering avenues for broadening their views; promoting their understanding of other nations in a cultural, political, and economic sense; strengthening their ability to think critically; and empowering them with professional
skills—all contributing to their sense of citizenship and engaging them in
pluriversity knowledge creation and application.

Although international graduate education holds the potential to provide
students with tools that facilitate the enactment of their responsibilities in a
variety of geographic settings, these contributions are possible only in the
presence of certain rights that are indispensable aspects of international educational exchange. At UCLA, foreign graduate students gain access to a
prominent public research university offering graduate degree programs in a
variety of fields. They can work within and outside their higher education
institutions. Foreign students pay local, state, and federal taxes and are able
to obtain a social security number. By virtue of their F-1 visa status, they gain
access to student health insurance plans. They are given the option of bringing family members with them.[78] If they are academic student employees—
tutors, readers, or teaching assistants—they are covered by collective bargaining agreements.[79]

Undoubtedly, these rights are limited in comparison to those afforded to
U.S. citizens, and regulations governing foreign students' activities in the
United States are considerable. For example, international students are re-
stricted in the number of hours they can work, and they have less access to
fellowships and scholarships. Beyond the ability to participate in collective
bargaining, other aspects of their political participation receive little legal support. Foreign students' cross-national movement is also strictly governed by
law, requiring complicated visa application procedures and frequent reporting of enrollment-related and other information through SEVIS. The impact
of the September 11, 2001 terrorist attacks on this latter area of regulations

cannot be overstated. However, despite the factors that distinguish international student rights from those afforded to U.S. citizens, it is crucial to underscore the availability of rights attached to the F-1 student visa, encompassing privileges that would not be automatically available to non–U.S. citizens on other forms of nonimmigrant visas.

The limited nature of international student rights, however, cannot be stressed enough. The volatility of the international student experience should not escape the attention of higher education institutions and policy makers. Many of the students participating in this study expressed serious concern over the insecurities they experienced in the years following the tightened visa and reporting regulations instituted after September 11, 2001.[80] The right to cross-national movement was at the forefront of these concerns, producing fears about continued access to graduate education at universities such as UCLA. International graduate students thus become members of U.S. society through their access to a set of limited rights, while at the same time remaining nonmembers because of restrictions and constraints that limit their participation. From the perspective of citizenship and the possibility to enact responsibilities in a collectivist fashion, feelings of being unwanted and excluded can lead to alienation on the part of the students, the offshoot of which may be a failure to make valuable connections to the host society and to promote greater intercultural encounters and understanding of transnational connections in politics and the economy.

The foreign graduate student experience thus raises important questions concerning the rights of transnational migrants. Considering the larger debate on citizenship in the context of globalization and immigration, international students present a special case. By no means are they permanent residents as Germany's guest workers described by Soysal in her framework of postnational membership.[81] Rather, they are long-term temporary residents, whose experiences reflect a set of rights that make it possible for them to meaningfully participate in many aspects of U.S. society. Although international human rights may play a role in shaping these privileges, the majority of rights are conferred by the U.S. government, in laws directing the foreign student visa program. The most critical aspect of the students' experiences, however, lies in the crucial presence of colleges and universities in supporting and, in a way, creating the need for international student rights. In the case of international educational exchange, then, education and citizenship are intertwined in providing a set of limited rights to individuals who would not otherwise have access to those privileges. Perhaps most importantly, these rights provide avenues for international students to engage in the creation and production of pluriversity knowledge at a U.S. university, with significant potential for applied contributions in the economic/occupational, social/cultural, and political/civic dimensions of citizenship.

CHAPTER 4

RESISTANCE TO NEOLIBERALISM:

North-South Tensions in Argentina

INSURRECTION IN THE STREETS AND FACTORIES

The 2004 film *The Take*, directed by Avi Lewis and written by Naomi Klein, presents the story of a group of some thirty Argentine metal workers who reopen a dormant factory through a cooperative worker-led project. "The take" of San Martin Forge was part of a larger struggle described as the Movement of Recuperated (sometimes "Recovered") Companies, whose battle cry was rather pointed: "Occupy, resist, produce."[1] The movement's goal was to reclaim factories and restore the livelihoods of the countless workers who lost their jobs following the December 2001 collapse of the Argentine economy. The takeover of San Martin Forge was one of many such reclamations organized to situate the means of production within the hands of those who typically produce much of the work—the workers.[2] In a broader sense, the movement, arising in key locations such as Buenos Aires, represents the growing challenge to forms of globalization advanced by wealthy countries such as the United States. Indeed, the economic, political, and social resistance deriving to a great degree from South American countries, including Argentina, Bolivia, Brazil, and Venezuela, defines to some extent the North-South divide separating developing countries and their wealthier counterparts to the north.

The Movement of Recuperated Companies presented significant challenges to a national system deeply implicated by global capitalism. In successfully expropriating workplaces in the face of "capitalist bosses," who later sought to reclaim their property once the workers had demonstrated their economic viability,[3] the workers powerfully revealed the possibilities of collective forms of ownership and production. The threat that a workers' movement poses to traditional structures of power is clear to see, as was noted in Lester Pimentel's review of *The Take*: "The rules of capitalism dictate that property rights are sacred, which is why the workers' movement poses such a challenge to the propertied interests in Argentina and financial institutions like the International Monetary Fund."[4]

What is captured by *The Take* is only the tip of the iceberg. The *piquetero* movement[5] (also described as the Movement of Unemployed Workers) that grew dramatically in size and scope following December 2001 touched nearly every aspect of Argentine life, eventually fueling powerful opposition movements targeting neoliberal global capitalism and the likes of intergovernmental organizations (IGOs) such as the International Monetary Fund (IMF) and the World Bank. The *piqueteros*, along with other grassroots organizations such as the National Front Against Poverty, forged a broad social movement that applied intense pressure to the nation's political leaders and core institutions. Due in large part to the strength of the oppositional movement, government officials like former President Fernando De la Rua and former Economy Minister Domingo Cavallo were forced to resign by the end of 2001 amid charges of complicity with the IMF. They were cast as traitors who led their country to the verge of economic ruin. Once De la Rua stepped down, the vacated office of president was filled by a succession of interim leaders until January 2002, when the National Congress selected Eduardo Duhalde of the Peronist Party.

Precipitated to a great extent by the economic decimation of the Argentine middle class, the grassroots rebellion was evident when we traveled to

Buenos Aires in the spring of 2002 and the summer of 2003 to conduct interviews with faculty and students at the University of Buenos Aires (UBA).[6] We wanted to learn more about the struggles of the Argentine people and the ways in which university professors and students addressed the growing crisis of neoliberal globalization. We also were interested in how their actions might advance notions of citizenship as well as how their engagement in the struggle might suggest a particular vision of the modern university. In years subsequent to our research trips, we followed events in Buenos Aires closely, saving newspaper and journal articles, interacting with UBA colleagues, and supporting a follow-up visit by a doctoral student a few years later. Hence, the story in this chapter represents the culmination of an extended analysis of the situation in Argentina and the role of UBA faculty and students as oppositional actors enacting globally informed forms of citizenship.[7]

There is much evidence from around the world of the complicity of universities in serving neoliberal globalization,[8] but what do we know of the ways in which university actors, as citizens with obligations to the broader society, engage in oppositional struggles, such as those that arose in the streets of Buenos Aires in December 2001? And what does this sort of "civic engagement" of university actors suggest as universities of the twenty-first century reconsider what it means to be socially responsible institutions? Can such endeavors fit within the vision and scope of university service to society? If not, then why not? And if so, then under what conditions and in what manner or form?

Certainly, few within the dominant economic institutions that shape world affairs are likely to challenge the role university actors play in supporting unchecked global capitalism, but is there a place for oppositional views and actions? What do we make of those actors and projects that seek to offer serious resistance to neoliberalism and the dominant economic order? How are such forms of resistance suggestive of models of citizenship or of global citizenship? And how might such views of citizenship help us reconsider universities and their role in society? What seems fairly clear is that globalization is producing a new reality in which world peace, perhaps even the survival of the human race, may depend on emerging notions of citizenship and what it means to be an engaged actor in a complex and shrinking world. These matters are central to the unfolding of this chapter.

By the spring of 2002, the massive grassroots movement was both visible and audible within and about the streets of Buenos Aires. Graffiti on the sides of buildings and walls revealed the target of the people's wrath: Argentina's political leaders and the IMF. The signs were everywhere: "Thieves!" "Criminals!" "Resign now!" "Down with corruption!" "We want our money back!" The sounds coming from the streets also told part of the story. In the evening, crowds of men, women, and children marched throughout the bustling thoroughfares banging pots and pans and demanding justice. These types of street protests, described locally as *cacerolazos*, were a powerful manifestation of the resistance movement that had formed within the communities and neighborhoods throughout the city. Interneighborhood assemblies became the heart and soul of the anti-neoliberalism movement that seemed to grow stronger every day. Not too surprisingly, the banking system became a central focus of the community-based organizing, especially after the implementation of banking restrictions in the fall of 2001, followed by the conversion of dollars to pesos and reports in the Argentine press that armored trucks had carted off some US$26 billion for safekeeping.[9]

The interneighborhood assemblies offered the economically marginalized of Argentina opportunities to contribute to decision making that held the potential to influence their lives in significant ways. Journalist Alfred Hopkins described their functioning at the height of the movement: "At the Interneighborhood assembly gatherings, local neighborhood groups send representatives to present proposals for popular vote. Anyone can speak; the only restrictions are that speeches must be limited to three minutes. After everyone has spoken, the group votes on the proposals on the basis of a simple majority. The leadership of the Assembly rotates weekly to prevent individuals or groups from seeking political advantage."[10] The democratic processes employed by the interneighborhood assemblies produced many proposals, including calls for nonpayment of the nation's foreign debt, reorganization of the banks, reform of the Supreme Court, job creation, salary reductions for politicians, and the "resignation of the entire government."[11] Obviously, some proposals had greater chances of coming to fruition than others, but nothing seemed beyond the realm of possibility. The spirit of "power to the imagination" truly was in the air.

The rise of the Argentine rebellion, as Latin Americanist Roger Burbach described it in a February 2002 article,[12] threatened the foundations of the society, as calls such as "Everyone has to be thrown out" signified rejection of the global imperatives that contributed to the nation's collapse, enacted largely under the direction of the IMF.[13] With little to hope for, the mass of unemployed protesters saw no good reason for the country *not* to default on its debt of some $140 billion, given the little to which they had benefited from such funds in the first place. The general conviction was that the nation's corrupt and self-serving political leaders and economic elites had been the only ones to gain from the IMF loans, as well as from the structural adjustment policies that came with them, and so why should the workers, the unemployed, and the economically disenfranchised suffer the heavy burden and brutal consequences of paying back the loans? As Burbach noted, the Argentine elite had been the beneficiaries of the nation's neoliberal push to privatize national enterprises:

Although Argentina captured the world's attention with the massive social explosion in late December [2001] that ushered in five presidents in less than two weeks, the crisis had been building for years. Its foundations are in the neo-liberal model that Argentina adopted in the early 1990's under Carlos Menem who served as president from 1989 to 1999. The head of the old Peronist movement, or *Justicalista* party as it is now called, Menem along with government and party bureaucrats grew rich as national companies ranging from petroleum and airline enterprises to telephone and water utilities were sold off to foreign interests.[14]

And so the rise of the Argentine rebellion was years in the making. However, in December 2001 economic hardship became so widespread that countless members of the middle class also were ready and willing to condemn the nation's leaders. Jose Luis Coraggio, rector of a Buenos Aires university, said it best: "The repudiation of the politicians and the economic elites is complete. None of them who are recognized can walk the streets without being insulted or spit upon. It is impossible to predict what will happen. . . . We could be in a state of chaos, or we could be building a new country that breaks with the neo-liberal and capitalist orthodoxy."[15] Coraggio's words portray a struggling nation in deep turmoil. But how had Argentina come to such a troubled point in its history, and what was to be the place of its universities?

THE BIGGER PICTURE: A NATION'S STRUGGLE

The ultimate irony of the economic crisis in Argentina was that for years the nation and its leaders, most notably President Carlos Menem, during the 1990s, had been held up as the IMF poster child. The nation had followed the neoliberal doctrine of privatization, deregulation, and marketization only to face its worst recession in decades, beginning in the fall of 1998. Economic crisis led to increased financial dependence on the IMF and further liberalization of the Argentine economy. Argentina was losing its autonomy as a nation-state, as it became increasingly dependent on global financial institutions.

At a Buenos Aires sidewalk café, not too removed from the street protests, UBA Professor Sergío Cuello,[16] a leading Argentine political economist, summarized his nation's struggle quite succinctly: "The IMF decides the nature of our daily lives. And there is no doubt about the impact and the consequence of this—for the poor, the middle class, and the rich. It is interesting to realize that all we have published, all we have said, is now all of a sudden the most cruel truth. We are totally dependent on what the IMF thinks of us. We depend on IMF policy positions." Professor Cuello was suspicious of the IMF's intentions and doubted whether the organization's interests really served Argentina—"They are a bank and after all banks are in the business of money." He added,

I'm really quite doubtful about what the IMF people say, doubtful in terms of their honesty, because in 1997, I think, President Menem was recognized and was awarded by the IMF as the best follower of IMF policies. So, to some extent they [the IMF] are really contradictory in terms of their own beliefs, because if they consider our country as the model for the rest of the world, how can they confirm that we were not following their recipes, because we were doing exactly what they asked of us?

Professor Cuello went on to argue that the cases of Argentina and Venezuela present problems for supporters of neoliberalism:

I think that from an international policy perspective, the Argentinean case and the Venezuelan case are kind of threatening the neoliberal reality. If you consider Argentina as the most important case in terms of achieving neoliberal goals, then I guess we have achieved exactly what they wanted us to achieve—54 percent unemployment! We have no state enterprises anymore, no public enterprises. We have sold everything. Our economy was totally left to the machinations of the market. Our economy was driven by global financial forces, not by national productivity. We stopped being an industrial country in terms of producing goods and now we're importing everything. So, we were the best student, the best pupil who faithfully followed the neoliberal model. And now, we are left to face the consequences of the model, the worst consequences in the world.

Comments such as the preceding were echoed by others with whom we spoke during our visits to Buenos Aires. Not too surprisingly, anti-neoliberal sentiment had grown quite powerful in Argentina as well as elsewhere in South America. This is one reason why the antiglobalization movement— which should really be read as anti-neoliberalism, because few people are truly opposed to the idea of globalization—has fostered such widespread support in the South.[17] This was most evident in 2002 at the World Social Forum (WSF) hosted in Porto Alegre, Brazil, when thousands turned out in opposition to the global hegemony of international organizations such as the IMF and World Trade Organization (WTO), calling instead for more democratic forms of globalization. Many in attendance had the chance to listen to Noam Chomsky deliver an excoriating attack against neoliberalism. In his talk titled "A World Without War," a number of Chomsky's points spoke to the North-South divide and the ways in which neoliberalism had contributed to economic inequality between rich and poor countries: "The rules of the game are likely to enhance deleterious effects for the poor. The rules of the WTO bar the mechanisms used by every rich country to reach its current state of development, while also providing unprecedented levels of protectionism for the rich, including a patent regime that bars innovation and growth in novel ways, and allows corporate entities to amass huge profits by monopolistic pricing of products often developed with substantial public contribution."[18] Under the direction of the "masters of the universe," a phrase Chomsky borrowed from Guy de Jonquières[19] to describe "the movers and shakers" who lead the international agencies and multinational corporations directing the global economy, democracy and democratically elected governments come under attack:

Under contemporary versions of traditional mechanisms, half the people of the world are effectively in receivership, their economic policies managed by experts in Washington. But even in the rich countries democracy is under attack by virtue of the shift of decision-making power from governments, which may be partially responsible to the public, to private tyrannies, which have no such defects. Cynical slogans such as "trust the people" or "minimize the state" do not, under current circumstances, call for increasing popular control. They shift decisions from governments to other hands, but not "the people": rather, the management of collectivist legal entities, largely unaccountable to the public, and effectively totalitarian in internal structure, much as conservatives charged a century ago when opposing "the corporatization of America."[20]

Because of the mounting criticism coming from the likes of Chomsky, as well as policy-making insiders such as Joseph Stiglitz,[21] international trade and governing agencies have had to launch counter campaigns, as part of an effort to retain their leading role in shaping the global economy. These counter campaigns are evident when one visits their organizational Web sites, where at one time the WTO listed "10 Benefits of the WTO Trading System," complete with cartoon characters, while the IMF sought to counter its adversaries in "Common Criticisms of the IMF."[22]

Not long after the 2001 economic collapse, the IMF, in the face of a growing wave of criticism, acknowledged some of its "little mistakes" in a report, *Lessons from the Crisis in Argentina*. In a section of the report titled "The Role of the IMF," the document explains, "In light of the gravity of the crisis that unfolded while the country was engaged in a succession of IMF-supported programs it is not surprising that the Fund has come under harsh criticism for its involvement in Argentina. Indeed, with hindsight, the Fund—like most other observers—erred in its assessment of the Argentine economy by overestimating its growth potential and underestimating its vulnerabilities."[23] But the report glosses over the most tragic of mistakes made by the IMF, mistakes consistently committed by global economic decision makers: The tendency to apply a one-size-fits-all model of economics—the neoliberal model, of course.[24] This fault, combined with the tendency to ignore or de-value social, cultural, and political differences across nations, contributed as much as anything to the economic calamity in Argentina.

THE IMPACT ON ARGENTINE UNIVERSITIES

Failure to understand the unique circumstances of Argentina in part contrib-uted to calls for reduced funding of public universities, including UBA. This was a nearly tragic mistake given the historic struggle of Argentine universi-ties and intellectuals to build vitality in the face of numerous military inter-ventions, and most notably, the nation's "Dirty War"—an ideological war against all forms of opposition to the military dictatorship that dominated the country during the 1970s. Only as recently as 1983, with the election of President Raul Alfonsín of the Radical Civil Union Party, did the country return to constitutional rule of law, this following nearly forty years of re-peated military takeovers and alternating attempts to install forms of demo-cratic rule, including the efforts of the popular Juan Domingo Perón.

Coming to terms with Argentina's cultural and historical circumstances is crucial to understanding the needs of the nation's universities. While many of the countries of North, Central, and South America were engaged in monu-mental efforts to reform their universities, including the massive expansion of the U.S. system during the 1960s and its increased alignment with business and industry, Argentine universities were struggling for survival in the face of military coups, the last one ruling the country from 1976 to 1983. A high-ranking academic administrator and faculty member at UBA, Pablo Azcona, offered his opinion about the impact of political instability in Argentina:

The Argentine universities should have been reformed in the 1970s, or even '68 or '69, when the universities of Mexico, universities of Brazil, UC Berkeley, and others were reformed. The Argentine university began to reform, too, but the military coup in-terrupted that. So, after the military coup, a reform did not take place. We only saw the liberalization of political life at the university. Thus, the Argentine university arrives at the age of globalization without having solved the pre-globalization prob-lems that it had. Argentine universities did not conclude the process of adapting themselves to the modern society.

One of the problems that Professor Azcona and others spoke of was the inability of the Argentine university to contribute in significant ways to scientific and technological development. This is a major reason why many of the faculty with whom we met were so opposed to IMF dictates aimed at cutting financial support for public universities. How is it possible for universities to develop the infrastructure to engage in meaningful scientific activity in an environment of drastic financial cuts? Reducing state support for universities and the research enterprise is akin to relinquishing any chance of competing in the knowledge economy as anything other than a consumer. Eliminating the capacity of universities to contribute to a technologically driven, knowledge-based economy may render the society dependent on wealthier nations for technological and scientific support. Professor Alejandro Ludena, a national expert on science and technology at UBA, explained it this way: "I believe that the policies that restrict scientific and technological research in Latin American countries are not accepted by the university communities. The Latin American countries and Argentina need research universities, and I am speaking of a university in which the idea of research is very important and cannot disappear." Professor Cuello addressed elements of this issue as well: "The problem is we had a dictatorship, a military dictatorship, that did not pay any attention to the university and higher education in general. Then we moved to a democracy in which one would expect the government to shift some of the public agenda in favor of science, scientific development, and higher education, but this never happened." The consequence is that at a time in which universities increasingly are seen as vital institutions to a nation's ability to compete in knowledge production, the Argentine university lacks the scientific infrastructure and financial support to compete with the likes of the universities to the north, those in the United States and elsewhere.

If Argentina were to completely follow the dictates of the IMF and other international financial organizations such as the World Bank, which repeatedly have recommended reductions to higher education in developing countries,[25] the nation likely would be destined to become a permanent observer on the sidelines of the knowledge economy. But resistance to the IMF and neoliberalism grew strong in Argentina during the early years of the twenty-first century. So much so in fact that in the spring of 2003 the Argentine people selected a president who openly opposed many of the IMF's policies. Peronist Néstor Kirchner, the governor of Santa Cruz province, defeated fellow Peronist and former president Carlos Menem,[26] who from 1989 to 1999 had played a central role in the country's IMF-guided efforts to privatize public resources and services. Kirchner took a different path from that of his predecessors. For example, he followed a political and economic agenda focused on solving social problems, often adopting strategies in opposition to IMF directives. This was evident during his first year in office, when he successfully rescheduled US$84 billion in debts with various international organizations. The reality that business as usual was about to end was evident during Kirchner's campaign for the presidency, when he visited Brazil's socialist-leaning President Luiz Ignácio Lula da Silva, made little effort to distance himself from his left-wing past, and often criticized neoliberal economic policies.

In actuality, resistance to IMF policies in Argentina had grown strong long before Kirchner's election, even before the December 2001 collapse. For example, many Argentine intellectuals saw the involvement of the IMF in their country as part of the larger U.S.-led project to shape the world in its own interests, or at least in the interests of Western economic powers, including the likes of Germany, France, and the United Kingdom. Criticism was often framed around a North-South divide in which many of the influential countries of the Northern Hemisphere were described as imperialistic in their intent to dominate poorer countries from the south.[27] Influences from the north, deriving mainly from the United States, and reflecting the economic interests of global capitalism, are believed to have had a major impact on efforts to reconstruct the Argentine university, including UBA. The push toward the privatization of UBA is seen as one such example in that calls for reductions in state support have been accompanied by increased efforts to supplant a social good model of the university with a more entrepreneurial or mercantilist vision.[28] For example, several reforms consistent with neoliberal ideology were included within the general Law on Higher Education, enacted in 1995, and then revised in 2000. Of particular concern to many UBA students and faculty was the law's focus on "assessment and accreditation," including the creation of the National Council for University Accreditation and Evaluation (CONEAU). Carlos Pujadas, an Argentine academic, pointed out that the assessment component of the law "means that the public universities will lose some of their autonomy, once they have submitted, for the first time, to greater control by government supervision."[29] This attempt by the Argentine government to gain greater control over the university is reflective of a global trend toward increased standardization and state assessment of higher education and to a great extent has been pushed by powerful intergovernmental organizations.[30] For Marcela Mollis and Simon Marginson, two noted comparativists of higher education, this trend clearly is rooted in neoliberalism and tends to promote a particular vision of the university—one based more on a corporate model of financial accountability and control (by professional managers) and less on pedagogical objectives guided by teachers and students.[31]

That the Argentine university would come under neoliberal assault is of course no big surprise. Indeed, the importance of the university in an increasingly global world cannot be understated, given the growing dominance of the knowledge industry and the broader economic context defined by Manuel Castells as "the information age" and characterized by "the network society." Castells expanded on this idea in the opening chapter to his book *The Power of Identity*: "Our world, and our lives, are being shaped by the conflicting trends of globalization and identity. The information technology revolution and the restructuring of capitalism have induced a new form of society, the network society. It is characterized by the globalization of strategically decisive economic activities. By the networking form of organization. By the flexibility and instability of work, and the individualization of labor."[32]

In the context of the network society, where information becomes a central commodity to be exchanged within the confines of the so-called free market, obviously organizations that produce and disseminate knowledge will be targets of neoliberalists and their efforts to fashion global networks in their own interests. The result is a neoliberal vision of the university that is twofold. First, the university has to be incorporated into the research and development interests of capital—as in the "academic capitalism knowledge regime," as described by Sheila Slaughter and Gary Rhoades[33]—often by tying the economic needs and motivations of university research to the private sector. Second, the university as a site of opposition and resistance must be minimized.[34] Along these lines, Boaventura de Sousa Santos noted that the World Bank, in its "reformist zeal" to refashion universities in a manner consistent with neoliberal ideology, often points to the "power held by the faculty" as one of its "main targets," and views academic freedom "as an obstacle to the responsibility of the entrepreneurial university vis-à-vis firms that wish to enlist its services. The power of the university must be wrested from the faculty and given to administrators trained to promote partnerships with private agents."[35] This is in part the argument offered by Rhoades when he described the restructuring of academic labor in the United States and the increasing treatment of faculty as "managed professionals."[36]

For Atilio Boron, a leading Argentine political economist, what has been most disappointing about IMF involvement in his country has been the direct assault on the university and a lack of recognition of the need for university development in such a network-based, information age. As Boron explained, "In the much celebrated 'knowledge society' and in an era in which the critical variables for international competitiveness in the global economy are science, technology, and knowledge and the key raw material is intelligence, the role of education in general and universities in particular can hardly be overestimated. Promotion of education at all levels and of scientific research and technological developments should be at the top of the governmental agenda of our countries."[37] Boron does not support an academic capitalist model of university science and technology. Although he sees the necessity of the Argentine university participating in the knowledge-based economy, such participation ought to be state supported to some extent and concerned with national interests. From his perspective, university science should not be at the beck and call of private capital, although such interests certainly have a role to play.

Based on the evidence, a strong argument can be made that the wealthiest countries of the world seek to advance economic policies through IGOs that ultimately limit the development of universities in poorer countries, thus strengthening their own dominance in a global economy increasingly driven by knowledge production and information management. Santos reinforced such a view when he pointed out that the "transformation of higher education into an educational commodity is a long-term goal" of organizations such as the WTO.[38] He also noted that organizations such as the World

Bank have advanced policies aimed at decimating public universities in developing countries, including, for example, those in Africa: "Unable to include in its calculations the importance of the university to the building of national projects and the creation of long-term critical thinking, the World Bank concluded that African universities do not generate sufficient 'return' on their investment. As a consequence, the African countries were asked to stop investing in universities."[39]

There certainly is ample evidence of neoliberalists seeking to refashion the university in Argentina. For example, a powerful movement in Argentina, essentially sponsored by the World Bank and other global financial institutions, aims to shift public universities toward operating more in line with private institutions, where a greater percentage of funding is to be based on user fees. As Professor Cuello explained, the privatization of the Argentine university "is becoming increasingly popular—the idea that the university is a business of the elites." Cuello went on to argue that such policies ignore the reality that in more developed countries

the financial help of the state is still very important. But here, in the context of the fiscal crisis of the state, and in light of structural adjustment policies imposed on the country in the last 15 to 20 years, there is the growing view that the university should belong to the private sector and the state should not mingle in its affairs and it should not devote resources to it. We should fund elementary and high school education, and forget the university. This movement is becoming stronger by the hour.

It was further suggested that such a policy will have disastrous long-term implications for economic development. A second professor put it quite succinctly: "We cannot survive as exporters of commodities and importers of technology."

Another form in which the neoliberal shift is manifested in the Argentine university is the turn toward a mercantilist model of the university. Mollis argued that "northern winds" associated with neoliberal ideology have transformed Argentine and Brazilian universities, along with "the knowledge they produce and disseminate."[40] She went on to explain, "Nowadays, Argentine and Brazilian universities—affected by neoliberal policies, budget restrictions, fiscal adjustments, and the transformation of the social contract between the state and the civil society—have denaturalized 'university knowl-edge' and turned it into 'mercantilist learning.'"[41] A professor with whom we spoke at UBA reinforced this view and described globalization as "economic hegemony from the north in terms of providing the sole economic model to be distributed among the nations of the globe. The global part of globaliza-tion is that we are dealing with all nations, but there is a strong feeling to-ward the inequality that globalization brings to the rest of the world. The notion of economic hegemony is really important in terms of how many Ar-gentine scholars understand globalization." This professor went on to point out that the academic capitalist model of the U.S. university, articulated so very well in the work of Slaughter, Larry Leslie, and Rhoades,[42] has had del-eterious effects on the Argentine university. A graduate student of philosophy and letters at UBA, Celía Rodríguez, also addressed these concerns: "There is the privatization of knowledge . . . there is the rise in graduate student tu-ition, there are more labor stipulations for professors. . . . We call this the labor 'precarious-ization' movement. That is to say in terms of professors there are fewer full-time professors, more contracts for part-time professors, and an emphasis on generating a larger quantity of publications." Similarly, Mollis, among others, has stressed this point repeatedly, noting that the neoliberal academic capitalist model has fundamentally altered the identity of the Ar-gentine university: "Our universities have suffered an alteration in their iden-tity as knowledge institutions and are constructing a new identity that equates them to a supermarket, where students are clients, knowledge is a piece of merchandise, and professors are salary earners who teach."[43]

The preceding comments help us consider the ways in which the Argen-tine university is being recast in a manner consistent with neoliberalism and some of the potentially dangerous side effects. These concerns are important to our analysis, as any attempt to reconsider the role of the university and its responsibility to society must ultimately come to terms with the vast commer-cialized pressures pushing it toward forms of public engagement wholly in line with capital and the global marketplace. But to understand the ways in which processes associated with neoliberalism are influencing modern universities, we find it useful to explore the development of universities and their relationship to the broader societies in which they exist.

THE UNIVERSITY AND SOCIETY: EXPLORING THE
MEANING OF PUBLIC ENGAGEMENT

Any effort to understand the modern university and its relationship to society must begin by recognizing that competing visions of the university have existed over the years. This matter was approached quite succinctly by Janice Newson and Howard Buchbinder in *The University Means Business*, published in 1988.[44] Newson and Buchbinder delineated three competing visions of the university, which should not be confused with Clark Kerr's notion of the multiversity and the commonly accepted idea of the tripartite mission of the research university—teaching, research, and service.[45] From the perspective of Newson and Buchbinder, the activities of teaching, research, and service may go on at any one university, but the ways in which such activities are carried out differ based on one of three overarching visions.

Newson and Buchbinder described one vision of the university as the "academic haven," which from their point of view is grounded in a fairly elitist view of higher education. From this perspective, the university stands above the society, serving as a cultural guardian of all that is righteous. The university as academic haven, as Daniel Schugurensky argued, is contingent on it being protected from four primary corrosive forces: the pursuit of utilitarian aims, the politicization of knowledge, massification, and low academic standards.[46] In other words, the university as academic haven must stand apart from society and the masses and be above the fray of politics and ideology. Images of the university as an "ivory tower" or as a "City Upon a Hill" offering light in the form of guidance and direction for the broader society come to mind here.

A second vision focuses on the university as a tool for economic development. This view primarily stresses two major economic contributions offered by universities: (1) the development of students from a human capital standpoint (students as prospective workers and managers) and (2) the development of science and technology in a manner consistent with an information- and knowledge-based economy (at least in the contemporary context). A vision of the university as a tool for economic development is of course a dominant theme in many public policy arenas; this was most evident in the work of the Bush administration's Spellings Commission on the Future of Higher Education in the United States. Indeed, a vision of the university as an economic tool has become such a widespread notion, especially within the United States, Europe, and Japan, that a small cottage industry seemingly has emerged around the criticism of this version of the academy. This is evident by the plethora of books—many of which are noted in Chapter 1—that have been published during the last decade and a half, including the work on academic capitalism.[47]

A third vision, perhaps less popular than the first two, centers on the university as an agent of social transformation. Proponents of this model maintain "that universities have an obligation to contribute not only to the equalization of educational opportunities but also to collective projects that promote social and environmental justice and ultimately alter existing social, economic, and political relationships."[48] This model of the university is far more common in Latin America than in the United States or Europe. The strength of this particular vision in Latin America in part explains why oppositional student movements have been so powerful over the years in the region, while they have been fairly dormant in countries such as the United States, with the exception of certain periods of time, including the 1960s, when student struggle took on new meaning and more socially transformative characteristics.[49] In fact, oppositional student movements at the University of Cordoba in 1918 helped shift the focus of the Latin American university from a model more closely resembling Newson and Buchbinder's academic haven (it was fairly elitist in nature) to a more democratic, socially responsible university having close ties to communities and their needs. The Cordoba reform movement of 1918 further solidified the role of students throughout Latin America in shaping and defining a more democratic and accessible university; in the years following the Cordoba reforms, universities throughout the region witnessed the power of students to organize around democratic concerns. A notable recent case is that of the National Autonomous University of Mexico (UNAM) and the massive protests by students over the course of an entire academic year (1999–2000) to preserve access to UNAM in light of proposed tuition increases linked to IMF structural adjustment policies.[50] But student activism is only part of the story. A university committed to societal transformation is an engaged university, and its key actors, students and faculty, actively participate in their communities and the broader society as socially conscious and concerned citizens. Such a vision of the university values transformative research over disinterested, socially disconnected inquiry and situates the university within the society. Indeed, the university is beholden to the society. This model exists in contrast to viewing the university as an entity or organ existing above or beyond the society (the academic haven model) and serving in some Minervan[51] form or fashion as guardian of the best of the society (including its "high culture"), which, of course, is more likely than not to be defined by economic and political elites seeking to protect their own culture or interests.

The three models outlined by Newson and Buchbinder, and further explored by Schugurensky, still contend within the context of today's higher education landscape, although we think it is fairly safe to say that the university as economic tool has come to thoroughly dominate the terrain (it also is likely to be the case that aspects of all three visions compete at the same institution at any one time). And although certainly the university as academic haven still has some sway, it is the university as agent of social change and the university as economic tool that we choose to focus on here, given the context of Argentina and the work of faculty and students at UBA to support the nation's oppositional movements aimed at challenging neoliberalism.

The university as economic tool is articulated today primarily within the discourse of academic capitalism and the increasing shift toward the commercialization of the university and its products and services. This view of the university is consistent with neoliberalism and the economic policies advanced by the IMF and World Bank. A professor at UBA addressed issues related to this trend: "Globalization affects the Argentine university in various ways. In the first place, globalization, in the neoliberal sense, implies a reduction of public monies. It implies that all of the public and private institutions should function like a business and generate their own resources to support themselves. . . . There also is large ideological contamination in the sense of seeing the country as a business and seeing everything from a point of view of economic efficiency. It contaminates thought." The university as a private business also introduces elements of elitism in that as a revenue-generating entity it tends to favor private user-fees over state-supported accessibility (the latter idea may be understood as part of the public-good mission of the university, to be funded by the state through tax revenue). Carlos

Valle, a professor of social science at UBA, spoke to this issue: "I believe that the impact of globalization for the academic community is very large. I know that the World Bank and its international policies affect us as a university, because there are many policies that resulted in the shrinking of large universities and in restrictions being placed upon us. I believe there is an intent to make the universities an 'elite class' and that this has to do with the policies of the global financial institutions."

In terms of service to society, the university as economic tool has a clear responsibility to serve the interests of capital, primarily by meeting the needs of corporations and industries. Consistent with the ideas of neoliberal globalization, the logic of the market is presented as the ultimate structure or solution in a long-standing Darwinian social play; hence, it becomes rather apparent to anyone supporting such a vision that the university ought to serve private interests. The political/civic aspect of universities and their role in preparing thoughtful and critical citizens cognizant of broad societal concerns is replaced by the role of indoctrinating students to free marketeerism and individualism.[52] Along these lines, Schugurensky argued that under the banner of neoliberalism, the university shifted from "service to society" to "service to industry" and from calls for "social relevance" to calls for "economic relevance."[53] He went on to make a critical point: "If a key mission of universities is to serve the public and to improve the communities and regions in which they operate, it is not self-evident that by serving business interests they are automatically serving the community."[54]

From the perspective of the university as agent of social transformation, economic interests still matter, but corporations are not the only entities worthy of the university's talents and resources. Other institutions and priorities also ought to matter, but many of these concerns are unlikely to be revenue generating. For example, addressing issues of poverty, homelessness, public health, and workers' rights ought to be issues of concern to the socially responsible university. And what of social movements aimed at restoring a nation's autonomy in light of massive global interventions? Such concerns, though, are likely to run counter to the more dominant model of the university as a vehicle for economic development. Indeed, the economic tool model casts the university as a fully commercialized project, relegating such public interests as workers' rights or social welfare to obscurity, while professors addressing the latter concerns are likely to be forced to eke out an intellectual existence in the hinterlands and boundaries of the academic capitalist regime, given their lack of revenue-generating potential.

As a key agent of social transformation, the university ought to be placed in the position of advancing national projects aimed at increasing social equality and further developing the nation's identity as a unique geopolitical space—as a nation-state. As Santos put it, national projects depend on public universities to generate and consolidate "the country's coherence and cohesion as an economically, socially, and culturally well-defined geopolitical territory."[55] But as Santos went on to posit, national projects—and necessarily public universities—exist in opposition to the transnational interests of neoliberalism and the global economic ambitions of organizations such as the IMF and WTO, whose central concern is erasing national boundaries in favor of the free flow of trade for the benefit of private interests and economic elites acting as global entrepreneurs and investors. This contradicts one of the basic functions of universities, especially public universities—advancing national interests through vital social projects. As Santos explained,

In the last 20 years, neoliberal globalization has launched a devastating attack on the idea of national projects, which are conceived as obstacles to the expansion of global capitalism. From the standpoint of neoliberal capitalism, national projects legitimize logics of national social production and reproduction that are embedded in heterogeneous national spaces and geared to intensifying such heterogeneity. Moreover, the operation of these logics is guaranteed by a political entity that is endowed with sovereign power over the territory, the nation-state, whose submission to global economic impositions is problematic from the start with regard to its own interests and those of national capitalism on which it has been politically dependent.[56]

In looking back at cases from Latin America, Asia, and Africa, Santos concluded that without a national project there really was no basis upon which to have public universities: "To question the national project was to question the public university. The reactive defensiveness that has dominated the university, namely, in its responses to financial crisis, derives from the fact that the university—endowed with reflexive and critical capacity like no other social institution—is lucidly coming to the conclusion that it is no longer tied to a national project and that, without one, there can be no public university."[57]

Like Santos, several of the professors at UBA with whom we spoke also raised concerns about the role of the Argentine university, given the growing influence of neoliberal globalization. As one explained, "I want to differentiate between globalization and internationalization. For us at the public university, and also for those at the private university, we have to defend the project to internationalize universities. But we must also respect national boundaries and the national social projects that the universities support. But under neoliberalism there is little respect for national boundaries." Another professor, Cristina Martino, argued that the Argentine university faces a crisis of identity, influenced to a great degree by pressures deriving from the United States:

What is happening to the Argentine university now is that its identity is changing. There are new universities that respond to the new, basically American model, because it is a model that sees the market as the guiding force in directing the university and university reform. It's the model of the North American university and the problem is that we've always had a more European-style university. We've always stressed the development of professionals who then go out and serve the public and social needs.

Such a model, of course, runs counter to the academic capitalist model and the centering of private economic interests.

Despite the growing dominance of the university as a means for economic development, the idea of the university as an agent of social transformation continues to survive, although it struggles for legitimacy. Indeed, the engagement of faculty and students from UBA in resistance movements offers evidence of the potential for universities and their key players to act in socially transformative ways, with the interests of marginalized peoples in mind. Given the importance this vision presents for challenging the hegemony of the university as economic tool, the actions of UBA faculty and students working in concert with workers and community organizations demand further exploration.

THE UNIVERSITY OF BUENOS AIRES

Located in the heart of Argentina's largest and most cosmopolitan city, UBA is a key component of a public higher education system accounting for roughly 80 to 85 percent of the nation's total student enrollment. UBA is one of Latin America's largest universities, offering courses to over 300,000 students, who mostly attend part-time and pay no tuition or fees. Founded in 1821, the university is the most prestigious in the country and is known for educating many of the nation's political leaders, as well as the leading professionals in fields such as law and medicine. A member of the League of World Universities, UBA offers extensive undergraduate and graduate programs in a wide variety of areas, most of which are offered through the following schools: law and social sciences, economic sciences, exact and natural sciences, meteorology, architecture, philosophy and letters, engineering, medicine, agriculture, dentistry, pharmacy and biochemistry, veterinary sciences, psychology, and social sciences. Many of the preceding schools are located in historic buildings (sometimes hidden along narrow side streets) in and around the heart of the city.

An interesting aspect of UBA is that it largely depends on part-time faculty to meet the needs of its burgeoning student body. The university employs thousands of part-timers who juggle their busy professional careers with teaching on the side. A senior professor of law, Julio Rodríguez Metayer, commented on the nature of academic work at UBA and the university's reliance on part-time professionals. He explained that UBA is staffed mostly by part-timers who envision their teaching as a form of "missionary work." The pay is quite low and the number of full-time teaching positions is limited. Professor Metayer added, "Faculty teach on the side and see their work at the university as a contribution to the betterment of society. Many faculty think that, 'Well, if I get paid, ok, but if I don't, I have to spread the word.' The problem is that this goes against the general tendency that we see overseas and in most countries in Latin America in which you have full-time professors." Metayer went on to point out that only about 13 to 14 percent of the faculty at UBA are full-time professors. The vast majority are "taxi cab professors," hustling and bustling between jobs, noted another professor and high-ranking academic administrator. He added: "They want to be exemplary professors, but they just don't have the time." A third professor offered insight into why Argentine professionals aspire to teach at the university: "First, the fundamental Argentine motivation is prestige. Also, teaching and professional exercise enrich one another. Teaching gives one a broader perspective." Cristian

Gómez, a professor of law, added to the discussion, while raising the possibility of losing scholars to the United States: "The professors have no choice but to take on a second job, because if they dedicated themselves to teaching alone, they would die of hunger. Therefore, they have to make peace with the idea of finding another source of income, because this income from the university wouldn't be able to support them. So, the U.S. absorbs Argentine intellectuals, it attracts them with economic conditions much more favorable than here."

Despite its high standing within the country, UBA faces many serious challenges. For one, rates of student attrition are quite high and students often get lost in the difficult and complex maze involved in negotiating program and graduation requirements. Part of the challenge UBA faces is that in embracing an egalitarian vision of open admissions, including no entrance examination requirements, the university attracts many students in need of serious academic support and yet offers very little. Higher education comparativist Philip Altbach commented about the university's problems in this area: "The university cares little about its students. It has no control over how many students enter each year. And it cannot control the quality of its entering students. Its only power is to eliminate students through examinations, attrition, or inattention. The students who do well tend to be those from well-off families. In this way, the university contributes to social inequality even though it has an ideology of egalitarianism."[58] Altbach also noted that the educational system at UBA seems to be based on "the Darwinian principle of survival of the fittest—everyone can enter, but only a small minority of the students who enroll eventually earn degrees—and they do this often by sheer persistence."[59] Many of UBA's students in fact depart during their first year of study, when they take their basic courses (similar to general education in the United States), often in overcrowded classrooms and "by all accounts not appealing to most students."[60]

A second concern is that facilities at UBA leave much to be desired, particularly in terms of the inadequacy of laboratories and libraries. This especially is a problem for advancing the university's and the nation's scientific and technological interests. Alejandro Ludena, a leading scientist with Argentina's CONICET (National Council of Scientific and Technical Investigations), shared stories of UBA scientists transporting much of their laboratory work back and forth from home to university in their cars. He went on to explain, "We need to give greater attention to developing intellect. The only way to export value is to cultivate intellect in the university and to support research, innovation, and put that creativity into the products that the country can sell." Other professors spoke of the ongoing loss of top scientific minds to countries to the north, given the limited support for science at UBA and throughout the country. Some argued that the economic strategy advanced by the IMF, of underinvesting in university science, has had devastating consequences for Argentina's long-term development.

A third challenge that UBA faces came to light during the course of conversations about university-society connections. There was a sense among several faculty members that some academic programs at the university lack a strong connection with the social concerns of the society and the actual career opportunities that exist for future graduates. Professor Martino addressed this apparent disconnect: "There needs to be an adaptation, an adaptation of the universities to the needs of society. We need to take into account how an understanding of global economics can better link the university with production, with the rest of the educational system, and with the grave problems Argentina has and will certainly have for many years to come. For example, we need to address high rates of unemployment and growing levels of inequality and poverty." Another professor noted that some academic programs at the university have not kept pace with the dramatic global changes in knowledge production and management. She felt that the university's computing systems and resources were largely outdated and offered little help to students seeking to participate in a knowledge-based economy.

On a positive note, several faculty members, and many of the students, spoke of important connections that had formed between UBA professors and students and key community organizations, especially in the aftermath of December 2001. These connections enabled many within the university community to contribute to movements challenging the neoliberal economic model that had so dominated the nation's decision making. Given UBA's long-standing associations with the more left-leaning political parties in Argentina, which oftentimes placed the university in opposition to the government, most notably when Peronists were in power, it should come as no major surprise that some members of the university came out in full support of the oppositional movements aimed at thwarting the power of neoliberalism.

A POPULAR MOVEMENT GROWS

The emergence of a movement in opposition to the IMF and neoliberalism took place well before December 2001, but the economic collapse served as a catalyst in escalating citizen involvement and the overall vitality of the struggle. The nature of engagement in the popular movement was quite diverse, and in many respects the movement itself represented a collectivity of smaller actions and activities with varying goals and objectives. For example, street protests had been present in the streets of Buenos Aires since 1997, during Menem's last months as president, when increasing unemployment fueled anger and resentment toward the nation's economic policies. In taking to the streets, as well as taking over the streets, protesters were the clearest manifestation of the broad struggle to restructure the Argentine economy in a manner more supportive of job creation and labor. But other movements also contributed to the growing challenge to neoliberalism including, most notably, the popular assemblies. This latter movement was strengthened in part by the middle class of Argentina and their declining lifestyle, a consequence of the nation's economic policies and its banking restrictions following the December 2001 crisis.

Marta Pérez, a professor of philosophy and letters at UBA, discussed the kinds of movements that emerged in the aftermath of the economic collapse:

You could say that there are two kinds of these new movements. One of them is monetary oriented. I mean people are trying to get some type of job. You have movements of unemployed workers (MTDs) all over the country.[61] In this category, you see monetary-oriented social organizations in which workers have taken over their own factories and workplaces. . . . The monetary-oriented movements often are small and entrepreneurial; they organize to produce something, anything, plates, drums, anything. They come from larger social movements. They may be a satellite of one of the recovered factories. Sometimes the workers with the factories have wives, so their wives and kids create these microbusinesses. I think that this is a very original form of organization within the broader social economy. They work on the cooperative side, but they don't overlook the cultural.

Professor Pérez and others described numerous ways in which faculty and students at UBA became involved in these sorts of movements, from providing expert advice and support, to assisting with organizing workers, to simply joining marches and protests. She also discussed a second type of movement: "You also have a wide range of non-monetary-oriented social movements. These are mainly social organizations; that is, they have political, cultural, and sometimes educational objectives and orientations. They really try to help the poorest of the poor to help them build a more positive future. . . . For example, you have neighborhood movements. But their main characteristic is that they are not organized by the state, not even by local authorities. They are organized by the people."

Neighborhood organizations mostly emerged in the face of a rapidly decomposing economic infrastructure. These organizations were most prominent in the poorest of neighborhoods throughout Buenos Aires and often functioned in conjunction with unemployed workers, sometimes operating outside of the Peronist-influenced labor unions. Of course, a key contribution to the broad popular movement came from the recuperated factory movement. The Movement of Recuperated Companies, like the street protesters, had been present in Argentina since the 1990s, but the events of 2001 only increased and intensified their presence. Drawing on the movement's battle cry—"Occupying, Resisting, Producing" (also "Occupy, Resist, Produce")—Andres Gaudin described the efforts of Argentine workers to take over abandoned factories:

It started timidly at first, in the mid-1990s, with workers occupying factories abandoned by their owners and getting them up and running again. But the phenomenon took off in December 2001, when the Argentinean economic crisis hit and massive street protests forced the country's president, Fernando de la Rua, from office. A decade of neoliberal policies had culminated in four years of recession, leaving thousands of domestically owned small and medium-sized businesses struggling or abandoned. Since 2001, in the face of growing unemployment and the state's failure to foresee or address the crisis, thousands of workers have restarted abandoned factories themselves. By taking over plant and equipment, these workers have put the right to work above employers' property rights, and have made some think that Argentina is at the beginning of a revolutionary process. While that is probably not the case, the takeovers do represent a remarkable form of action by Argentinean workers under conditions of harsh economic crisis.[62]

In pointing to the dramatic shift taking place throughout the country, Gaudin went on to cite a key statement from the constitution of the National Movement of Recuperated Companies: "We are a new social actor; we're creating a new consensus."[63]

The recovery of closed factories has greater legal standing than may be immediately apparent. First of all, the factories that are reclaimed typically fall into one of three categories: (1) the owner of the factory faces lawsuits from creditors, or (2) the factory has been declared bankrupt by the Argentine Department of Justice, or (3) the owner simply has abandoned the factory in light of marginal profitability.[64] In some cases, the workers have won the right to operate the plant and pay off creditors, or rent the plant and equipment from the owner. In other cases, the government has taken over the factory and handed it over to the workers. The latter has been precedent setting, as Attorney Luis Caro, legal adviser to many workers at recovered plants, explained: "We have been able to get many judges to agree that when the destiny of the society is in the balance, private property should come after the right to work."[65] Although the workers who engaged in the recovery of closed factories primarily based their actions on economic survival and not on some larger ideological challenge to capitalism, or global capitalism for that matter, the implications of their actions nonetheless pose a serious crisis for neoliberalism. Such actions also suggest alternative models of citizenship beyond those typically advanced by diehard free-market advocates and their tendency to define the ideal citizen as an individual entrepreneur.

A GLOBAL MOVEMENT

Although our focus centers mostly on the Argentine context, it is noteworthy that the cause of the popular rebellion in Argentina was also taken up elsewhere around the world. A notable example was the Argentina Autonomista Project (AAP), which originated in the United States and was founded by Graciela Monteagudo, an Argentine human rights activist and community artist living in Vermont. The AAP was founded to support the grassroots organizations of Argentina. As the movement's Web site explains: "The purpose of the argentina autonomista project is to bring news about events in Argentina to North America and Europe, through people-to-people exchanges and the internet (web and e-mail) and to facilitate non-hierarchical communication within Argentina, especially among groups with a minimum of resources."[66] The AAP engaged in a variety of actions to increase awareness about the struggle in Argentina, including the development and implementation of an eight-unit study abroad program complete with an internship at a recovered factory. Another example was the 2003 "Autonomista Caravan" in which a group of Argentine and Brazilian activists traveled from Montreal to Miami, using puppetry to dramatize events in Argentina before audiences up and down the East Coast. They closed their road trip with an "outlaw performance" described by Joseph Huff-Hannon on *ZNet* and posted at the AAP Web site:

What better way to end the caravan than with an outlaw puppet show? Right as the cardboard police came to evict the cardboard workers from their cardboard factory in the show, flesh and blood police officers showed up to tell Graciela Monteagudo, the Argentine "puppetista," that they had come to evict the audience. According to them, capacity had been exceeded in the hotel conference room. But this particular audience was not your typical passive crowd. They had all come here this weekend, to Columbus, Georgia, to protest against the infamous US Army School of the Americas. And in typical activist fashion the show went on, until it was forcefully moved outside and performed in the hotel parking lot. When the police threatened to arrest the crowd for trespassing on private property, the show continued on the sidewalk.[67]

Huff-Hannon went on to explain that the caravan's goals were to "expand people's knowledge of grassroots social movements in Argentina and Brazil, and to let people know about ways to visit, get to know, and work with movements down south." Huff-Hannon's "down south" most likely references any of the economically marginalized nations south of the U.S.-Mexico border and brings to mind once again the dramatic economic divide separating the United States and the many poorer nations of Latin America.

Raising awareness about the nature and significance of the struggle in Argentina certainly is an important task for those removed from the day-to-day crisis that is life in Buenos Aires and elsewhere throughout the country. But for the purposes of this chapter, it is most important to understand the contributions of UBA faculty and students and the potential role universities might play in supporting oppositional struggles. Consequently, the role of the university and its key actors in supporting social movements, as well as the implications such actions may have for advancing a more transformative vision of global citizenship, are central concerns of the remainder of this chapter.

UNIVERSITY ACTORS AND OPPOSITION TO NEOLIBERALISM

UBA faculty and students found many ways to involve themselves in supporting the grassroots movement in Argentina.[68] Students and professors constituted an important force in organizing and advancing protests and demonstrations in the streets of Buenos Aires, but they also participated in ongoing movements and organizations aimed at reconstituting Argentine society. At the heart of the grassroots movement was resistance to a form of society deeply influenced by powerful external forces acting upon Argentina. As Celía Rodríguez, a doctoral student, explained, "If we understand globalization as imperialism, then we are anti-globalizers. If we think that in order for many of these movements or for some part of these movements to arise, then they must connect with other international movements and form a part of an alternative globalization." Relatedly, Raúl García, a professor of social science at UBA, spoke of different levels of consciousness that arose in Argentina and that enabled movements to gain strength: "I think there are different levels of consciousness. I think that there are people that have greater consciousness than others, but that all the people involved in the movements, at this moment in history, have a consciousness that it [neoliberalism] doesn't work. They want it to change. I mean I think that they have an important role to play." Professor García went on to suggest that the struggle against neoliberal globalization is really not a new phenomenon, but is essentially a struggle against "a continuation of imperialism."

García's position that neoliberalism reflects the ongoing process of imperialism is supported to some extent by David Harvey, who argued that neoliberalism of the post–Cold War era actually contributes to new forms of imperialism, or what he termed the "new imperialism":

The end of the Cold War suddenly removed a long-standing threat to the terrain of global capital accumulation. The collective bourgeoisie had indeed inherited the earth. Fukuyama prophesized that the end of history was at hand. It seemed, for a brief moment, that Lenin was wrong and that Kautsky might be right—an ultra-imperialism based on a "peaceful" collaboration between all the major capitalist powers (now symbolized by the grouping known as the G7, expanded to the G8 to incorporate Russia, albeit under the hegemony of US leadership) was possible—and that the cosmopolitan character of finance capital (symbolized by the meetings of the World Economic Forum in Davos) would be its founding ideology.[69]

From Harvey's perspective, physical occupation of another nation is no longer necessary to enact forms of imperialism—it is simply a matter of imposing a global capitalist system that mostly benefits those nations holding the power of imposition. Although neoliberalism may constitute key elements of a new imperialism, this is not to suggest that it is advanced globally without much resistance. Indeed, UBA faculty and students have found numerous ways to be engaged in oppositional movements throughout Buenos Aires.

Forms of Engagement. The most basic form of engagement in various grassroots struggles is simply taking to the streets with other Argentine citizens. Mabel López, a graduate student specializing in economic and social development, discussed her involvement in this most basic but important act: "I participated a lot in protests in 2001 and even before 2001. Over here we have a tradition. Every March 24th we take to the streets to remember the coup d'etat of '76. . . . We commemorate this date and we embody this manifestation that perhaps is the most important one that Argentina has." López specifically discussed her participation in December 2001 and its significance: "During 2001, I did indeed participate in what was the social protest involving the fall of the streets on December 19th. I went out to the streets and I found myself with people. I went to protest and I found myself with my neighbors. I participated in the *cazerolazos*. I took to the streets with my own frying pan."

Other students and faculty also spoke of their involvement in the demonstrations in the streets and the powerful sense of unity that formed among many Argentine citizens. Professor Gómez explained it this way: "In 2001 there was a confluence of union members and strikers. It was a moment full of energy, where union members joined with the picketers. There was a famous song sung in the streets that talked about 'Picket, frying pan, the fight is one and the same.' "[70] Professor García also captured elements of the camaraderie evident in the streets: "I am involved in a leftist party and also the Workers Socialist Party. . . . It's a Trotskyist organization. And as a part of this militant organization, I anticipated a range of political manifestations and everything in-between. Then, on the 19th of December, the night when we occupied the city, we were all neighbors, together in the streets. All of Buenos Aires was a party."

A second common form of engagement involved assisting with the recuperated factory movement. Professor Pérez spoke of her past and present involvement with recuperated businesses and other community organizations such as soup kitchens: "One of the things that we do with factory workers is helping them to discover how to self-organize. They have been workers for generations, and then all of a sudden they were on their own. The university can help by providing them with some of its social capital." Pérez went on to note other ways in which UBA's faculty helped the workers' movement: "We have a rather large project focused on knowledge transference. It includes the faculty of engineering, sciences, social work, humanities. We have a project working with the workers of recovered businesses, teaching them organizational skills, but also teaching them how to keep their factories running."

Faculty and students in this study tended to believe that they could make a difference and that social movements held the potential of advancing the concerns of workers. As Professor Gómez explained,

I think you can say that a people united can change politics and the economy. They can change as much globally as they can at the city or local level. For example, globalization affects all of us through the work force. I believe that workers united, working together, can indeed block processes that might threaten their work, like the shrinking of the job market and diminishing salaries. Individuals cannot do anything, but they have to have an awareness of what affects them. The people with awareness who do nothing will explode. They have to recognize that they have the power to change their situation, to change their whole lives. They can fight.

This professor was quite optimistic about the potential of workers, students, and regular people to change society: "Yeah, I think they can change it. And not only can they change it, but they can rule their society. They make the society every day. The workers, the students, the peasants, they can rule. They make change every day. The economy of our society is made from all we have and do. Our clothes, our food, they are all made by the workers, the working class."

A third key form of engagement by many students and faculty concerned the Higher Education Law and efforts to overturn it. Ivan González, the president of an important student organization, elaborated: "The Higher Education Law was important. It was highly questioned by the students. We wanted to reverse the neoliberal forms of higher education that were being advanced. This implies that among other things the universities could regain some of the autonomy that they had lost." Professor Gómez also spoke to these concerns: "In the '90's the entire educational arena was changed at the high school level by the Federal Education Law and at the university level by the Higher Education Law. There were an enormous number of protests, marches, and rallies, against this law." Mabel López (a graduate student) had participated as an undergraduate in such protests: "When I was a student at UBA, I participated in university marches concerning the Higher Education Law. Mainly because there wouldn't be much of a budget for higher education anymore."

The Higher Education Law of 1995 was part of the broader privatization push aimed at shifting the role of the Argentine state from one of "provider and subsidizer," as Mollis argued, to one of "regulator."[71] This was in part accomplished through the creation of CONEAU, the National Council for University Accreditation and Evaluation (as noted earlier), combined with various efforts to increasingly shift the nation's universities from one of service to the broader society to one of service to the labor market and economic competitiveness. Mollis elaborated, "This new 'common sense' acknowledges the social value of higher education—but primarily for its role in meeting labor market demands and enhancing national competitiveness. The traditional knowledge-based responsibilities of universities—such as research, teaching, and community service—have increasingly been located within the demands of the labor market."[72] She went on to point out that, as part of the accountability movement, which she saw as being linked to the privatization trend and neoliberalism in general, both public and private universities must collect data from their graduates regarding their earnings. The outcome of this assessment process is, "Universities are considered to be successful to the extent to which their graduates earn high salaries."[73] Mollis described this broad shift as a movement "away from the idea of the university as a social institution toward the idea of higher education as an 'industry.'"[74] In light of these trends within the broad landscape of the nation's higher education system, the efforts of faculty and students at UBA to support various grassroots movements thus run contrary to the university-as-industry model critiqued by Mollis (the university-as-industry model more or less conveys the same idea as the economic tool model introduced earlier in this chapter). Given the form of university advanced by the Higher Education Law of 1995, it is fairly easy to see why those faculty and students most likely to support the grassroots movement also might be involved in opposition to the law; these individuals place great value on the university as a socially transformative institution and see their engagement with oppositional movements as an appropriate way of applying what they have studied and learned over the years.

A fourth form of oppositional engagement was tied more directly to the intellectual life of students and professors at UBA. For example, Mabel López, a graduate student, spoke of her involvement in organizing a conference on globalization:

April of 2002, or thereabouts, is when I started to participate in the organization of the first Global Social Forum in Argentina. In the Porto Alegre meeting of that same year it was proposed and decided to have a thematic forum in Argentina, given that there had been the economic disaster here. So I participated in the development of that forum and from there it turned into a global event. There was a global protest with all the renowned icons of the movement against the IMF and the other multilateral organizations, the WTO, World Bank, etc. . . . It had other themes tied in with globalization having to do with gender, agriculture, food supplies, and the environment. . . . At that moment in history there were connections being made with everything that has to do with people and organizations that work globally.

In discussions with UBA faculty and students, it was clear that many valued the opportunity to connect their intellectual work to social change efforts. Along these lines, Celía Rodríguez (a doctoral student in the Faculty of Philosophy and Letters) discussed her engagement in various intellectual activities: "We organized a congress two years ago where we brought together experiences from 20 universities from all over the country. . . . And we are publishing a book about the activities that the university is doing for society." Rodríguez went on to discuss the place of academic work, suggesting that getting individuals and groups together at conferences or assemblies is foundational to organizing ideas and joint forms of resistance: "We reflected and created theory in order to better understand and to more effectively transform our reality."

Marta Pérez spoke of the opportunity and responsibility that students and faculty at UBA have for linking the struggles of Argentina to larger issues and ideas tied to globalization. She pointed out that many workers lack the opportunity to forge such links: "I don't think globalization comes into their thoughts. They are preoccupied more with their daily lives. Anti-globalization movements are a luxury of the university students, although not all of the university students. Mainly the middle class. . . . I think that the most important thing to recognize is that we are free to do it. We have the possibility to do it. I can devote part of my research to this." Pérez went on to argue that this ought to be part of the function of the university: "There is an obligation of the university. I'm not asking whether or not we make a difference. That is a very difficult question to answer. But then I begin to think that in general we do make a difference. Anything makes a difference." Ivan González, a student leader, echoed Pérez's thoughts: "This sector has the privilege to think and have an intellectual relationship. We have an ethical responsibility to the people, to bring all the students and professors together to help with the challenges in our society."

UBA faculty and students also became involved in a variety of intellectual movements specifically in opposition to neoliberalism. One example is the women's movement. For example, María José Lubertino, president of the Women's Social and Political Institute and Professor of Human Rights at the Faculty of Law at UBA, offered the following observations about the crisis in Argentina:

The causes of the crisis are political and economic. There are factors and political responsibilities at both the national and international level. The political paradigm that is collapsing is partisan, patriarchal, vertical, authoritarian, misogynist, patronage-based and corrupt. After the dictatorship, this model prevailed in the power structures and it was maintained for twenty years with popular support, sometimes with good intentions and at other times with the worst intentions, but always with bad results for the majority of the population. The destruction of representation in politics put democracy itself at risk. But the implementation of an economic model that has resulted in the gravest concentration of wealth in Argentinean history is probably as bad or worse than the anti-democratic and corrupt political system. This model has resulted in 59% of children living under the poverty line and 18 million poor people within a total population of 40 million people. Ten years of Menem were central to an economic transformation encouraged by the world power centers. Today we are living with the consequences of that false bubble, of the superficial appearance of a first world economy.[75]

Professor Lubertino went on to describe the contribution of the women's movement: "The women's movement in all its diversity is contributing, as usual with its energy, creativity and free labour in order to solve the most pressing issues: hunger, poverty, education and health. A lot of women's energy is also going into spaces of citizenship participation, social rebellion, and popular activism."[76] She explained that since December 2001, the women's movement in Argentina has been involved in every social movement of significance. Professor Lubertino concluded by calling for global engagement and a challenge to the existing power structures that so dominate countries such as her own: "It is my hope that feminists all over the world will raise their voices about the situation in Argentina. Not only to ask for humanitarian assistance but also to say that enough is enough, to say that the democratization of [the] United Nations is indispensable—no more veto power to the Security Council, no more full members—no more power to the World Bank and the World Trade Organization, and the repolitization of the international funding agencies so they could return to the goals for which they were created."[77]

Many academics at UBA take seriously their intellectual contributions to the struggle against unchecked global capitalism and its deleterious effects on Argentina. These individuals tend to believe that although actions are critical to the success of oppositional movements, they do not want to ignore the fact that ideas matter too. They believe that the work of leading intellectuals at UBA, and throughout the country, has played a key role in the fight against neoliberal domination. For example, one professor addressed the contribution of Argentine and Latin American scholars to the anti-neoliberalism movement: "On the whole, I would say that we have a pretty good staff of people in the humanities, people who write a lot, write books, publish in America, Europe, and also of course, Argentina. Their contributions to the globalization debate are relevant. I wouldn't say that it is the most important thing, but these people are doing serious work in their fields, in social science, political science, sociology, anthropology, philosophy, literature."

The forms of engagement discussed in this section tend to suggest a particular vision of the university—one that sees the need to connect intellectual life and academic knowledge to social change efforts. Indeed, many students and faculty referenced a vision of a more transformative university, one committed to addressing the social and economic needs of broad segments of the society, as opposed to being bound by the concerns of an elite class of powerful decision makers.

Linking the University to Social Concerns. A key theme emerging from discussions with faculty and students was a strong belief in the need to embed the university in society for the purpose of addressing social needs. For example, María Torres, a student in the Faculty of Philosophy and Letters, discussed a course she took that focused on social movements. Torres was particularly enthused about the ways in which the professor linked the course to investigations of actual movements in Buenos Aires and how such a praxis-oriented strategy enabled the students to contribute in meaningful ways. She spoke passionately about the need for links between the university and society. Torres chose to focus her academic work on the relationship between universities and recuperated businesses, because she believed universities have a lot to offer such organizations. Torres also decided to work in this sector because she saw recuperated businesses as a more egalitarian way of functioning in a capitalistic world.

Roberto Silva, another student in the Faculty of Philosophy and Letters, addressed a key issue that occasionally was missing from the conversation about university-community ties—building a more egalitarian relationship between the university and the community, whereby the university is not simply positioned as the keeper of knowledge, in a Freirian sense, and the community is seen as something more than a passive recipient. Silva explained, "There is the need to think of these relationships as something other than the banking concept of the university. . . . So this work surrounds itself in the matter of how to think about a more horizontal relationship, one that breaks the barriers between society and the typical university." He explained that because of the success of some initial partnerships, which were grounded in egalitarianism, new collaborations have emerged and the university's engagement has surged as a consequence. There has been much success, but, as Silva noted, "the connection cannot be vertical." He concluded that a space within the university must exist to serve the society; the university must be free to reach out to "the people, social organizations, the popular sectors, those that don't have easy access to education." One professor pointed out that the kind of egalitarian relationships suggested by Silva may occur more naturally within the Argentine context, given that the nation's professors do not for the most part constitute a paid professional class and may see themselves as more connected to workers and the plight of the working class. This professor argued that this reality makes building less hierarchical ties to workers much easier. But he also concluded that the disadvantages of relying on so many part-time faculty members far outweigh any advantages and that in the end service to society suffers from lack of a full-time academic workforce.

Like Silva, many students and faculty involved in grassroots organizing took seriously the idea and practice of enacting more egalitarian pedagogical relations with communities of workers and activists. A professor with the Faculty of Social Sciences, Carlos Valle, spoke of organizing investigative projects with factory workers as a means of enhancing their bottom line and increasing the likelihood of the factory's survival. Some of these investigative projects led to the development and implementation of academic conferences, and on at least one occasion a major sociological conference was hosted by a recuperated factory.

Many of the individuals interviewed spoke passionately about the need to maintain the university's autonomy, in terms of governance, so that faculty and students would be free to engage the society. As Professor Pérez explained, "The most important thing is that we are free to do it. We have the possibility to do it. I can devote part of my research to this." Celía Rodríguez echoed these sentiments, arguing that the university must be free to use its intellectual resources to provide support and direction for the larger society: It should offer "critical analysis and think up alternatives. This is the duty of the university." Rodríguez added, "Presently, the students are working hand in hand [within society]. This is also important. But I also think that fundamentally the university has to say something, something with respect to what has happened, about what is happening, and about what should happen. The university should make some type of contribution in this area." Roberto Silva (a student) commented as well, "The university has to be financed through the state and it has to be free to serve those in need."

At times, though, there appeared to be some contradictions in assessing the connections between the university and society. Some still saw major barriers existing between UBA and the broader Argentine society, although they acknowledged that there have been improvements. Ivan González (a student leader) explained, "Yes, the relationship between the university and society has changed. There used to be a wall between the university and society. It was a different world from within the university, when compared to the outside." But González also noted that completely eliminating the wall would take time. Celía Rodríguez supported such a position, noting that many within the broader society continue to see the university as a "distant, foreign space." As Rodríguez explained, "Other people see the university as a place where those with money study for free, and that doesn't seem fair to them." She added, "With respect to the link between the university and social movements, I believe that the majority of the population doesn't know that there are bonds between these movements and the university; they don't know that people in the university are working with the movements, mainly because the communication is poor." Structurally speaking, at least one professor felt that there was something missing in the manner by which knowledge is transferred to various interested parties and organizations within Argentine society. Mabel López (a graduate student) elaborated on this: "We have a high level of political involvement. We have a high level of self-reflection concerning the broader society. We are interested in society's needs. But, as an institution, it seems to me that we are lacking in our ability to transfer knowledge to social organizations, not only in the social sciences, but in all departments." López saw some individuals and departments as being actively involved and highly successful in knowledge transfer, but at the university level, she saw major shortcomings.

One professor was highly critical of UBA for its lack of engagement in the community and in the broader social and economic needs of local citizens. Speaking mostly from a historical perspective, this professor explained,

> In the U.S., people see the university as the key institution in helping to advance corporate interests, community interests, regional development, and so forth. Is this the case in Argentina? No. We see very little of this. In Argentina, I would say that the dominant idea is that the university is an autonomous body, to be kept separate from the broader society to some extent. We've had to struggle for many years against the intrusion of political power. The consequence of such a concern for autonomy is very, very low-level connections with firms and even with the community.

But this professor went on to express a degree of optimism regarding the grassroots movement and the growing opportunity for UBA to take a stand in support of restructuring the society around a more democratic economic model. Indeed, this professor had assumed a leading role in opposing neoliberalism. His pointed remarks highlight a paradox with regard to the Argentine higher education context. Many faculty and students want and expect greater institutional autonomy, while at the same time they see the need for stronger ties and connections to the society. Many of these same faculty members fear the privatization of UBA, including the possibility of increased ties between the university and potential corporate sponsors. For these faculty members, increased corporate ties to the university threaten the social-movement ties that they prefer to build. Consequently, these individuals see state funding as a necessity for maintaining the degree of institutional autonomy necessary for meeting the needs of what they define as the broader social good. Of course, such a view exists in opposition to many of the policy positions of the IMF and World Bank, and of neoliberalism in general.

The actions and views of the faculty and students in this section speak to a different notion of the university than that of economic tool or the university as industry. These individuals mostly envision a university firmly planted within the community and directly involved in addressing social needs. This is not the ivory tower university, nor the dominant U.S. version heavily framed by academic capitalism. It is in fact quite unlikely that many of the activities described in this section would ever generate streams of revenue for university actors or the institutions they represent. But what *is* likely is that their engagement may contribute to something bigger than an immediate economic return: a restructured society based on more democratic economic practices along with perhaps more politically engaged citizens knowledgeable of globalization and its localized effects. Clearly, the lessons we can take from these professors and students have implications for how we think about the modern university and the challenge of advancing more globally minded citizens.

TOWARD AN EMANCIPATORY UNIVERSITY AND TRANSFORMATIVE CITIZENSHIP

Neoliberalism suggests a particular vision of society and the role of citizens. In *The Third Way: The Renewal of Social Democracy*, Anthony Giddens listed the essential characteristics of a neoliberal model of society, one he also described as "Thatcherism," reflecting Margaret Thatcher's role in advancing such a model: minimal government, autonomous civil society, market fundamentalism, moral authoritarianism, economic individualism, acceptance of inequality, traditional nationalism, welfare state as safety net (social support only as a final resort!), linear modernization, low ecological consciousness, realist theory of international order, acceptance of a bipolar world view (good vs. evil, dominant vs. the dominated, etc.).[78] At the center of such an ideology is, of course, market fundamentalism—a blind faith in the power of the market to solve all major social problems. Market fundamentalism suggests that any problem that cannot be solved by the free market must be accepted as a basic element of social existence; in essence, citizens must be realists and accept that social inequality is a fact of life. Giddens expanded upon this type of thinking in his critique of Thatcher's reign as prime minister of the United Kingdom:

Thatcherism characteristically is indifferent to inequalities, or actively endorses them. The idea that "social inequality is inherently wrong or harmful" is "naïve and implausible." Above all, it is against egalitarianism. Egalitarian policies, most obviously those followed in Soviet Russia, create a society of drab uniformity, and can only be implemented by the use of despotic power. . . . A society where the market has free play may create large economic inequalities, but these don't matter as long as people with determination and ability can rise to positions that fit their capacities.[79]

Of course, Thatcherism paralleled a U.S.-led version of the same movement under Ronald Reagan, often described as Reaganism. Whatever the name, the fundamental (and fundamentalist!) views of Thatcher and Reagan came to dominate global economic policy during the 1980s, and their influence continues into the present century; for example, Thatcherism and Reaganism helped shape the policy perspectives of NGOs such as the WTO, World Bank, and IMF.

Universities, acting in accord with neoliberal principles, have come to formulate academic programs, research, and service largely along the lines of an academic capitalist model fairly consistent with Giddens's delineation of Thatcherism. The consequence is that the social contract between societies and universities largely has been refashioned in a manner consistent with the market—a global market to some extent. Given that many public good endeavors—such as providing access to quality higher education for the poor and working class—are not revenue-generating activities, these objectives, associated to some extent with the Keynesian welfare state, are either dropped altogether or targeted for massive reductions in terms of financial support. Practically speaking, and in reference to U.S. higher education, this is obvious in the way that merit scholarships have replaced need-based financial aid. Such a trend clearly reflects the individualism inspired by academic capitalism, and is hardly an issue under regimes of power associated with neoliberalism, Thatcherism, or Reaganism. As Slaughter and Rhoades pointed out, "The neoliberal state focuses not on social welfare for the citizenry as a whole but on enabling individuals as economic actors. To that end, neoliberal states move resources away from social welfare functions toward production functions."[80] They went on to note, "The academic capitalism knowledge regime values knowledge privatization and profit taking in which institutions, inventor faculty, and corporations have claims that come before those of the public. Public interest in science goods are subsumed in the increased growth expected from a strong knowledge economy."[81] This position, of course, should sound familiar to anyone who has followed world politics and economics over the past thirty years or so. It is rooted in the thinking of neoliberal monetarists such as Milton Friedman (and his followers—the Chicago Boys) and, in essence, suggests that governments need to support individual and corporate entrepreneurial activity, because in the end such endeavors produce "trickle down" effects for the rest of society. The general belief is that a "rising tide lifts all boats."[82] But somewhere on the river to riches, economic and political elites failed to notice that not everyone was wealthy enough to own a boat. Or perhaps they did notice, but just did not care.

The forms of citizenship promoted by the academic capitalist knowledge regime are of course consistent with those envisioned by the neoliberal state. That is, students of the academic capitalist university are trained to be economic individualists who accept social inequality because, according to Thatcher, the free market is bound to produce vast economic differences given that personal qualities of determination and ability differ dramatically. A professor at UBA addressed this issue in the context of her critique of changes in undergraduate education taking place in Argentina:

Public universities used to train students for public service, but with the growing impact of privatization policies, students are no longer trained to enter the public labor market anymore. So, given that the public labor market is being dismantled, students of course are not willing to be educated in terms of public roles. Nowadays, corporatization is totally overwhelming the purposes of universities. So, for students there is no possibility of demanding some kind of public specialties. Take architecture for example. There is no urban architecture anymore because it is not marketable. The same thing happens when you look at lawyers and doctors; there is no public health, and it used to be really, very important. For me, the best way to explain exactly what marketization is is this: It is the privatization of minds. Students are being trained to belong to corporate enterprises.

Oppositional themes to the academic capitalist model certainly exist in academe, and whether one examines cases in Argentina or the United States, for example, it is readily apparent that neoliberalism and academic capitalism face resistance. The fact that opposition exists is quite consistent with Michel Foucault's work on power and disciplinary regimes, and this also helps to explain a key theoretical element of academic capitalism in the writing of

Slaughter and Rhoades. Although Slaughter and Rhoades stressed the power and penetrability of the academic capitalist regime in academe, they also noted that other regimes of power exist as well.[83] However, given the strength of academic capitalism, alternative regimes mostly exist as subordinate discourses, as marginal sources of power. For example, it may be argued that the academic capitalist knowledge regime supplanted the public good knowledge regime, but the latter continues to assert influence from time to time and offers ongoing resistance to the dominant model. Santos noted as much in his global analysis of the university of the twenty-first century: "The transformations of the past decade were profound and, despite having been dominated by the mercantilization of higher education, they were not reduced to only mercantile interests."[84]

Even though alternative conceptions of the university continue to operate, it is a mistake for progressive thinkers to seek a return to former dominant models. Santos made a strong case for a progressive vision of university transformation that "confronts the new with the new," as opposed to looking back on a university that was never in actuality so public-good oriented in the first place. As he explained in discussing the global context of higher education reform: "The new [the neoliberal or academic capitalist model] cannot be viewed as the problem and the old as the solution. Besides, what existed before was not a golden age and, if it was, it was just for the university and not for the rest of society, and, within the bosom of the university itself, it was for some and not for others."[85] As part of Santos's vision of meeting the new with the new, he described a movement toward a more democratic and socially conscious university, characterized by a shift from university knowledge to pluriversity knowledge. University knowledge defines the forms of knowledge produced for the better part of the twentieth century, firmly rooted in disciplinary regimes and distanced to some extent from society and the public good. When university knowledge served society, it did so on its own terms and through its own self-selected methodologies. In contrast, "pluriversity knowledge is a contextual knowledge insofar as the organizing principle of its construction is its application. Because this application is extramural, the initiative for formulating the problems to be solved and the determination of their criteria of relevance are the result of sharing among researchers and users. It is a transdisciplinary knowledge that, by its very contextualization, demands a dialogue or confrontation with other kinds of knowledge."[86]

Although the movement of the university to pluriversity knowledge has created the potential for stronger connections between the university and society and, in effect, introduced democratizing elements to the academy, the simultaneous push of neoliberalism over the past thirty years or so has made the university astutely concerned with the revenue potential of its knowledge production. Thus, the university of the twenty-first century is confronted with two opposing pressures: On the one hand, there exists the pressure that comes with a shift to pluriversity knowledge to increasingly answer to public demands and better serve societal needs. On the other hand, neoliberalism pushes the university to concern itself only with knowledge production leading to the generation of revenue—"the ultraprivate pressure to commodify knowledge displaces the social responsibility of the university with a focus on producing economically useful and commercially viable knowledge."[87] Although both of these pressures exist simultaneously, obviously neoliberal pressures to commodify knowledge severely limit the potential for pluriversity knowledge to serve societal needs beyond those of corporations and big business.

To rectify the problems confronting today's university, Santos pointed to "democratic and emancipatory university reform" involving a "counterhegemonic globalization of the university-as-public-good."[88] Such a vision stresses a return to national projects and identities, but in a nonnationalistic manner. For countries faced with economic marginality at the global level, including countries such as Argentina, this counterhegemonic struggle demands resisting neoliberal globalization. Thus, as neoliberalism pushes the erasure of nation-states and national projects and identities—this is especially the case with peripheral and semiperipheral countries—a counterhegemonic struggle calls for the elevation of a national project in which the university plays a critical role. Again, Santos addressed this issue:

The difficulty and, often, the drama of university reform in many countries reside in the fact that reform involves revisiting and reexamining the idea of the national project, something that the politicians of the last 20 years have hoped to avoid, either because they see such an idea as throwing sand in the gears of their surrender to neoliberalism or because they truly believe nationhood is outmoded as an instrument of resistance. The public university knows that, without a national project, there are only global contexts, and these are too powerful to be seriously confronted by the university's resistance.[89]

The challenge, then, is to rebuild the university in peripheral and semiperipheral nations in a manner supportive of neoliberal opposition and consistent with a national project capable of situating the society within a global context, but not as victim or puppet of global power brokers such as the IMF and World Bank, or the United States for that matter. In this light, the engagement of faculty and students from UBA in the grassroots resistance movement in Argentina is wholly consistent with a more democratic and emancipatory view of the university of the twenty-first century and suggests a particular understanding of global citizenship.

The democratic and emancipatory university offers a challenge to the widespread neoliberal model of citizenship by envisioning citizens as actively engaged in social struggle for the benefit of the broader society and not simply serving their own interests. Although neoliberalism emphasizes an economic view of citizens—citizens idealized as potential entrepreneurs and corporate/industrial men and women—the democratic, emancipatory university recognizes the role of citizens not only in terms of the economic dimensions of social life but also in terms of the cultural and political dimensions. Students educated in a manner consistent with the democratic, emancipatory university ideal are to be concerned about the well-being of others and interested in addressing social inequality. They offer a challenge to the logic of Reaganism and Thatcherism and instead of accepting vast levels of economic inequality as part of the natural evolution of societies, they revolt against them, as the citizens of Argentina and many of the faculty and students at UBA have done. Indeed, the actions of UBA faculty and students who participated in oppositional movements suggest important points to consider as we seek to advance global citizenship in increasingly complex times.

One obvious lesson to be learned from a study of the Argentine grassroots rebellion and the engagement of faculty and students is that local action ought to be informed by a critical and complex understanding of global processes. Related to this point, universities are needed to prepare citizens for this complex sort of engagement. One professor alluded to these issues in a discussion of university reform:

Citizenship is a central theme that is not on the general reform agenda and it should be. For our part, we are talking about promoting some university studies, but we've done little up to now in the area of citizenship, especially given the powerful global forces acting upon Argentina. I think that the study of the construction of the citizen is indispensable. In the reconstruction of a new democratic contract among Argentines, the role of the local is going to be even more relevant than it was in the past.

Clearly, any conception of global citizenship must take into account what it means to exist within a particular local context, including concerns for the needs and challenges of local communities. The democratic, emancipatory university envisioned by Santos must also recognize these concerns. As Professor Cristina Martino argued,

Each distinct area of thought that the university has, each distinct discipline, must support the community. Each has to start with small things. For example, what is done in architecture should not only be dedicated to the problematics of engineering and construction, but also to the possibility of affordable housing and the materials of urbanism. All this makes the social vital to the university. I think that all disciplines have to forcefully motivate themselves to try to solve the types of social problems that our country has.

Another point deriving from the comments of UBA faculty and students concerns the role of the university in serving the public good and the challenges in helping the general public to understand the breadth of such a role. Universities around the world often come under suspicion from ethnic minorities, women, and the lower and working classes, in part because universities have at times been ivory towers removed from the daily lives of less privileged folks. Universities have not always been so democratic, even when the public good regime supposedly took precedence (it was really a public good regime as defined by elite classes of people). Consequently, the new democratic, emancipatory university must work to build connections with the people, including those who have been most excluded from the university on the basis of race, ethnicity, class, and gender, among other defining characteristics that have formed the basis of discrimination.

A third point suggested by this study concerns the challenge of building financial support and infrastructure for the university, given the goals of a democratic, emancipatory vision and its dependence on state support. The democratic, emancipatory model does not reject private capital per se, but it clearly does not give precedence to privatization. Business and industry also have interests in the university, and they too must be included in the definition of society and in any deliberations about what is meant by the broader social good. But unlike the neoliberal model, the democratic university does not place the interests of business and industry above all else. The ability to resist such pressure depends on adequate public support—that is, financial support in the form of state monies. This means making the public-good contribution of the university clear to the broader public. Part of the challenge involves connecting the university to a national project, a national identity, but at the same time coming to terms with an increasingly global world and its influences. This is no small feat. A professor in medical education at UBA addressed the challenge of building such an institution, while also noting the importance of a national project:

We lack infrastructure, budgetary support, so it's better for us to associate ourselves with other universities in the form of a network. What is important is to define the project. Now, we should not copy models, but instead rescue our own national identity. This is important because at times globalization implies adaptation to another world, and we have to form our own culture, but knowing what happens outside and seeking support, but not copying everything from the outside.

This professor went on to argue that part of the challenge involves addressing the general public and helping people to see the value of the university to the society in general. A big challenge is countering the views and policies of global organizations that may not see the value of the university as a public-good model. As he maintained, "They do not see higher education as a public service provided by the state. . . . The IMF, for example, supports the development of private universities, because they require that the services come with fees. I believe that this is an erroneous perspective. We have to change the public mentality a little and find new ways to support public education."

CONCLUDING REMARKS

The challenges confronting universities are many, but one overarching issue continues to divide students, scholars, practitioners, and policy makers: the fundamental tension between a social vision of the university versus a more economic-oriented and market-driven perspective. Each of these perspectives is suggestive of a particular version of citizenship and the choices students and faculty must make as they enact academic lives and commitments. Given the significant tension between a market-driven perspective and a more socially transformative orientation, many have portrayed the challenge in either/or terms, implying that a final resolution to this tension must necessarily conclude with a momentous victory by one side and annihilation of the other. In terms of the forms of citizenship suggestive of such a resolution, universities are to promote either economic entrepreneurs acting in their own self-interests or socially engaged citizens mindful of the broader good. This chapter, like others in this book, favors a more hybridized view of the ideological battle before us. Given the economic reality of the modern university—in Argentina and elsewhere—the push and pull of market economics cannot be ignored. By the same token, a nation cannot afford the social consequences of turning over its universities, and indeed its entire higher education system, completely to the market. But the trend toward marketization is growing by the hour, and to a great extent this book seeks to challenge this trend. The intent here is not to eliminate entrepreneurialism, commercialization, and some forms of privatization, but to support a counterbalance by suggesting a more hybridized, socially transformative university. The model of the university advanced in this chapter, and throughout the book as well, is one that incorporates in its model of service to society a commitment to private enterprise, but not at the expense of a democratically negotiated public good.

The social vision of the university advanced in this chapter highlights a form of citizenship in opposition to the neoliberal, capitalist model founded on individualism and the pursuit of self-interests. The UBA faculty and students who became involved in the Argentine rebellion saw the benefit of a university embedded in service to the needs of society. The model of citizenship they embraced was one that values a spirit of collectivism and a view that everyday people—factory workers, the unemployed, students, professors, and neighbors—can challenge the global movers and shakers of the IMF and other intergovernmental organizations, but only when they organize and stand in solidarity with one another. Their challenge to neoliberalism and global capitalism reveals the power of the people and the social movements they create to forge a more socially conscious society, one that recognizes the importance of preserving local jobs and opportunities, impacting communities and neighborhoods, and challenging antidemocratic actions by political and economic elites. Although their concerns were primarily about local issues, they clearly saw many of the global connections and sources of influence that had brought Argentina to her knees.

The view of the university suggested by the faculty and students introduced in this chapter is one that emphasizes social obligations, as opposed to stressing an opportunistic vision of the university tapping into any revenue stream available. The socially responsible university, with its commitment to the broader social good, is in a sense a model for individual behavior as well and suggestive of a more community-minded form of citizenship. This spirit of collectivism stands in sharp contrast to the model of citizenship advanced by neoliberalism, in which a calculus of personal economic gain is the strategic ideal and individualism the defining quality of social existence. The consequence for societies when citizens come to define their relations to others only on the basis of personal gain may be devastating for a world that increasingly demands global cooperation. Universities must stand as more than beacons of hope and actively enact forms of social responsibility fitting the struggles of communities and the challenges of preparing citizens for an increasingly complex and conflicted global environment.

CHAPTER 5

POSTCOMMUNISM, GLOBALIZATION, AND CITIZENSHIP:

The Case of Central European University in Hungary

INTRODUCTION

The enormous political changes sweeping through Hungary in 1989 transformed the streets of Budapest. The fall of communism and the introduction of a capitalist economic system brought Western advertising, multinational companies, U.S.-style malls, and even a new, sassier sense of fashion, especially among the younger generations. As the present suddenly became a part of history, the city returned to the use of precommunist street names and removed many of the symbols that defined its almost half-century of existence under communist rule. Missing from the streets of Budapest today are the towering statues of a Soviet Army Liberation Soldier and of Lenin, Engels, and Marx. Gone are the Hungarian-Soviet Friendship Memorial and the Hungarian Communist Party Memorial Plaque. Although these monuments are now absent from the city's life, much of the communist past lives on in

Szoborpark (Statue Park), an outdoor museum tucked away in a Budapest suburb, a thirty-minute bus ride away from Budapest.[1]

Every year, forty thousand tourists—both Hungarian and foreign—visit Szoborpark, displaying forty-two communist-era statues, monuments, and plaques gathered from the streets and squares of Budapest. Upon passing through the gate where larger-than-life statues of Lenin, Engels, and Marx vigilantly stand guard, the visitor is taken on a powerful pathway of symbolism: "The park is arranged in the form of a straight path, from which 'figure-of-eight' walkways lead off (so that the wandering visitor will always return to the true path!), around which statues and monuments are displayed. In the centre of the park is a flower bed in the form of a Soviet Star. Eventually, the path ends abruptly in a brick wall, representing the 'dead end' which state socialism represented for Hungary: visitors have no choice but to walk back the way they have previously come."[2]

Symbolism, however, is not only apparent in the park's physical design. The mere existence of Szoborpark is a powerful statement of Hungary's approach to dealing with the transition from communism, a process that began in 1989. Indeed, preserving the street monuments and statues in the setting of a park was just one of many solutions considered. One extreme proposal campaigned for the monuments' destruction, while another advocated for leaving them untouched in their original locations as continuing reminders of past communist rule.[3] The creation of Szoborpark is a carefully planned middle ground, both acknowledging the historical significance of the statues and hiding them away from the public eye on the edge of the nation's capital.[4] But, above all, Szoborpark represents the transition of forty-two emblems of communism to a democratic society. In the words of Ákos Eleőd, Szoborpark's architect: "This Park is about dictatorship. And at the same time, because it can be talked about, described and built up, this Park is about democracy. After all, only democracy can provide an opportunity to think freely about dictatorship. Or about democracy. Or about anything!"[5]

Thinking freely about dictatorship, about democracy, and, most importantly, about postcommunist transitions in a broader political, cultural, and economic sense also became the focal point of conversations among a group of intellectuals during seminars organized in April 1989 in Dubrovnik, in today's

Croatia.[6] Sponsored by the Soros Foundation, a U.S.-based organization headed by George Soros, the Hungarian-born U.S. financier and philanthropist, the seminars focused on the idea of creating a university aiming to train a new elite that would help along Central and Eastern Europe's and Central Asia's transition from communism to democracy and capitalism. In 1991, a new institution of higher education came into being and was named Central European University (CEU). The university's founding ideals were built on a vision of an open society defined by CEU as "the recognition that no one has a monopoly on truth, that different people have different views and interests, and that there is a need for institutions to protect the rights of all people to allow them to live together in peace. . . . Reliance on the rule of law, the existence of democratically-elected governments, diverse and vigorous civil society, and respect for minorities and minority opinions" were also important determinants of the view of an open society adopted by CEU.[7]

The transition from one-party rule to democracy and from a state-controlled economy to one based on the free market, however, was not the only transition that has shaped CEU's existence. The integration of several formerly communist countries into the European Union—a process that began with the accession of the Czech Republic, Estonia, Hungary, Latvia, Lithuania, Poland, Slovakia, and Slovenia in 2004—has also had a profound impact, both shifting the university's emphasis and raising a host of new questions concerning its role in society. At the same time, as the countries in the region have completed the most crucial period of political and economic transition, the very meaning and relevance of postcommunist transitions have changed, also redirecting CEU's emphasis. Equally importantly, along with other colleges and universities in the world, CEU has not been immune to the forces of globalization that have come to significantly shape institutional functioning, goals, and practices regardless of a university's location, mission, and years in existence. As István Teplán, CEU's former senior vice president, stated succinctly, depicting CEU as a university in transition, both acting upon and being acted upon by forces in the external world:

An important feature of CEU is that it's constantly changing and its management necessitates a level of flexibility that is rarely seen at other universities. CEU came into being at the time of system change: Around the year 1989, Central Europe was a very important, interesting region, some of the world's best professors came here to teach, to do research, because their academic interests attracted them here. By now, this period has come to pass, we have a market economy, and so the primary focus of research on "transition" issues does not concern this region either. At CEU as well, problems following the "transition" have become increasingly important: the distribution of income, inequality, poverty, the EU, the expansion of the EU. Therefore, on the one hand, critical social science is no longer new in the region and, on the other hand, the region itself is increasingly faced with the same problems as other European countries. These developments take away from the uniqueness of CEU; for this reason, we need to concentrate on quality, the one characteristic of CEU that makes any university truly attractive.[8]

CEU, during its brief existence so far, has thus undergone a variety of transitions, shaping its functions, mission, and values. This chapter brings into focus the significance of these transitions at CEU, a university whose very existence was built upon its role as a change agent in societies undergoing major political, economic, and social transformations. What role has CEU played in Hungary, Central and Eastern Europe's and Central Asia's former communist states, the European Union, and a global sphere? In what ways have the original goals changed with the progress of the postcommunist transition and as a result of other external political and economic forces—mainly those related to globalization? What opportunities and challenges do CEU and its faculty face? In what ways have the university and its faculty approached their role in addressing issues of democracy in the region's emerging free-market economies? Finally, how have these societal and institutional transformations shaped CEU faculty's conceptions of citizenship? Questions such as these were at the center of our discussions with twenty-one faculty members at CEU, discussions that focused on how faculty members have interpreted both the university's role and their own roles within CEU. Our conversations with professors representing departments of political science, history, gender studies, environmental science, international relations and European studies, economics, and public policy were complemented by a review of primary documents and secondary literature related to CEU, documenting the progression of the university from its creation through the early years of the twenty-first century.

THE FOUNDING OF CENTRAL EUROPEAN UNIVERSITY

CEU was founded in 1991 as a U.S.-style, English language, graduate school offering education primarily in the humanities and social sciences for students arriving from the countries of Central and Eastern Europe and Central Asia. First accredited by the Commission on Higher Education of the Middle States Association of Colleges and Schools in the United States, CEU operates with a charter from the Board of Regents of the University of the State of New York. In April 2005, CEU also received legal status as a Hungarian institution of higher education under the name Közép-európai Egyetem (the literal translation of Central European University), accredited by the Hungarian Accreditation Committee and the Higher Education and Research Council. The majority of funding for the university has been provided by George Soros, whose annual contributions of $20 million were followed by a $250 million endowment gift in 2001. The donation was to become the largest gift amount that a university in Europe had ever received. Soros commented on the purpose of the gift in a 2001 interview with the *New York Times*: "This replaces my annual contribution. . . . It's the cutting of the umbilical cord. This university is the brain center of my foundation network."[9]

In its 1990 yearbook, the Soros Foundation pointed to CEU's intention "to bring back the network of universities that reached their zenith during the late Middle Ages and whose academics traveled between various locations, in search of enlightenment."[10] These ideals were the driving force behind the founders' original plan to create a multicampus institution in several countries, reflecting the strong regional—rather than national—focus in the university's mission. Political pressures and related problems with accreditation, however, preempted the founders' intention to establish a campus in Bratislava, Slovakia.[11] Although later plans involved creating "a university with three legs: Budapest, Prague and Warsaw,"[12] this plan also failed to materialize when the Prague and Warsaw campuses closed after a few years of operation.[13] Today, CEU firmly stands on one leg, the campus in the heart of Budapest.

The history of CEU in Prague, documented by Jiři Musil, the academic director of the Czech campus from 1991 to 1994, provides an insightful glimpse at some of the attitudes surrounding the creation of a private U.S.-sponsored university in Eastern and Central Europe. Writing with the voice of clear frustration in 2002, Musil described an initially supportive environment in the Czech Republic that, brought on by political changes and a new administration in 1992, "slowly transformed into an effort to get rid of the university."[14] During this period, opponents expressed concerns about the "unfair competition" that CEU represented for existing Czech institutions of higher education, pointed to the inability of the Czech Republic to contribute financially to the university's functioning, and underscored the absence of a legal basis for the founding of the type of university embodied by CEU. But the greatest opposition, according to Musil, had strong philosophical-political underpinnings: "The liberal concept of an open society represented by the university was unacceptable" for the newly formed government of Václav Klaus.[15] The Czech government then proposed cuts in funding for the university, recommended that Soros find a location for the school outside the capital, and drew upon Czech law in claiming that CEU could not become a part of the country's higher education system and, therefore, should not have the power to award degrees. In short, CEU would not be accepted as a university in the Czech Republic. By 1996, CEU Prague was left with no students or professors and the Czech campus ended its operations.

Support for CEU proved considerably stronger in Hungary, where the institution functioned first as a U.S. entity and today forms a legal part of the Hungarian system of higher education as well. Writing in 2002 about CEU Prague's history, Musil reflected on the dynamism of the Budapest campus: "The school has a large library, publishing house, conference center, exhibition gallery and dormitory. Its annual budget is approximately 21 million USD. But these are dry facts—what's more important is that it has undeniably become one of the liveliest and most influential intellectual centers in Europe. All this could also have been in Prague. Unfortunately, it's not."[16]

Although the plan to establish a multicampus institution of higher education was not successful in the long run, CEU has focused its attention on a broad range of countries since its establishment. In the 1990 Yearbook, the Soros Foundation outlined four specific goals driving the creation of the new university, focusing on the region in its entirety. The four goals consisted of (1) creating a new curriculum that can be taught at CEU and other universities in the region, (2) assisting in the training of new leaders in Central Europe, (3) raising the standards of education and research in the whole region, and (4) promoting cooperation and understanding among the region's citizens and nations.[17] Most importantly, all of these goals were to take shape in the context of the major transitions that societies in Eastern and Central Europe, as well as the former states of the Soviet Union, were undergoing beginning in 1989, with the onset of the postcommunist transition.

A REGION IN TRANSITION

The years 1989 and 1990 marked the beginning of a new era in the lives of the countries that made up the communist bloc of Central and Eastern Europe and Central Asia. Country after country succumbed to a wave of mostly non-violent revolutions deposing the one-party political system and ushering in principles of democratic governance and a capitalist economy. Although a reform movement transforming communist regimes was under way in a number of the region's countries, the revolutionary events took many by surprise. Ronald Linden's famous exclamation on Radio Free Europe, proclaiming that "our jaws cannot drop any lower," has become a widely cited commentary of the changes that took place in the region.[18] Geoff Eley commented on the impact of each revolutionary event on the next: "The revolutionary transitions, through which Communists surrendered their monopoly, were generic. They were linked in a single chain, each sparking and inspiring the next. This connectedness came partly from common belonging to the Warsaw Pact and partly from regional circuits of opposition from the 1980s. But it also resulted from the communications revolution apparent in 1968. These revolutions were televised."[19]

No doubt, events followed each other in rapid succession: In June 1989, the Solidarity Party in Poland, after almost a decade of struggle against the Communist Party, claimed overwhelming victory in the country's parliamentary elections. In October 1989, Hungary passed legislation allowing democratic parliamentary and presidential elections and adopted the name "Republic of Hungary," replacing the former designation of "People's Republic." In November 1989, the Berlin Wall fell, making it possible to travel freely between East and West Berlin. In November and December 1989, during the

Velvet Revolution, hundreds of thousands of protesters gathered in Prague, demanding change in the political system. By December 10, Czechoslovakia saw the establishment of its first noncommunist government since 1948. In December 1989, Nicolae Ceauşescu, the leader of the Romanian Communist Party, was executed along with his wife, Elena. In 1990, democratic parliamentary elections were held in Romania (May) and Czechoslovakia and Bulgaria (June). On October 3, 1990, East and West Germany were unified. In 1991, Albania conducted free elections, temporarily keeping communist rule but turning to a coalition government with noncommunists in response to popular pressure. The year 1991 also witnessed the disintegration of the Soviet Union into fifteen states, following free elections and declarations of independence. The Warsaw Pact, the organization to which the communist states of Bulgaria, Czechoslovakia, Hungary, Poland, Romania, the Soviet Union, and East Germany had belonged beginning in 1955, was officially disbanded in July 1991.

The enormity of the revolutions that toppled communism and brought in some of the most significant societal changes of the twentieth century has been repeatedly analyzed by social scientists. Reflecting on the significance of 1989, Padraic Kenney wrote: "As the years have passed, the term 'revolution' often disappears; people even in Central Europe speak of the 'changes,' the 'transition,' or just '1989.' But the scope of change—political, economic, social, cultural—plus the speed at which it took place make any other word a strange and even tendentious fit."[20] In a similar vein, Eley's work highlighted the wide variety of transformations resulting from the revolutions: "What did the 1989 revolutions achieve? These were democratic revolutions in a strict sense. Primary demands recurred: free elections, parliamentary government, civil freedoms, multiparty competition. Conditions of pluralism were secured, not just by party competition in free elections but via rule of law and a guaranteed public sphere. Party and state were to be separated, as were state and civil society. So too were the state and economy: the biggest future agenda was marketization."[21]

On the tenth anniversary of 1989, Vladimir Tismaneanu referred to 1989 as precipitating "an irreversible transformation," explaining that "the upheavals in the East, especially in the Central European core countries, were indeed a series of *political revolutions* that transformed the existing order decisively and irreversibly. They replaced autocratic one-party systems with emerging pluralist polities. They allowed the citizens of the former ideologically driven despotisms to recover their principal human and civic rights and to build new open societies. Instead of centrally planned command economies, these societies have begun to create market economies."[22] Tismaneanu added,

> Some have succeeded better and faster than others in creating political pluralism, a market economy, and a civil society, but throughout the former Soviet bloc the once-monolithic order has given way to political and cultural diversity. While we do not yet know whether *all* these societies will become functioning liberal democracies, we do know that in all of them, the Leninist systems based on ideological uniformity, political coercion, dictatorship over human needs, and suppression of civic rights have been dismantled.[23]

Open society, democracy, and political and cultural diversity, however, are by no means the only ideals that come to mind when thinking about the legacy of the fall of communism and the years of transition that followed. Widespread nationalism, violent ethnic conflict, even instances of ethnic cleansing have haunted several areas of the region, especially the former Yugoslavia and the newly independent states of the former Soviet Union, such as Georgia, Armenia, and Azerbaijan.[24] Economic and political instability also continue to be prominent in a range of nations emerging from the communist era. Indeed, remaking the societies of Eastern and Central Europe and the former Soviet Union has proven to be an arduous task, often fraught with nationalism, inequality, instability, and violent conflict. Important to recognize, however, is the complexity of the postcommunist transition in the region, an experience that harbored widely varying processes and outcomes reflecting the individual societal context and history of each nation. Tismaneanu described the process of transition in the following terms:

> A struggle between the friends and foes of an open society is being waged in all these countries. . . . Economic hardship, growing unemployment, and the disbanding of the socialist state's welfare system have generated discontent, anger, and rampant disaffection with the new order. . . . Some countries have better prospects than others in their efforts to democratize and create successful market economies. These opportuni-

ties are directly related to the learning of deliberative procedures, the development of pluralist institutions, and the maturing of a political class committed to the values of an open society. In some countries liberal views and practices will prevail, in others civil society and pluralism will remain weak, problematic, and beleaguered.[25]

The transition from communism to democracy and a free-market economy has thus been marked by significant national differentiation, bringing about a wide variety of economic, social, and political conditions.

CEU: THE ORIGINAL MISSION

Recognizing the complexities and variation of the region plays a key role in efforts to understand the nature of CEU's self-imposed task to help along the process of postcommunist transition in the countries of the region. In fact, the role embraced by CEU was no less than providing the types of educational and research structures that, in turn, can not only address the country-specific transformations but also train a new elite that comprises the leadership of the region's countries with the goal of promoting the emergence and maintenance of open societies. In the words of Gyula Révai,[26] a professor of economics: "So the traditional mission statement of CEU was to spread the idea of an open society and Western and European values in Central and Eastern Europe. . . . Really to bring what the rest of the world was doing in the last 50 years into these countries. I think this is still an important mission and I think basically all faculty members would agree this has been important, but there is another goal, which is to really start research within this region, so it's not just to bring the education and bring the ideas, but to somehow influence the economic environment."

What approaches has CEU adopted to achieve these goals? And what specific activities reflect the early mission of CEU? A March 2000 report from the university's rector provides a useful summary of the goals embraced by the various academic units of CEU in the ten years following its founding in 1991: "Many of the newly established Departments and Programs saw their central role in teaching and promoting the mission of the University, primarily in the region of Central and Eastern Europe and also in the other further lying post-communist countries. Other Departments preferred to understand their mission in the region to be that of becoming the best possible disciplinary followers of Western Universities. Some units succeeded in finding a genuinely scholarly answer to being both of high quality and of regional relevance."[27]

A key manifestation of CEU's mission to address issues of postcommunist transition is reflected clearly in the university's curriculum. A sampling of CEU's early syllabi strongly reflects this emphasis: In the years 1992 through 1996, for example, the political science department offered classes with the titles of "Breakdown of Dictatorships," "Comparative Democratic Government," "The Concept of Civil Society," "The End of the (Post) Cold War?" "Political Economy of Stabilizations and Structural Adjustment," and "Post-Communist Transition in Historical and Comparative Perspective." In the same period, some of the classes offered by the Department of International Relations and European Studies bore the titles of "Comparative Democratic Transition in Europe" and "Privatization in Eastern and Central Europe." The legal studies department's offerings included courses on "Freedom of Speech," "Legal Institutions of the Market," and "Constitutionalism and Rights in Post-Communist Central Europe."

The Department of International Relations and European Studies' winter 1996 course on "Privatization in Eastern and Central Europe" provides one example of the approach adopted to offer a critical analysis of the transition. As the syllabus described:

Five years after the tumultuous events of the winter of 1989, when the "realities" of the world seemed to change before our eyes, observers have learned to be more cautious in their expectations for the future. Gone are the confident predictions of rapid change from state-controlled economies to efficient systems based on private property, replaced by a grudging acceptance that "privatization" in Eastern Europe has little in common with a large garage sale, or some other process of distribution. In 1994, participants and observers speak of privatization as a contingent process, replete with complexities both theoretical and technical. This course will examine some of these complexities, focusing on the concept of what is property, and how it is possible for a functional and efficient property system to develop.[28]

Taking a comparative approach, the course placed special focus on four countries in the region: the Czech Republic, Russia, Hungary, and Poland.

Postcommunist countries, however, were not the only geographic emphasis of the courses taught at CEU during its early years of existence. Instead, nations from around the world were frequently featured in the topics discussed in the curriculum. For example, in a course on "Comparative Institutional Federalism," taught in the fall of 1995, the instructor described the goal to "explore constitutional democracies that adopted a federal system of government (with the focus on the USA, Canada, Switzerland, Germany, and India)."[29] Several courses in the Department of Environmental Sciences and Policy considered environmental issues from a global perspective, comparing the experiences of Central and Eastern Europe to other countries of the world.

The university's curriculum has also focused on presenting theoretical and methodological frameworks, many of them taken from recent and contemporary Western thought. During the 1994 and 1995 academic years, students in the gender studies department, for example, took courses on "Theory and Method in Contemporary Gender Studies." In 1997–98, the curriculum was broadened to include courses on "Gender and Nationalism" and "Social Science Methodologies from a Feminist Perspective," among other new courses. Econometrics, microeconomics, macroeconomics, and theories of market economies were important offerings of the economics department in the years 1992–96. The departments of medieval studies and history have focused on presenting historical perspectives, primarily based on the countries of the postcommunist region of Central and Eastern Europe and Central Asia.

The preceding examples of courses offered at CEU in the early years of its existence point to a curriculum intent on raising students' awareness and understanding of some of the most critical issues facing the postcommunist region. The university made this initial goal clear: "CEU was to be an unusual graduate school for this region, an independent international institution offering a curriculum in the social sciences and the humanities, committed to promoting a new model of learning: serious and morally responsible intellectual engagement inspired by, and in the service of, pressing and challenging social needs."[30] But who were the students participating in the "serious and morally responsible intellectual engagement" described as a major goal of the university? Instruction at CEU began with one hundred students, arriving primarily from Central and Eastern Europe and the former Soviet Union. Although students from other parts of the world also attended, it was only in 2000 that the university's recruitment efforts were expanded to nations outside the postcommunist region.[31]

In the early years of its existence, then, CEU and its faculty made a conscious effort to fulfill the mission to train the new elite of formerly communist countries. As reflected in the comments of Anna Meier, a professor of international relations and European studies: "Of course, the mission statement in the beginning was to promote open societies and to educate a new generation of leaders, including politicians, journalists, activists, professors, lawyers, to educate them and inculcate them in the values of democracy and civil freedom, so they will go back to their countries and sort of spread this into this big huge mission, which I think is great. Already our first generation of students are sending more students here." Andrea Hóka, a professor of political science, expressed enthusiastic affirmation to our question of whether CEU has accomplished its goal to train the leaders of the region: "Yes. The short answer to that is yes. Yes, yes, yes. I bump into CEU graduates everywhere."

The university's engagement in the issues of political, economic, and social transition and introducing Western traditions of research and education have been evident in other aspects of CEU's functioning as well. In one important example, the university hosted a conference examining the legacy of the 1989 revolutions. The conference, held in March 1999, bore the title "Between Past and Future: The Revolutions of 1989 and the Struggle for Democracy in Central and Eastern Europe" and brought together public figures, scholars, and journalists from a range of countries representing both the postcommunist region and the Western world.[32] Throughout the university's existence, emphasis has also been placed on the recruitment of faculty both from the region and from other parts of the world, especially Western Europe and North America.

NEW TRANSITIONS—A NEW MISSION

Although many of CEU's original goals have remained crucial as the university entered its second decade of existence, strong forces of change became evident in the early years of the twenty-first century. These changes were well reflected in our conversations with CEU faculty:

Hungary has joined the European Union, as have a number of other countries, and traditional students from Poland and the Czech Republic, Slovakia, that used to come here can now go to universities in Germany or Denmark or Britain, or wherever, and they're willing to pay to go to Britain to do their degree rather than have a free education at CEU.

James Wilkens, Professor of Public Policy

I see a big challenge in the expansion of the European Union, we have competitors, various competitors from European universities, which are more accessible to our students now, the students who apply to CEU. So we really have to compete more on the basis of our own merits and quality, which may face us with bigger problems. And just the places [where students can study]. . . . You know, it's nicer for a student to live in Paris. So globalization has good and bad effects. The good effect is that we can have really better faculty, more diverse faculty, better trained, more known faculty, and we can have better students. The difficult aspect to it is that we have to compete more for this.

Ernő Papp, Professor of Political Science

The whole idea of focusing only on post-communist countries was a little bit outdated already because the whole region ceased to be homogenous, had become quite diverse. So the Board of Trustees decided that CEU should really go global, it should look at all countries, on the whole idea of transition, democratization. We have Iraqi students, Iranian students, so we are really going global, and our department this year got this large new grant from the European Union, Erasmus Mundus, which directly gives us a mandate to invite people from all over the world. This is a list of students who were admitted and they are coming from countries as diverse as Australia, Canada, U.S., Brazil. Of course, from the Soviet countries, China, India, Malaysia, it's really global.

Erik Jones, Professor of Environmental Science and Policy

I think the university had a clearer goal in the past as the first Western-style education system for the students from this region, I think in the early 90s they played an important role. I think nowadays, it has lost some of that original mission. Countries like the Czech Republic and Slovakia or Hungary are no longer countries that need help from CEU. Perhaps the country that needs some sort of help would be, I don't know, Kyrgyzstan and Georgia and so on, and on that front, maybe the university still has mission goals there. . . . I don't know if this is a formal change in mission, but I think the university is becoming more like an international graduate school where fee-paying students are encouraged to apply and professors are judged more on their research and publishing record rather than their ability to teach students.

John Singer, Professor of International Relations and European Studies

What is apparent from the preceding faculty comments is that toward the end of its first decade of existence, CEU started experiencing considerable challenges to its identity and was confronted with the task of reframing its mission in an attempt to sustain its relevance as an institution of higher education. Some of these challenges arrived with the progress of postcommunist transition, making its very focus on transition issues less and less pertinent for some countries of the region. CEU's response in this regard was to cast a wider net, addressing issues of transition and democratization in a range of countries beyond the former communist bloc. The enlargement of the European Union, including the accession of the first eight countries in Central and Eastern Europe in 2004, followed by Romania and Bulgaria in 2007 and continuing negotiations with countries in the Western Balkans, also presented novel conditions for the university: Recruiting students from these countries simply became more difficult given the opening up of new, and more easily accessible, opportunities for graduate education in Western Europe. And although Central and Eastern European students maintain an important presence at CEU, students from Central Asia have increased their representation, as have students from other countries, including those in Western Europe, North America, Africa, and Asia. Today, CEU enrolls students from over eighty countries, and students from no single country form a prevailing majority.[33] CEU's location in a member state of the European Union has also brought new opportunities for the university, as reflected in the success of the Department of Environmental Sciences and Policy to obtain Erasmus Mundus scholarships directed at diversifying the student population. Faculty perceptions of the university's functioning within the European Union, however, were also linked to fears about increased competition from other European universities, an experience that CEU had not had to confront to a significant degree during its first decade of existence.

Adjustment to the new European environment and becoming part of the supranational structure represented by the European Union has also become an important aspect of scholarly inquiry, among both faculty and students. Describing his experiences in interviewing prospective students, Samuel Johnson, a professor of political science, explained: "It's a joke among the professors that when we go and interview the students, so many of them say, 'My country's joining the European Union. . . .' It's not such an interesting question when you've read so many different papers about it. . . . I suppose if you come from a country joining the European Union, it might be exciting." Although Professor Johnson's comments harbored some sarcasm in depicting students' affinity to undertake their studies focused on issues related to European integration, his statement underscored the existence of enormous interest in the topic. Responding to this interest, CEU established the Center for EU Enlargement Studies, a center focusing on both the past and future of European integration through research and related policy work.[34]

Many of the aforementioned changes have emphasized finding a unique niche for a graduate-level higher education institution within the context of challenging and new societal conditions. Parallel to these changes, the university underwent other equally significant transformations that began to emphasize research, fundraising, a clearly articulated agenda to attract more fee-paying students, and quality control encompassing different standards of faculty evaluation. These initiatives were promoted and embraced by Yehuda Elkana, the university's new rector, assuming CEU's leadership in 1999. Strengthening the research function of CEU, thereby turning the institution into a full-fledged research university, was foremost among these goals. The October 2001 rector's report elaborates on this development, underscoring the importance of a strong emphasis on research, whose contributions were to be judged based on criteria including its disciplinary, interdisciplinary, and policy relevance, as well as its role in the creation of new knowledge.[35] In order to achieve this goal, CEU reconstituted its research board, expanding the board's task from awarding grants to also instituting programs to train faculty and graduate students in writing effective and fundable research proposals.[36] The introduction and strengthening of doctoral programs, expanding the university's traditional emphasis on granting master's degrees, also received much attention.[37]

In a related development, raising funds for university functioning began to assume an increasingly important role. Since CEU depended primarily on one benefactor's gifts to sustain itself for a number of years following its establishment, bringing in external revenues from other sources became a new focus. These sentiments were expressed with striking honesty by Rector Yehuda Elkana in 2002:

None of us in the Administration is experienced in fundraising. . . . Yet, we do realize that an infrastructure for intelligent fundraising has to be set up, and before all else an atmosphere at the university had to be created, where most of the faculty and staff show some minimum interest, realize the need, and believe in the feasibility of doing so. Much too long has there been an exclusive reliance on the munificence of the founder, and the faculty got used to being passive. I think that this stage is behind us.[38]

CEU's involvement in efforts to obtain external funds thus became a key institutional undertaking, with fundraising efforts directed at individual donors, alumni, foundations, and corporations.

New sources of funds were also sought from the students. In 2001, CEU provided full fellowship packages to 700 students attending degree programs offered by its various departments. Up to that point, the practice of providing a free education was central to the university's mission. In his October 2001 report, however, the rector proposed a plan to increase student enrollment to 1,000 while, at the same time, departing from the university's traditional commitment to fully funding the education of its students. Specifically, the report recommended the introduction of a new admissions policy that would offer options for enrollment on both partially and fully funded bases. Further, the report outlined an allocation plan for financial aid packages based on student merit, as opposed to need. Although recognizing the unequal nature of such distribution of aid, Rector Elkana presented merit-based aid as the only manageable policy for financial support: "Since in this region of the world it seems to be hopeless to have a need-based allocation of funds (there are simply no means to ascertain income of students or their families), we must revert to a purely merit-based allocation. This is not only difficult for all of us with sensitive social antennae, but it also makes it imperative for the departments to grade all their applicants according to merit. Many find this task daunting, if not impossible."[39] Today, a system of financial aid based on full and partial fellowships and tuition waivers continues to define the mechanisms of student support at CEU. Important to note, however, is that the majority of CEU students receive financial aid packages from the institution. In the academic year 2007–2008, for example, out of the 969 students enrolled, 710 received some type of financial aid.[40]

With the weakening of CEU's mission in the former communist region and the goal to attain research university status, the meaning of the term *quality* was also cast in new light, receiving more and, to a large extent, different emphasis. Attracting scholars intent on making a long-term commitment to a career at CEU and to research became an important institutional goal. When it came to the evaluation of faculty work, in 2002, the university established new guidelines regarding publications. Although the institution has never offered tenure, the academic ranks of assistant, associate, and full professor do exist, with faculty evaluation and promotion decisions based increasingly on research and publications. In his March 2000 report, Rector Elkana described the importance of quality control in the following terms: "The task of the University Administration is first of all to exercise quality control (without breaking contracts), replacing the less suitable faculty with carefully selected and very good new faculty, and to seek to introduce disciplinary areas which are not yet present at CEU."[41]

As CEU transformed itself in response to the transitions occurring in Central and Eastern Europe and Central Asia, the societal forces at play in facilitating these institutional changes become readily apparent. After all, at the beginning of the twenty-first century, CEU was not alone in its efforts to introduce stricter criteria for quality control, a strengthened emphasis on revenue-generating research and activities to obtain external funding, and the move in the direction of attaching a higher price, to be paid by the student, to the education attained within its walls. Indeed, these are some of the most significant signs of a growing worldwide trend at institutions of higher education today. Although CEU's related activities are not as deep-seated as at some other universities that have been in existence for longer periods of time, the connection to wider trends in higher education is evident.

The increased emphasis on fundraising, for example, depicts CEU as an institution intent on engaging in entrepreneurial activities. This aspect of the university's functioning bears resemblance to Sheila Slaughter and Larry Leslie's description of an academic capitalist model of higher education, where universities increasingly undertake marketlike activities to obtain external moneys. According to Slaughter and Leslie's definition, "*marketlike behaviors* refer to institutional and faculty competition for moneys, whether these are from external grants and contracts, endowment funds, university-industry partnerships, institutional investment in professors' spinoff companies, or student tuition and fees."[42] It is clear that CEU has placed growing emphasis on this aspect of institutional functioning, with the involvement of both faculty and administrators. Interestingly, however, despite these goals, some of the faculty mentioned that they did not feel strong pressure to obtain funding for their research. One professor stated: "I feel pressured to publish at CEU, but I haven't felt the monetary pressure, but I'm also not ambitious enough." Another professor explained her own experiences in somewhat different terms, focusing on the fact that her work itself required monetary support: "They expect me to publish. If I could publish just sitting in the library and reading, then that would be fine, but even that's hard to do because in the type of work that I do, I do need research funding, so there is some pressure. I don't feel much pressure, but there is some pressure to get some funding." These faculty comments may reflect the relatively mild, although increasing, emphasis— especially in comparison to research universities in the United States—on faculty entrepreneurialism at CEU. Also important to underscore is that fundraising is a new goal of the university, coinciding with George Soros's statement that his $250 million endowment signified the "cutting of the umbilical cord," thereby making CEU an independent institution.

Stronger quality control and international competition with other institutions have also been described as part of worldwide developments in higher education, although the motivations at CEU both follow and depart from these general trends. Carlos Alberto Torres and Robert Rhoads linked accountability, quality control, and competition to a form of neoliberal globalization promoted by organizations such as the IMF and World Bank, emphasizing standards-based reform and the achievement of those standards at the lowest possible cost.[43] Presumably, these standards enable institutions of higher education to more effectively compete with other universities in an international sphere. Undoubtedly, CEU has made competitiveness with other universities and achieving a higher degree of excellence through quality control important goals. In this regard, the university conforms to a worldwide trend in higher education, a phenomenon insightfully depicted by Nelly Stromquist: "The competition that operates in higher education positions university against university, department against department, and professors against each other. While competition has always existed, today the concept has been extended to new frontiers. This competitive ethos characterizes both faculty and students."[44]

It is also true that CEU has established and maintained strong connections with multilateral agencies traditionally linked with the promotion of the goals of neoliberal globalization. In his article on philanthropy and CEU, Nicolas Guilhot provided a detailed analysis of these connections:

The relations with the [World] Bank have been continuous and intense. At the founding of CEU, the World Bank actively participated in creating seminars on privatization. It organized a student program in 1991, a joint conference on corporate governance in 1994, and more recently, in April 2002, its aid was sought for the management and financing of the CEU business school. These institutional exchanges ensure that teaching and research are attuned to the global agendas of economic reform and that the policy prescriptions of international financial institutions are circulated and discussed in academic environments.[45]

The influence of multilateral agencies has thus been important at the university, reflecting a model of academic capitalism that portrays the university as an entity with some degree of networks to major actors in the new, global economy.[46]

In another important example, CEU's business school has as its major goal to provide "a continuous source of networking opportunities through our close ties with the local and regional business communities."[47] Although these linkages are more prominent in certain aspects of the university's functioning than others, the connections with both multilateral organizations and corporations have much in common with a conceptualization of academic capitalism that "focuses on networks—new circuits of knowledge, interstitial organizational emergence, networks that intermediate between public and private sector, extended managerial capacity—that link institutions as well as faculty, administrators, academic professionals and students to the new economy. New investment, marketing and consumption behaviors on the part of members of the university community also link them to the new economy. Together these mechanisms and behaviors constitute an academic capitalist knowledge/learning regime."[48]

For CEU, as a private institution of higher education, the implications of these connections might be conceived in a different light than in Slaughter and Rhoades's original conceptualization of networks taking place mainly between the public sector of higher education and the new economy.[49] The theory of academic capitalism primarily was developed with reference to public higher education, leaving many unexplored issues relating to private higher education's involvement in networks with the new economy. Along these lines, it is crucial to recognize the many ways in which private institutions of higher education have embraced societal involvement, accompanied by a strong commitment to social justice goals and objectives to promote the public good. These institutional missions thus make academic capitalism a concern of high importance at all institutions of higher education. What happens to the public good mission of private colleges and universities in a climate of academic capitalism has significant implications for the functioning of the higher education system.

CEU provides an interesting example in which an increased emphasis on market-driven, entrepreneurial activities has been accompanied by actions motivated by the importance of institutional support for faculty productivity and the significance of continued commitment to the public good. On the one hand, in its efforts to live up to its aim to function like a U.S.-style university, CEU has been careful to approach its competitiveness goals by increasing faculty salaries, allowing for faculty time devoted to research through the granting of sabbaticals and other methods of reducing faculty teaching load, and a continued emphasis on excellence in teaching, policy work, and community-building activities.[50] On the other hand, CEU has maintained a strong emphasis on engagement in socially relevant problems, democracy building, and the development of open societies. The influence of globalization has been at the center of this continuing and, at the same time, shifting emphasis. Rector Elkana made this connection clear in his March 2003 report:

CEU is contemplating becoming a "global niche" in the next decade, with a cutting edge impact on the former Soviet Union, Central Asia, South-East Asia, and eventually even on China, while continuing to be relevant for the region of Central and Eastern Europe. CEU has developed a distinctive expertise on transition problems and could develop high quality research and teaching in other areas most relevant for new democracies in the non-Western world. Among these are: transition economies, issues of human rights, political developments, socio-anthropological and legal knowledge, different approaches to history, environmental studies, nationalism studies, gender studies, business and public administration—all these along the lines of the *shifting boundary between the local and the universal.*[51]

Finding a niche in a world shaped by the processes of globalization and juxtaposing the local with the universal have thus become central goals of CEU. This emphasis is prominently featured in the university's strategic plan for the years 2003–2013 as well: "With globalization of markets, information, knowledge and values, the local comes inevitably to the fore, often contradicting the universal, and there is a constant need to weigh and juxtapose the local against the universal on most of the issues in our lives. This process is a fundamental aspect of intellectual life at CEU."[52]

As CEU entered the twenty-first century, it made becoming part of the global network of research-intensive universities a primary goal. This process meant homogenization through the establishment of standards common at Western universities driven, on the one hand, by CEU's affiliation with the United States and, on the other hand, by the application of the Bologna Process, representing a set of regulations aimed at standardizing higher education in member states of the European Union. It also meant the recruitment of fee-paying students and increasing enrollments and a greater emphasis on entrepreneurial activities, competitiveness, and quality control. But this process also implied a renewed interest in heterogeneity by adopting a distinctive mission in examining universal processes in light of a variety of local realities and vice versa. Democracy building and the promotion of open societies, addressed on both the global and local levels, became the unique niche to be fulfilled in the university's research, teaching, and service activities.

The notions of global homogenization and the continuing relevance of the local in interaction with the global have been described as some of the most important facets of the globalization of culture.[53] In the case of CEU, the term *culture* bears a distinctly academic connotation, with special emphasis on the meaning-making processes that individuals and groups of individuals engage in within the context of the production and application of academic knowledge. John Tomlinson's account is particularly helpful in highlighting the multifaceted nature of cultural globalization, depicting globalization as "complex connectivity," a concept that refers to "the rapidly developing and ever-densening network of interconnections and interdependencies that characterize modern social life."[54] Within this framework, in a particularly intriguing analogy, Tomlinson likened the phenomenon of cultural homogenization to the various ways in which people, particularly individuals on business trips, approach traveling by air outside their countries of origin. As Tomlinson stated: "The assertion of global homogenization of culture is a little like arriving by plane but never leaving the terminal, spending all one's time browsing amongst the global brands of the duty-free shops."[55] Tomlinson added that globalization "doesn't make all places the same, but it creates globalized spaces and connecting corridors which ease the flow of capital (including its commodities and personnel) by matching the time-space compression of connectivity with a degree of cultural 'compression.'"

However, once the traveler ventures outside the globalized space of the airport terminal and beyond the world of five-star hotels and business centers, an entirely different picture, the picture of the local, emerges. Stressing the overwhelming importance of "localities," Tomlinson noted that entering the local streets, houses, churches, workplaces, and shops "means entering the order of social life which feels the sway of local affairs more than the demands of globality, and which exhibits the particularity—the cultural difference—of 'locality.' When discussions of globalization raise (as most do) the 'global-local' relationship, this is the vast order of everyday life that they invoke."[56] This, of course, is not to say that the local survives side-by-side global spaces of existence. Rather, the global transforms and interacts with the local, holding far-reaching consequences for all areas of life. As Tomlinson suggested, "the paradigmatic experience of global modernity for most people—and this is not of course unrelated to the correlation between income and mobility—is that of staying in one place by experiencing the 'displacement' that global modernity *brings to them*." Such interconnections between local and global spheres of existence have been emphasized in numerous scholarly accounts of cultural globalization, even resulting in the adoption of the term *glocalization*.[57]

How do theories of cultural globalization apply to CEU? First and foremost, CEU is a highly globalized place of academic culture. It is a globalizing force, bringing Western values to the education of its students, many arriving from Eastern and Central Europe and Central Asia, and to the conduct of research and service by its faculty. This focus is more than apparent in the mission of the university, and even when CEU's scholarly and teaching emphasis concerned mainly the postcommunist region, the introduction of Western practices and values contributed much to the globalization of academic life in Central and Eastern Europe. This view was also underscored by the comments of a faculty member:

You can find critical voices [of globalization] but, in general, CEU is an institution that is benefiting coincidentally from globalization. . . . We represent here a small world, especially from the region, from the new democracies. . . . There's a small microcosm of the region and also that's a broader world in terms of inviting a spectrum of professors, and of course the faculty members are traveling a lot. Sometimes they accept invitations from foreign universities, so they benefit a lot from globalization. CEU as such must be pro-globalization by its mere existence.

By bringing the Western into the educational sphere of the postcommunist region, what CEU, in effect, accomplishes is a form of Westernization of university life.

The university is also acted upon by global forces, as reflected in its strategies to broaden its applicant pool, to find a niche in addressing democratic development in countries beyond the postcommunist region, and to adopt an agenda of competitiveness, fundraising, and stricter quality control. In all of these aspects of its functioning, CEU is reacting to global forces shaping higher education in all parts of the world. Yet, elements of the local are easy to recognize. Perhaps most importantly, in many ways, the university reaches beyond the globalized space of the airport terminal, to adopt Tomlinson's analogy,[58] into the streets, homes, workplaces, banks, and governments of the societies experiencing transitions to democracy. Its newly adopted mission to juxtapose the local and the universal brings into focus the reality of glocalization in its research, teaching, and service activities. A central goal of this chapter is to examine the ways in which CEU faculty approached the global and the local in the highly globalized academic environment present at CEU. The remainder of the chapter explores the views and experiences of the faculty within the model of higher education offered by CEU, with special emphasis on their views and experiences of citizenship.

AN INTERNATIONAL FACULTY

Accompanying the significant national diversity in the university's student population are the international origins of the faculty, representing approximately thirty countries, from both the postcommunist region and other countries of the world. Perhaps the most significant unifying theme in faculty members' backgrounds is the tremendous level of international experience that they bring to their work at CEU. The majority of the faculty members had studied or worked in a variety of other countries prior to joining the university. Many of the Hungarian and other Eastern European professors obtained their Ph.D.s in the United States or had considerable professional experience abroad. Taken together, these experiences contributed to the faculty's expertise and knowledge of research and teaching traditions in the West. Gyula Révai explained his decision to return home after obtaining his Ph.D. in the United States by highlighting the value he attached to an advanced degree from a U.S. university: "Someone with a U.S. education would have a much bigger impact here than in the U.S. We are approached by many more students. Occasionally, not always, but occasionally our opinion counts more than it would in a U.S. university, so there is also this other dimension of having a bigger influence or a bigger impact on the academic environment." Professor Révai also underscored the importance of his decision to return to Hungary by referring to his notion of citizenship: "I think it's a different attitude towards the home country maybe and it's a different notion of citizenship. I wouldn't call it a weaker citizenship. It might actually be stronger because you had the choice of going to another country and you made the choice of returning and you made the choice of wanting to integrate your experiences into your local economy and not the other way around."

Other factors, such as the importance of living in a traditional European city like Budapest, the difficulty of finding an academic position in the United States, and being close to family were also among reasons that faculty mentioned in explaining their decision to return from abroad. In terms of what these international experiences meant at CEU, the faculty members discussed a broadened understanding of their professional fields; an increased familiarity with Western academic culture, including teaching practices; an exposure to different lifestyles and ways of thinking; and even a chance to enrich their libraries with books that would enhance their research and teaching at the university. Obviously, all of these experiences and the knowledge they helped to spawn were very much in line with the mission of CEU.

Accompanying our interviews with faculty from Eastern and Central Europe, we had the opportunity to talk with professors who arrived from countries in Western Europe, North America, and the South Pacific region. The majority of these professors expressed considerable commitment to their professional endeavors at CEU and to their continuing research on the region. In fact, this research emphasis was a major draw for many when they accepted their positions at the university. For them, living in Eastern Europe was not a novel experience. Rather, working in Hungary presented an opportunity to maintain an immediate connection with their areas of research in a variety of Eastern European countries.

This connection to the region, however, did not always translate into high levels of participation in Hungarian society. Faculty from countries other than Hungary often depicted their everyday experiences as linked primarily to CEU. Some even described the university as a "bubble": "Working at CEU is like being in a bubble because it's an English-language institution, it's a foreign institution, it's composed largely of ex-pats, so it's kind of like this bubble. It's not really well integrated into the rest of Hungarian society." Strong professional and personal connections to CEU were thus the cornerstone of many of the international faculty's experiences. In some instances, then, especially for foreign faculty, CEU as a globalized space had broader significance than the introduction of Western values, also acting as a place of global belonging, accommodating faculty members from a range of countries outside of Hungary.

Although a number of professors discussed their positions at CEU as longer-term professional engagements, some pointed out that their stay was temporary. One faculty member in the latter category even referred to himself as a "flying professor," having taught in a number of countries. In response to what attracted him to the life of a "flying professor," this faculty member explained: "Travel. I get bored in one place. I lived in [a West European country] for a number of years and after a while I found it a little too parochial and inward looking and I got tired of it and I wanted a change. So yes, it's self-inflicted." Another young faculty member from North America, having spent just a portion of one academic year at CEU, also related his plans to assume an academic position in another country the following year. Although this experience was not widespread among the faculty, one professor expressed concern that the university might be seen as a stepping-stone among some of its newest recruits: "CEU is quite good at attracting young bright people who recently finished their Ph.D. They come here for four or so years, get teaching experience, get the opportunity to turn their dissertation into a book, and then they get snapped up by other institutions in Europe or America because CEU can't keep them, it can't keep them because of the pay and conditions." Interestingly, the two faculty members who discussed their soon-to-be-accomplished plans to assume professional responsibilities in other countries held academic interests that were either very theoretical in nature or concerned with issues in countries outside the postcommunist region. Such emphases, however, were also present in other professors' research interests as well, providing an indication of CEU's increasing global focus.

Despite the various levels of commitment professors showed toward the university, the international backgrounds of faculty laid an important foundation for CEU in accomplishing its mission. A professor arriving at CEU from a West European country summed up the utility of his own international experiences: "CEU wants to be both Western and Eastern. When it comes to drawing up a course, drawing up a class, or carrying out a research project, I have connections with English universities that can be so useful both for them and for us. So that's perhaps why I enjoy being here, so I engage in work that has a purpose to it and it's useful, so that's what drives me." Many of the professors from Eastern and Central Europe possessed a strong understanding of Western notions of academic life, and many faculty members from Western Europe, North America, and the South Pacific held a long-standing interest in the postcommunist region.

How did this international body of faculty approach the mission of CEU in their work as scholars and teachers? What opportunities and challenges has CEU, as a private, highly international institution of higher education with a strong regional and increasingly global mission, presented to its faculty? In what ways were the faculty members' notions of citizenship expressed in their research, teaching, service, and policy work at CEU? The ensuing sections address the significance of questions such as these in the lives of CEU faculty members.

FACULTY WORK AND CITIZENSHIP

In Chapter 1 of this book, we described a model of citizenship that is reflected in the political/civic, economic/occupational, and social/cultural dimensions. Our discussions with CEU professors focused primarily on notions of citizenship in faculty work, as expressed first and foremost in the occupational/economic dimension. However, in alignment with our citizenship model (see Figure 1.1 in Chapter 1), many of our findings depict significant overlaps among the three dimensions of citizenship. In fact, the vantage point of faculty work highlights several notions of citizenship faculty members held not only in relation to the economic/occupational dimension of citizenship but also in relation to the political/civic and the social/cultural dimensions.

Such overlaps are also powerfully expressed in the literature on faculty engagement and the notion of faculty as engaged scholars. One strain of this literature is rooted in the groundbreaking publication of *Scholarship Reconsidered* by Ernest Boyer.[59] Responding to criticisms pointing to the disengagement of faculty from societal concerns,[60] Boyer proposed a new direction for faculty work: "We believe the time has come to move beyond the tired old 'teaching versus research' debate and give the familiar and honorable term 'scholarship' a broader, more capacious meaning, one that brings legitimacy to the full scope of academic work. Surely, scholarship means engaging in original research. But the work of the scholar also means stepping back from one's investigation, looking for connections, building bridges between theory and practice, and communicating one's knowledge effectively to students."[61] Following in the footsteps of Boyer's contributions, in the United States a new understanding of faculty work emerged and began to shape theory and research, bringing into focus the notions of the engaged scholar and teacher in a model of the "scholarship of engagement."[62]

Similar efforts to reshape understandings of knowledge production have also been proposed in the landmark work of Michael Gibbons and his coauthors, *The New Production of Knowledge: The Dynamics of Science and Research in Contemporary Societies*.[63] Suggesting that the contexts and manner of knowledge production have changed radically, the authors proposed that a shift is taking place from "Mode 1 knowledge" to "Mode 2 knowledge," where "in Mode 1 problems are set and solved in a context governed by the, largely academic, interests of a specific community. By contrast, Mode 2 knowledge is carried out in a context of application."[64] The authors added that "Mode 1 is disciplinary while Mode 2 is transdisciplinary. Mode 1 is characterized by homogeneity, Mode 2 by heterogeneity. Organisationally, Mode 1 is hierarchical and tends to preserve its form, while Mode 2 is more heterarchical and transient. Each employs a different type of quality control. In comparison with Mode 1, Mode 2 is more socially accountable and reflexive. It includes a wider, more temporary and heterogeneous set of practitioners, collaborating on a problem defined in a specific and localised context."[65] An unprecedented proximity to the societies surrounding academic life and an emphasis on application and collaboration among researchers, practitioners, and policy makers thus defines the new, Mode 2, type of knowledge production.

The notion of citizenship advanced in this study builds on these images of faculty work with significant engagement in societal concerns, encompassing a conceptualization of citizenship that has broad implications in the economic/occupational, political/civic, and social/cultural dimensions. Notions of citizenship in the experiences of CEU faculty members, however, also add to these images of the engaged scholar and Mode 2 knowledge producer by emphasizing the connections between the local, national, regional, and the global, representing localities that are indispensable in understanding faculty work in the globalized environment of CEU.

FACULTY VIEWS ON CEU MISSION

As an important indication of the continuing strength of CEU's original mission, the majority of faculty had formed strong opinions of the goals that drove the establishment of the university. Most also spoke at length about the changes that, with the onset of the new century, began to shift the institution's identity from a regional to a more global reach in its activities. However, although many faculty members expressed support for the original objectives, voices of critique were also present. Professor Samuel Johnson described his perceptions of the academic environment: "Well, CEU isn't very coherent. I mean, every department is different. . . . There was something in the initial mission that sounds like spreading liberal democratic ideas, but it doesn't happen because all sorts of ideas end up getting spread from here." Professor Alexandra Hulse echoed these sentiments. Focusing on the example of faculty views on globalization, she noted that some departments, for example, sociology, present mostly critical views of globalization. Many faculty members in the economics department, by contrast, tend to espouse much more supportive views.

Several faculty members raised the issue of CEU's original mission, to bring Western ideals of democracy to the postcommunist region, questioning the relevance of this goal in their work and offering alternative perspectives. These professors focused on translating their own professional goals into practice while, at the same time, presenting a critique of a Western model of democratization. George Miller, a professor of political science, offered his reflections by linking the issue to larger debates about democratization: "This is the old debate of whether you think that democracy is good. How far can you go to impose it on others? I think if you go abroad, then it becomes highly questionable whether you should do it." Another professor offered a nuanced perspective concerning public perceptions of the university's goals: "Now here, in this country, CEU is seen as a force that should be bringing East Europeans together, democratizing the region, having a liberal education system. The same guy [George Soros], who is seen as a sort of a democratizer here is seen as sort of a capitalist banker in [North America]. The thing is, he's probably both and that's the thing, right? So I think we're not talking about different things because I think they co-exist." Interesting to note in this comment are the differences among the variety of possible meanings, depending on one's geographic location, attached to CEU's mission.

Several faculty members expressed acceptance toward what they perceived to be the university's model of democratization and Westernization and supported the maintenance of those goals in the face of the institution's efforts to become more global in its emphasis. The successes of CEU in providing high-quality education and a strong belief in the increasing openness of formerly closed societies formed the center of these faculty views. Professor Anna Meier referred to the tremendous opportunities she saw CEU offering to students from poor countries of the region: "That's why I'm not really critical of the students who are kind of starry-eyed, you know, they believe in capitalism and they want a little piece of the dream too. . . . The countries are so poor. Not all of them, but a lot of them, most of them, and places where we're recruiting are desperately poor. There's no bright future for them, so this is mostly why I believe in CEU, because I think that any institution that will give someone, a bright, hard-working person from a place like that an opportunity, is good." Echoing these thoughts, several other faculty members depicted CEU as a stepping-stone for students to pursue more advanced degrees after they attain a master's degree at CEU.

A professor originally from a formerly communist country also stressed his support for CEU's mission, emphasizing the university's work in the creation of open societies:

I think we were created as a part of globalizing efforts because George Soros is quite an open-minded person and he thought that the major threat for the post-communist world is to be closed. So in a way, I'm working in this globalizing environment from very early on, so for me, I never thought about this as being something hostile or something which encroaches on my sphere of interests. Quite the contrary. I consider myself as working in the institution which is in fact a tool of globalization. From the point of view of opening borders and making Western education available for people from outside Western Europe, I think that was our major input.

Explaining the reasons behind his views, this professor drew on his own experiences, which led him to his strong belief in democratic, open societies.

Many faculty members who supported CEU's mission were interested in maintaining its geographic emphasis on the postcommunist regions of Central and Eastern Europe and Central Asia, referring to these areas as the regions in which CEU has developed expertise. Professor Alexandra Hulse noted: "I think we are not big enough to be a global university which has broad global programs, so I think we probably should really stick to this idea that we are attached to the region." Another professor explained: "Honestly, I feel like CEU should stay the course. I think that they still have a role to play in the region. They should just focus on what they do well, which is politics in the region." Although the preceding faculty views reflect both support and critique of CEU's developing identity, what links them together is a deep-seated concern for societal engagement in the university's work. The ensuing sections detail the ways in which this concern and other issues related to conceptions of citizenship were reflected in three areas of faculty work: research and publishing, societal engagement and policy work, and teaching.

RESEARCH AND PUBLISHING

As an institution of higher education working to strengthen its research productivity, CEU has placed considerable emphasis on supporting the research activities of its faculty. Within this growing research infrastructure, the faculty members described a wide variety of research foci, representing interests in a range of geographic areas that encompassed nearly all continents of the world. Not surprisingly, several professors indicated a continuing interest in studying issues related to political and economic transition in Central and Eastern Europe and Central Asia. Others were more driven by their goals to make contributions to theories of democratization, globalization, and global governance. Yet others stressed the importance of developing a comparative understanding of societal issues, for example, examining the implications of a capitalist economic system around the world. Overall, our conversations with CEU faculty members revealed a wide-ranging mix of interests in studies of locally, nationally, regionally, and globally relevant phenomena, with local interests often examined from a global perspective and global processes investigated in a local or national light.

Venturing into the local from the global space of CEU was an especially important element of the research undertaken by most of the faculty. A professor in the Department of International Relations and European Studies described these intersections of the local with the global succinctly: "I'm most interested in the region, but I always try to figure out what is regional, what is specific to the region, and where it is that the variance you observe in the region is the variance of global capitalism." Professor Andrea Hóka in political science explained the various sources of influence in the development of her research interests in the postcommunist region: "It started out with a keen interest in Hungary and improving things here, but I also got to know the U.S. system since quite a bit of my teaching was about that, and also because of my cultural and other geographical links to the United States. So then I got to have this mix of theory and hands-on knowledge that was kind of honed in on Hungary and it turned out that this combination was useful for other socialist countries as well."

Reaching into local realities, however, was not at the center of all faculty's research. Some professors pursued highly theoretical work or were interested in understanding larger processes of globalization and global governance. Interestingly, one of these faculty members had been considering a research project focusing specifically on Hungary, only to be discouraged from the research by her weak knowledge of the Hungarian language: "And the language barrier is one thing inhibiting to me because I'm more sociologically and anthropologically trained and my attitude is, 'I don't speak Hungarian, I just can't understand anything.'" Several other professors who arrived from English-speaking countries, however, were very much engaged in locally relevant research projects in a number of countries in Eastern Europe. These faculty members used their skills in one of the region's languages to conduct research activities focusing on local or national issues, while at the same time drawing on the globalized academic environment of CEU.

Use of language was also a prominent concern among some faculty members with regard to making their research findings and writing publicly available. Foremost among these concerns were questions of individual professional advancement and the types of local and global audiences that professors wanted to reach. Teaching at an English-language, U.S.-affiliated university with a globalized academic culture created an environment where publishing in English, for an international audience, became a natural undertaking. A North American professor with continuing research interests in the postcommunist region stressed the importance of publishing in English from the perspective of her career: "I sort of feel like I'm writing about this region for a North American audience or an Anglo-American audience, largely because, you know, my image in the eyes of people in that kind of universe is what really matters for my career advancement."

Along similar lines, several faculty members indicated that English-language publications were more valued by CEU. Professor Hulse noted: "What is expected from us is to turn towards a market which is not a local market, right? So this has no ties to the local market. So this is one concern. The other one is something else. I think that this is not only about language. It's only on the level of language where it's discussed. This is about a certain type of hegemonic view of what science is about." What is evident in these comments is Professor Hulse's recognition of a deeper issue about the Western-style standardization of knowledge, reaching beyond the language of publishing. Perhaps as an indication of how seriously Professor Hulse took this concern, she chose to publish her writing both in English and in her native language.

Other faculty simply found it easier to use English as the language of their publications. Angelika Horváth, a professor of history, noted: "The language of what I'm doing is more established in English, so that's the one that I know I can do. . . . If you are very good linguistically as well, then you can [write in more languages]. So I'm not saying you can't do it. For me, it's easier to write in English." Professor Ernő Papp explained that despite his strong interest in research on issues affecting East Central Europe, he had not published anything in Hungarian for several years: "The intellectual material, my work, is still strongly connected to the region, not only Hungary, but to the region and I have very positive feelings about the region, but still . . . You know, some people manage to do both. . . . I don't have the capacity to do that and then I had to make a choice and my choice was more the international arena." As many of the faculty publishing mostly in English indicated, reaching an international audience and remaining connected to the region by publishing the same pieces of research in two or more languages was a difficult undertaking.

Not all faculty shared these views. In fact, several professors spoke of a strong responsibility they felt in making their research available both internationally and locally, in the countries that were the subjects of their writing. One Hungarian professor noted in reference to a research project with important implications for Russia: "We will insist on translating this book at least into Russian because we know that in the Russian hemisphere, people don't speak English and if something is not printed, just posted on the Internet, especially in English, they would not use it." András Kis, an economics professor, explained his decision to publish in both English and Hungarian: "Obviously, from the economic point, it's more interesting to publish it in English, but then because I work on Hungarian issues, I want that Hungarians know about it and I want to make them aware of what my results are and obviously when I write it in Hungarian, more people will read it here." Importantly, these faculty members were successful at resolving the tension between an increased workload of writing in two languages and the responsibility they attached to contributing to the knowledge base in local languages that are not typically at the center of globalized academic environments. This responsibility, although it is primarily occupational in nature, also held significant implications for the political/civic dimension of citizenship, highlighting the importance of faculty's civic and political engagement in local societies.

SOCIETAL AND POLICY-RELATED ENGAGEMENT

CEU faculty members expressed various degrees of enthusiasm about the potential for societal and policy-related engagement through research. Some emphasized the importance of making their findings available to policy circles, identifying such practical linkages as the driving force behind their work. Perhaps the most striking example of such societal engagement was reflected in the comments of a professor in the Department of Environmental Sciences and Policy: "The only reason why our department is here is that we are trying to build a bridge. We are not doing hardcore environmental science research. A lot of things which can really improve the situation are very well-known. No new scientific discoveries are needed. What is needed is to find the ways in which these well-known discoveries can be implemented." Another professor described the work of the Center for Policy Studies: "The Center was created to make academics more interested in policy, to get them to think that you can do a piece of research about something related to policy. It's one thing to make a conclusion, but there's a next step that you can take. You can use this to make a strong case for a particular policy, a particular approach. You can take it to the problem-solving stage. I am interested to see how far academics do have a useful role to play in policy making." Reflected in these examples is a focus on establishing linkages between research, policy, and practice on the departmental and center levels, where the occupational dimension of citizenship in faculty work was consciously brought in line with the political/civic dimension.

Similar linkages were also relevant in the work of individual faculty members, several of whom reflected on the value they placed on their own societal engagement and policy-related work. Professor Andrea Hóka explained her increasing interest in policy, even referring to her most recent work as "something that you might not even call research, but it is more working on public policy." Professor Hóka related an especially important example of her policy-related activities, an example with significant local implications in the post-communist region in the context of globalization:

I have been discussing the issue of supra-national labor. And the main message that I have been trying to relate to [successor states of the former Soviet Union] was that they should be very careful because joining certain supranational arrangements might result in increased brain-drain from these countries to Western Europe. And they should not believe most of the high talk that they get from the Western Europeans because one of the main reasons for this sort of unification of the European higher education system is to make it easier to actually get bright people from here to German and French universities to work for them, and so it is not clear at all that they should be so happy with this.

A critical understanding of local-global and local-regional relations, with a heightened emphasis on policy implications at the level of national governments, took center stage in this specific project. Other professors also spoke of their involvement in work with national ministries as well as international organizations and task forces bringing together academics and policy makers from a range of countries to address societal problems.

One professor approached the question of societal engagement from a different perspective, placing more emphasis on her contributions to her field in the East European country where she conducted her research: "When I was there, when I was doing research, I let them know anything I can do I'm happy to do it. I was translating for them, cleaning up the English, things like that. When I had other contacts and information that would be useful, I would share it. There's a group of people trying to put together a little edited volume of essays on gender, which is hardly out there at all. People don't even know what gender means for the most part, so I'm writing something for that."

Other professors recognized the potential of their writing endeavors to increase public awareness of societal issues, but did not put much emphasis on direct involvement in policy work. Professor Samuel Johnson highlighted the personal responsibility he saw in making the public aware of controversial topics, mainly concerning individuals and organizations in power: "I keep trying to recycle the facts just so they get more widely spread whatever my actual article is about. So I guess that is part of wanting to contribute to keeping the issue on the agenda and in the public eye." Another professor, engaged in mostly theoretical work, focused on the impact of his contributions to local media outlets in the postcommunist region: "I used to publish more, but I do publish journalistic pieces. I think this is needed . . . in terms of the better self-understanding of the people involved." Several faculty members thus recognized multiple forms of societal engagement through their research and writing activities. On a number of occasions, bringing their knowledge from the globalized environment of CEU and their individual international backgrounds to bear on local issues was at the center of these endeavors.

Not all professors indicated interest in linking their occupational responsibilities with direct involvement in societal and policy-related matters. Professor John Singer identified a sharp distinction between research and policy work: "I don't have the time, the energy, or the knowledge of applying my work. I think it's all specialization, so it's a division of labor and my responsibility I think is to do research." Professor Anna Meier, who referred to the invitations she sometimes received to be involved in government projects as a "waste of time," stated: "It's sad that I'm not more politically active, but I think some of this has to do with maybe the academic personality, which is more about thinking, writing, and reading, and less doing." Professor András Kis explained the difficulty of translating his work into immediate policy implications: "Sometimes I work with Hungarian ministries or things like that, but I'm not involved in policy-making and I don't want to be involved in that, so if they ask me, I can tell them my opinion, but because I use past data, I can really study what happened in the past and see change, particularly in Hungary and in the region altogether. I cannot really offer any advice on my research because it's not up-to-date in that sense."

Societal engagement—or lack thereof—was also a topic of conversation in relation to faculty members' everyday life. Many of the professors arriving at CEU from other countries spoke at length about their lack of engagement in the immediate society in Hungary, despite their choice to reside there for extended periods of time. George Miller, a professor of political science, related his lack of societal participation to his experiences of living abroad: "Among those of us who claim that they're so flexible to live in so many countries, many of us would also claim that we are so socially engaged, but in fact we are not, and this is one of the costs of living abroad and being mobile and being able to adapt quickly. You never take any roots, which would mean that you're not showing any association to the society." Others attributed the difficulties they experienced in participating in society to their weak knowledge of the Hungarian language and one professor highlighted the irony of having to pay taxes in Hungary, yet at the same time, not possessing certain rights that would enable her to become involved politically: "I don't have a choice about paying Hungarian taxes, but yet I don't have any say in how they're spent. Even if I did have a say in how they're spent, it would be very hard for me to exercise that right, whereas I have lots of opinions about what the U.S. government is doing and I was a taxpayer there for a long time so I do feel like I can complain about how that money is being spent." For these faculty members, working at an English-language private university with significant ties to the United States often translated into an experience with little civic, political, and social involvement in their everyday lives. Important to emphasize, however, is that most of these faculty members were significantly engaged in issues relevant to a variety of localities in the region.

TEACHING

Engagement in local, national, and regional issues in a highly international environment was also at the center of the faculty's teaching activities. The majority of the professors stressed the unique classroom climates created by the international student body, where individual student backgrounds played a key role in shaping class discussions. Professor Anna Meier spoke enthusiastically of her classes at CEU: "The students are completely international and I think it's wonderful. I think it's wonderful that in my classes, I have no more than three people from the same country. I mean, you'll never find another university like that. It's totally unusual, and, you know, it's intentional." Although other professors mentioned that they had taught similarly diverse student populations in their classes at UK and U.S. universities, the lack of a dominant national origin in the student body was a significant characteristic of CEU.

Although many CEU students continued to arrive from the regions of Eastern and Central Europe and Central Asia, recent recruitment efforts brought a number of students from other continents and countries, representing both Western and developing nations. Along with these diverse national origins came a variety of experiences and viewpoints lending a distinctive flavor to instructional practices at the university and giving rise to significant expressions of the social/cultural dimension of citizenship. Professor Julia Erikson, in gender studies, emphasized the pedagogical opportunities inherent in diverse student perspectives: "It's amazing to have people from different places and to have different perspectives, but also just being able to reflect on the different experiences. . . . They're making realizations and comparing across countries." In many cases, students' diverse backgrounds provided fertile ground for such comparative analyses across cultures and national traditions and values. Oftentimes, faculty members, in their occupational roles as teachers, acted as cultural mediators in the classroom.

A number of professors discussed the strong emphasis they placed on local and national realities when discussing issues of global significance. Oftentimes, this focus was prompted by student interest in examining issues relevant to their home countries. Professor Olivia Doros, in the Department of Gender Studies, noted: "We try and think about gender issues in a global perspective. Students tend to be interested in what's going on in their country, but I do try and make them think about how their country is linked to a global network of political interests basically and see how those global interests shape what's going on in their country and vice versa." Seeing globally relevant phenomena through local occurrences often led to eye-opening experiences. Professor Anna Meier reflected on some of the larger teachable moments in her classroom: "You see politics happening in the classroom, you know, and you see your own national biases, you become more sensitive to those of others. You know, you stop seeing your viewpoint as normal patriotism and national pride and theirs as nationalism." For Professor Meier, then, teaching at CEU also meant a reevaluation of her own belief systems.

The coexistence of national origins and experiences in CEU's student body sometimes presented challenges as well. Professor Angelika Horváth described these challenges through a specific example of a workshop where two students engaged in a discussion about a highly controversial issue with considerable personal significance: "I was at a workshop once when a student was presenting her thesis synopsis, and she was writing about Chechen refugees, refugees in refugee camps. It was quite a challenge to handle the fact that she was there and then there was a Russian man in the same group who was also writing about refugees and they had very different ideas on the whole issue and when you feel that there is tension and, of course, you don't know where the woman is from and you don't know where the man is from, but you have to handle all this somehow. There are lots of instances like this." Conflict in the classroom, in this example, stemmed from the students' different views—and perhaps even personal experiences—of ethnic conflict.

Most of the professors embraced the notion of creating an environment that is conducive to critical thinking and reflection as the primary goal in their teaching. Promoting their students' skills to think critically was relevant to these faculty members in a number of ways, from critiquing students' assumptions about their own cultural traditions, values, and practices to critically evaluating Western values, democratization, and globalization. Professor Samuel Johnson related an example of a student who, in the course of writing a class paper, was led to a realization that made her question her beliefs about the relevance of feminism in her country of origin: "I had one Polish woman once who was interested in why feminism is not relevant for Polish women and she argued that this was a Western idea. And I said: 'Why don't you write a paper about that?' And so when she did actual research, she found out that her ideas about what feminism is were completely wrong and that she got that from Polish media because in the Polish media, they have this really anti-feminist discourse and so she ended up writing about why Poland has this anti-feminist discourse. So it's things like that, to get them to think about where their different ideas are coming from and to do research to find out for themselves."

Critiquing Western values and ways of thinking was also at the center of some faculty's teaching practices. As Professor Julia Erikson noted: "I've always tried to encourage more discussion, and also to be more critical about just taking these Western theories and applying them here. It doesn't necessarily mean they can be applied. Maybe they're assuming things that aren't universal, so we need to think about how they can be applied." Political science professor Endre Hargitay discussed his emphasis on students' critiques of the Western literature he uses in his classes: "Most of the literature that I use is on Western Europe or on the United States and I mention at the beginning of my courses that they should criticize or comment on this literature, incorporating their own experience."

The diversity of student backgrounds was also a tool that Professor Samuel Johnson used in challenging his students from the postcommunist Eastern and Central European and Central Asian regions to think more critically about liberal capitalist values:

They sometimes seem to me incredibly uncritical of liberalism and capitalism and all those things. They really believe the American dream sometimes and they say: "In the West, everything is perfect and in my country, we're just dreadful and corrupt." So that's something I always try and challenge actually and that's why I like to have some Western students and also if we have African students and Indonesian students, they bring in other perspectives to the classroom. Because it used to be more predominantly East Europeans, Central Asians coming from the post-Soviet experience and they had a really particular view of the world that it was East and West— West was good, East was bad. And so if you bring in people from Africa, that immediately disrupts that way of thinking, or people from Indonesia and even, you know if we have some Americans and Brits who also don't think the system they're coming from is good. It's always good to have an American that says, "No, America is no Utopia," just to surprise people and undermine those sorts of assumptions.

Other faculty members took a more general approach, focusing on an open-minded attitude to all subject matter in their classes. Along these lines, Professor Angelika Horváth emphasized similar goals in stating that "everything that I teach is really trying to somehow emphasize the diversity of things, perspectives and then theories and then trying to make sense of unity amongst diversity." Professor John Singer stressed his effort to leave his own political views outside the classroom: "I mean, I have to be honest. I don't have explicit political concerns in what I teach. I have very academic concerns. I want students to have an open mind, to be aware of the number of theories, to critically examine the material, but in doing so, left, right, pro or contra globalization sentiments are not an issue that I want to influence students on."

A different approach to teaching was presented by some professors who put clear emphasis on the responsibility they felt for introducing students to Western frameworks. As Professor Gyula Révai explained: "I think that's also true in all of the countries where these students come from, that they have a very different view and idea about economics based on what they learned there as an undergraduate and I think we have an important, well, we don't want to enforce it, but I think it's important to give this other approach, these other aspects, then it's up to them how they do it, what they keep and where they proceed, but I think this approach is becoming more and more dominant in the world." Some faculty members went further, defending CEU and its instructional practices in the face of criticisms for promoting Western ideals: "There are a lot of ways in which this is a very sort of neocolonial project, you know, but it's meant well and it has actually had very important effects." Another professor noted, "I know there are these charges leveled against CEU in all kinds of traditional Eastern European settings that claim that CEU is somehow taking people from Eastern Europe and then turning them against their own people by teaching them all kinds of wild Western ideas. Yes, to some extent we are. People can judge, people can come, and they will learn stuff from us, not just explicit academic knowledge, but also the mechanisms and attitudes." A generally positive outlook toward the role of Western values in the educational experiences of CEU students was evident in these faculty comments, presenting a counterpoint to other professors' commitment to presenting critical evaluations of values, traditions, and practices whether from Western or other perspectives.

Faculty work at CEU took shape amid a highly international and global academic environment, with constant connections to national, regional, and local realities. The faculty's activities to connect these diverse geographic spheres of existence were a powerful representation of the process of academic glocalization, where most faculty, as teachers, researchers, and policy makers, ventured into the local and national, while drawing on the globalized resources and support structures of CEU. These geographic connections also presented a crucial context for the expression of citizenship in faculty work in the economic/occupational, social/cultural, and political/civic dimensions. For these professors, CEU provides a unique academic climate that challenges its faculty members to think and act both globally and locally, traversing national and regional boundaries in all aspects of their work.

CONCLUSION: CENTRAL EUROPEAN UNIVERSITY, ITS FACULTY, AND CITIZENSHIP

CEU is a distinct and distinctively global university. Its identity is built on the cross-border mobility of students, faculty, and administrators and the offering of Western-style and, in part, foreign-affiliated education at the postsecondary level. Despite its focus on achieving a global presence, however, CEU in its current state does not belong in the circle of universities that form the Emergent Global Model (EGM) of higher education outlined in the work of Kathryn Mohrman, Wanhua Ma, and David Baker.[66] The eight characteristics of EGM institutions—defined as "global mission, research intensity, new roles for professors, diversified funding, worldwide recruitment, increasing complexity, new relationships with government and industry, and global collaboration with similar institutions"—are represented among CEU's activities and aspirations on only a small scale. CEU, with a relatively modest operating budget, a primary focus on the humanities and social sciences, and an enrollment of just over 1,500 students, among other features, has a long way to go to be among the universities identified as representations of the EGM of higher education institutions.

However, the global nature of CEU is evident in many of its characteristics, from its highly international body of students and faculty, through collaborations with a range of institutions across national borders, to the identification of a mission centered on democracy and the building of open societies in the postcommunist region as well as other areas of the world.[67]

Worldwide trends in higher education are also apparent, reflected in its intensified emphasis on research, quality control, and revenue-generating activities. CEU, then, is a distinctive kind of global university, a small institution that has presented a unique way of addressing the local, the national, the regional, and the global, as well as the entrepreneurial and the socially responsible. The central goal of this chapter was to explore the ways in which this unique academic environment shaped faculty members' conceptions of citizenship, as expressed in their values, professional activities, contributions, and the approaches they took in addressing the challenges and opportunities they faced in their work.

In the experiences of the faculty members participating in this study, citizenship was tied intimately to a high level of autonomy reflected in both faculty attitudes toward the university's institutional mission and their research, teaching, and societal engagement and policy work. Faculty autonomy was especially evident in relation to CEU's mission, expressed in voices of acceptance and critique, with most faculty members taking the institution's call to engage in and promote critical thinking quite seriously. Some of the faculty members shaped their activities in alignment with their perceptions of CEU's mission and focused on bringing Western values and frames of reference to societies undergoing processes of democratization in the postcommunist territories of Eastern and Central Europe and Central Asia. Many others, however, presented a critique of what they perceived to be the university's mission and pointed to the importance of critical examinations of values originating from all societal contexts, including those from the West and societies undergoing democratization. Many of these faculty members presented their work as driven by their own individual missions, shaped in the globalized environment of CEU, but also building on their experiences, goals, and values toward what constitutes meaningful academic work and education. Interpretations of the role of Westernization and democratization in faculty work were thus present on a continuum from enthusiastic support to application framed in critical analysis and a healthy skepticism.

What is especially important to underscore is that the varying viewpoints concerning the university's goals survived side-by-side, giving way to a democratic educational environment that brought CEU's mission of promoting democracy in larger societal contexts to the level of the institution and faculty work. True, the democratic character of faculty life at CEU functioned within certain limits. Comments from a professor of political science shed light on these constraints:

Well, if you read the official document, then you see many references to values. If you look at actual practice, then you also see many values. I don't know whether the two are closely related. I think there is a little bit of coincidence, that most of the faculty and most of the students are kind of liberal cosmopolitans simply because these are the sort of people who speak languages and who are ready to work or to study at this sort of institution. Also there is a big emphasis at the university on human rights, there are many events that take place here that connect to that. So yes, I do think that there are values and these are sort of progressive liberal values. If I compare CEU to Hungarian universities, what we don't have is the kind of conservative Christian nationalist orientation and if I compare CEU to a typical Western European or even an American university, then what you don't have is this radical leftist orientation.

Within such boundaries, set by the parameters of the recruitment and hiring of faculty members, however, the existence of varying values and practices reveals a faculty culture open to a democratic vision of university life, with significant implications for citizenship.

In the realm of citizenship, then, the culture of CEU gave way to significant engagement in larger societal concerns in the work of a number of professors, reflected in their approaches to teaching, research, and policy involvement. Some faculty members emphasized the responsibility they felt in tailoring their research and other professional activities in a manner that facilitated their efforts to address societal issues. These faculty members indicated the importance of their contributions in the areas of governmental policy, engagement in practice-oriented research, working on disciplinary issues at the local level, and making their research and writing available to audiences in local languages, as opposed to using just English as the language of scholarly communication. These faculty commitments reflected the confluence of the dimensions of citizenship we outlined in Chapter 1 of this book, pointing to the importance of the political and civic dimensions of citizenship within larger occupational considerations in faculty life.

Others, by contrast, showed less inclination to don the hat of the socially engaged scholar, refuting the personal relevance of directly reaching out to practitioners and policy makers. Some faculty members, for example, emphasized the importance of publishing in English, directing their research to an international audience for reasons of career advancement, ease of language use, or to continue an established habit of writing in English. Some of these faculty members also identified a division of labor between academe and the policy world, preferring to maintain their focus on research and writing without substantial direct societal engagement. This emphasis did not mean that these professors showed no concern for the public good. Instead, they saw their contributions as researchers and writers and attributed the responsibility to implement their work in practice to others.

The coexistence of academic work removed from direct societal involvement with more socially engaged forms of scholarship should not be surprising. These disparate conceptions of faculty work reflect two perspectives on academic life, one of which is rooted in a more traditional understanding of the public good, built on the logic of serendipity in making research findings available for societal application. Referring mainly to the sciences, Slaughter and Rhoades explained this focus:

The cornerstone of the public good knowledge regime was basic science that led to the discovery of new knowledge within the academic disciplines, serendipitously leading to public benefits. . . . The discoveries of basic science always preceded development, which occurred in federal laboratories and sometimes in corporations. It often involved building and testing costly prototypes. Application followed development and almost always took place in corporations. The public good model assumed a relatively strong separation between public and private sectors.[68]

According to this conceptualization, knowledge produced in the public good knowledge regime thus lacks an immediate connection to application and is defined by the distance existing between the sphere of the public university and the private sphere of corporations. Put in other words, this notion of faculty work lacks significant overlaps between the economic/occupational and political/civic dimensions of citizenship.

By contrast, faculty members with significant commitment to direct engagement in societal and policy-relevant concerns adopted a vision of academic work that established a clear connection between research and practice. In the various conceptualizations existing in the literature, such academic engagement has been referred to as the "scholarship of engagement," or the production of "Mode 2 knowledge."[69] CEU faculty members who embraced the notion of societal engagement and the application of the knowledge they produced adopted a view of citizenship that built on the intersections between the economic/occupational and political/civic dimensions. In their teaching, the majority of the CEU faculty members made it clear that their practice as instructors was embedded in a highly multinational and multicultural environment, where they often emerged not only as cultural mediators but also as critical observers of their students' and their own cultural practices. The overlap between the economic/occupational and the social/cultural dimensions of citizenship was especially apparent in this aspect of faculty life.

The geographic foci of faculty work also put a clear mark on the reach of citizenship adopted by CEU faculty. CEU and its faculty are, no doubt, significant forces of cultural globalization. In the work of its professors, concerns attached to local and national spheres of existence were represented alongside interests in the regional and global aspects of political, cultural, and economic life. A few CEU faculty members adopted a regional or global approach to their work, focusing mainly on contributions in the realm of theory. Their work, in many ways, maintained a global emphasis within a global university.

Other faculty members were local or national actors, whose work was informed by the values and practices they drew from an internationally relevant system of knowledge production. These professors used a glocal lens in their work, connecting the local and national with the global and venturing into local and national realities from the globalized space of CEU. Importantly, after failed attempts to establish a multicampus institution of higher education in three Eastern European countries, CEU's most immediate geographic surrounding is just one country, Hungary. Reflecting the importance of this geographic location, the local and national realities represented by Hungary were often at the center of faculty members' professional activities. What is important to recognize, however, is that Hungary was not the sole nation-state that shaped the professional activities of professors. Although a focus on a variety of national realities is common at any university, the lack of a dominant national origin among CEU students and the wide range of geographic foci of faculty work bring a distinct flavor to the form of cultural globalization and glocalization advanced by CEU professors both in the classroom and in their research, societal engagement, and policy work. Indeed, reaching out to multiple local and national realities was a cornerstone of faculty work. Even more importantly, the culture of CEU acted as a constant source of regional and, more recently, global inspiration, informing the work and societal engagement of its faculty.

These elements of faculty's professional lives highlight CEU as an institution of higher education whose reactions in the face of globalization are not easily predicted. Faced with financial pressures, increased competition from other universities, and new global realities, CEU—and by extension, its faculty—could have easily turned away from its democratic vision and socially relevant engagement. True, the university has reacted to external pressures by adopting competitiveness, revenue-generation, and quality control as important goals. Yet, CEU has also maintained a clear emphasis on its socially relevant mission and has provided a democratic academic culture supporting its faculty in their efforts to embrace their own professional missions within the larger setting of the university. The resulting form of citizenship pays tribute to the possibility of the emergence and survival of socially relevant institutional values in the face of overarching societal transitions and pressures driven by an increased emphasis on entrepreneurial, academic capitalist cultures in higher education.

As the finishing touches were put on this chapter, the twentieth anniversary of the fall of communism in Hungary was fast approaching. Given what has come to pass during the last twenty years or so, visitors to Szoborpark experience the trip to the outskirts of Budapest as not only a rendezvous with the past but also a brief excursion away from the reality of the present, a reality shaped so powerfully by the forces of globalization. Yet the postcommunist societal transitions represented by the existence of Szoborpark continue to capture the imagination of faculty affiliated with CEU, an institution of higher education whose very existence hinges on the events that rocked the region in the late 1980s and early 1990s. As the statues and monuments of Szoborpark become no more than a part of history for a growing number of the park's visitors, CEU faculty have responded to new opportunities and challenges by taking their interest in democratization and societies in transition to a new global plane, turning their attention to an ever-expanding range of countries. This shift in the university's emphasis, bolstered by the democratic academic environment supporting faculty citizenship, depicts CEU as a socially conscious entrepreneur, a university that has remained true to its original mission by adapting to the new, global realities of the twenty-first century.

CHAPTER 6

GLOBAL CITIZENSHIP AND CHANGING TIMES FOR UNIVERSITIES

GLOBAL COMMUNITIES, GLOBAL CHALLENGES

Recently we heard the story of a Chinese immigrant mother and her young daughter, living in one of the eastern suburbs of Los Angeles. Walking together along the street one day, the child turned to her mother and in a somewhat disappointed tone asked her when they were going to move to the United States. This area of the Los Angeles region is dominated by Chinese immigrants, and it is quite common for stores, restaurants, and businesses to advertise and conduct their commercial activities in Chinese Mandarin or Cantonese. The child's confusion was based on a simple yet basic assumption: In the United States, people speak English.

Evidence suggests that a particular region to the east of downtown Los Angeles has replaced the older downtown Chinatown as the heart of Chinese culture in the region. A 2008 *Los Angeles Times* article documented the profound influence of Chinese immigration on the area known as the San Gabriel Valley: "Much of the eastern San Gabriel Valley has more in common with Taipei, Beijing or Shanghai than it does with neighboring Los Angeles. Here, Asian-immigrant entrepreneurs have transformed once-sleepy suburbia into a Chinatown like no other."[1] A simple drive down Main Street through one of the many communities in this area tells the story of Chinese influence. Indeed, an employee at a high-end sneakers store lamented, "I never get to practice my English. Sometimes it feels like I'm still in China."[2]

Although certainly Chinese immigration to California (both from mainland China and Taiwan) has had a major impact on shaping the cultural landscape of the greater Los Angeles region, it somewhat pales in comparison to the impact of immigration from Mexico. For example, according to the Migration Policy Institute, Mexico accounts for some 30 percent of all U.S. immigration, and Los Angeles is a preferred destination for both documented and undocumented Mexican immigrants. To give some perspective to this, immigration from Mexico to the United States is seven times greater than immigration from the second greatest source—the Philippines.[3] The influence of Mexican migration to Los Angeles is widely evident, especially in communities to the east (East Los Angeles) and north (San Fernando Valley). Data from the Los Angeles Unified School District (LAUSD) also tell the story in that Hispanics represent nearly 74 percent of the district's student enrollment (2007–08 school year).[4] Adding to the complex challenges posed by immigration, 33 percent of all students in the district are English learners, and although Spanish-speaking English learners (the vast majority from Mexico) account for 94 percent of this aggregate group, the fact is that students report 92 different primary languages.[5] Such diverse cultural and linguistic backgrounds certainly present challenges to educators and policy makers involved in Los Angeles schools, colleges, and universities, and yet that same diversity also offers a cultural richness upon which to build vibrant and hybridized institutions and social systems.

On the opposite coast of the United States, in the city of Boston, similar cultural changes may be observed.[6] The once quintessential English and Irish settlement is now a significant immigrant destination for people from over 100 countries around the world. Echoing this major influx of immigrants, in the year 2000, 33 percent of Boston's residents spoke a language other than

English at home, including languages as diverse as Spanish, Haitian Creole, Chinese, Portuguese, Cape Verdean Creole, Vietnamese, French, Italian, and Russian.[7] As a result, Boston has made "the transition from what used to be one of the most lily-white regions of the country to one that is rapidly becoming multiracial and multicultural."[8] In fact, Boston's population has already reached the realities predicted in the near future for the entire United States: People of color now represent a slight demographic majority within the city's boundaries.[9]

Immigrants also make up substantial proportions of Boston's Public School system, where in 2004, 54.4 percent of students reported speaking only English. In the same year, 10,150 students participated in programs for English-language learners, and every year around 200 to 300 new Boston public high school students are first-generation immigrants.[10] Such diversity is reflected in the academic excellence and achievement of the city's top public school students. For example, according to the *Boston Globe*'s yearly reports, close to half of the city's high school valedictorians have been foreign born in several recent years. In 2009, 16 out of 37 valedictorians were born outside the United States.[11] In 2007, 18 of 38 valedictorians originated from Albania, Bangladesh, Cape Verde, China, the Dominican Republic, Haiti, Morocco, Peru, Tibet, Uganda, Venezuela, and Vietnam.[12]

Brief quotations from Boston's immigrant valedictorians published by the *Boston Globe* in 2007 reflect a variety of dreams and aspirations, some of them expressing a longing to make significant contributions outside the United States. Samenta Abraham, a student originally from Haiti, wrote: "My dream is to travel around the world and build shelters for people who are less fortunate, especially in my country." Abadur Rahman, from Bangladesh, noted his future professional plans: "I grew up seeing the need for doctors and the impact of malnutrition. I am going to try to open a hospital back home." Although others expressed gratitude for the hardships their parents endured in coming to the United States, intergenerational conflict over the importance of cultural influences was not absent from the students' accounts. As Tenzin Yangchen, a first-generation immigrant from Tibet, explained: "My parents worry that I am falling into the American way of living. I try to Americanize them, because we live here."[13] What is most provocative about Yangchen's comments is the expression "the American way of living." Given the changing cultural landscape of the United States and cities such as Boston, "the American way of living" is not an easy idea to decode. The fact is that the cultural realities of Boston increasingly are defined as a project linked to globalization, where cultural forms coexist and interact in everyday life. Tenzin Yangchen's support for her notion of "Americanization" and her parents' resistance to what they believed to be the American way of life thus most likely reflect a hybrid form of cultural reality, one that is located at the intersection of various cultural influences, of which "American" and "Tibetan" form only a part.

Cultural changes in Los Angeles and Boston as well as elsewhere in the world also are impacting universities, which, of course, is a central concern of this book. At our own universities—the University of Massachusetts, Boston (UMass Boston) and the University of California, Los Angeles (UCLA), we see these changes nearly everywhere we look. UMass Boston identifies itself as a "multi-bordered community, one not so much defined by the location of the physical buildings . . . but the multiple and diverse locales from which its students come. Those boundaries are local, regional, national, and global. We have students from over 140 countries who, at home, speak 90 different languages."[14] UMass Boston's recognition of its role both within and beyond Boston's diverse urban environment is well reflected in its strengthened institutional commitment to issues of globalization: The recent economic crisis did not prevent university officials from establishing the new Office of International and Transnational Affairs in 2009, an endeavor deemed a crucial undertaking in positioning the university as a major player in a global world. And UCLA's role in a globalizing world, as highlighted in detail in Chapter 3, reaches from its strongly international and recent immigrant student body, through research and activism focusing on issues in an international sphere, to efforts to bring a more global emphasis to its curriculum, as reflected in its establishment of the major in Global Studies. Indeed, UCLA is perhaps one of the most significant examples of a global research university, well reflected in the Paul Simon Award for Campus Internationalization it received from NAFSA: Association of International Educators in 2005.[15]

The preceding discussion calls to mind the extensive debates about whether or not globalization marks the end of local cultural forms or whether local forms are simply reshaped in light of global forces.[16] Some, of course, argue that globalization amounts to the Americanization or Westernization of the world. However, the examples that we introduce in preceding paragraphs, deriving from the cities of Los Angeles and Boston, reveal not the Americanization of the world, but the multifaceted influence of global processes on U.S. cities and universities. Although we recognize the power of the United States in particular and the West in general, we tend to side with Allan Luke and Carmen Luke in concluding that globalization and related influences must be understood in terms of the interplay between and among global and local forces.[17] Indeed, in highlighting four universities in different parts of the world, our intent was to provide rich details about this interplay.

We opened this book by noting the influence of American pop culture in China, resulting in the emergence of rappers such as Black Babble. But the beginning of this chapter highlights how Chinese culture, especially through immigration, is altering the cultural landscape of the United States, and particularly suburban areas of Los Angeles. Similar cultural transformations are taking place in Boston and its surrounding communities. In one striking example, the public library of Quincy, a town bordering Boston, regularly offers trilingual story-times—in English, Cantonese, and Mandarin—to its young patrons. Cultural changes and the adaptations that people and locales undertake in response to these changes are becoming more and more widespread around the world. To a significant extent, these changes are reshaping and redefining not only what it means to participate in societal life but also what it means to be a citizen both within the broader society and within the context of the modern university.

LOOKING BACK, MOVING AHEAD

One of the goals of this book was to take readers on a journey—from southern China, to the United States, to Argentina, to Hungary—and throughout that journey raise interesting and provocative points about the changing context of university life and the opportunities and challenges confronting university actors as citizens in these global times. Of course, a key objective is to advance a broader conception of citizenship that we think of and describe as global citizenship. The four case studies embodied diverse ways in which the countries and their universities not only experienced but also re-acted to globalization. Elements of citizenship were evidenced on the part of faculty and students, encompassing local, national, regional, and global dimensions.

The journey began in southern China, along a gentle stream flowing through a teaching university known as Guangdong University of Foreign Studies (GDUFS), or Guangwai to locals. Against this tranquil backdrop came to light the lives of GDUFS students and professors, striving to connect with the world within and beyond their young, international university. Students and faculty spoke of globalization as a coin with two sides, highlighting numerous opportunities and challenges that have come to shape the realities of China, the Guangdong region, and their university. Set within the contradictions of China's "socialist market economy," foremost among the opportunities were enhanced economic prospects, growing political freedom, a sense of improved human rights, and the two-way movement of new ideas between China and the outside world. However, challenges are also paramount, reflected most significantly in fears about the weakening of Chinese culture in the context of growing international influences, environmental degradation, and China essentially becoming the factory of the world.

In a very real sense, GDUFS sits at the intersection of these challenges and opportunities, adopting a potent role in advancing, opposing, embracing, and critiquing the benefits and drawbacks of globalization. In doing so, the university and some of its faculty and students stressed the growing importance of English, reliance on foreign and foreign-trained academic talent, the influx of Western-influenced teaching styles, enhanced connections between China and the West, and an increasingly competitive academic climate, where a "publish or perish" culture and revenue-generating pressures are beginning to challenge the more traditional focus on teaching as the primary task of professorial work. At the same time, GDUFS is also home to faculty and students whose concerns over increased international influence, the perceived abandonment of Chinese cultural norms, and the difficulties presented by brain drain to Western nations provide powerful critiques of the challenges of globalization.

Implications for citizenship are readily apparent in the ways in which students and faculty choose to resolve the paradoxes of globalization. Or, in other words, their decisions about how to respond to each side of the proverbial two-sided coin have immense implications for the future of GDUFS and the future of their identities as citizens in the face of growing global influences. A faculty member's decision to resist or support the spread of English as the language of instruction, for example, will have wide-ranging implications for the academic culture of the university. A star professor's choice to pursue professional opportunities abroad, taking advantage of the global connections available at GDUFS, might have the potential to take away significant talent from the university's offerings. In essence, whether the university is able to "seek harmony out of differences" depends to a large extent on the resolution of globalization's contradictions, a task that no doubt requires concerted and conscious approaches to citizenship on the part of both faculty and students.

Our journey continued in Los Angeles, in one of the most bustling, global, and culturally diverse cities of the United States. Even a passing glimpse at the city's major public research university, the University of California, Los Angeles (UCLA), provides a powerful image of global influence, reflected in a commitment to furthering internationally relevant issues in health care, politics, and culture; active engagement in economic development with an ever-widening geographic reach; and a student population defined significantly by the high representation of first- and second-generation immigrants and international students. Within this immense diversity, we turned our attention to Brazilian, Chinese, and Italian graduate students, a group of long-term, albeit temporary, transnational migrants, whose experiences in international graduate education separated and, in many cases, reconnected them with their home societies and regions.

Throughout the students' sojourn in Los Angeles, questions of citizenship centered on the juxtaposition of various locales, challenging them to reevaluate their roles in relation to their countries and regions of origin, the United States, and a more global sphere of existence. Through intense intercultural encounters and exposure to a variety of academic, social, economic, and political experiences in the United States, these students were actively engaged in the creation of a contextualized form of knowledge—in Boaventura de Sousa Santos's terms, pluriversity knowledge—that included emancipatory and, at times, mercantilistic applications.[18] Perhaps most importantly, the context of pluriversity knowledge creation gave voice to the expression of citizen rights and responsibilities that substantially defined the ways in which the students identified their future economic/occupational, political/civic, and social/cultural challenges in relation to a variety of geographic locales.

The experiences of the Brazilian, Chinese, and Italian graduate students also raise a multitude of questions regarding the nature of rights afforded to this class of transnational migrants in the United States. The availability of rights to holders of the F-1 visa undoubtedly supports a level of participation in U.S. society that few other nonimmigrant visa holders enjoy. At the same time, the volatility of the international student experience is reflected in a number of recent challenges evident in the students' comments about insecurities regarding their rights to movement in a post-9/11 environment and the availability of professional opportunities. These issues underscore the importance of considering questions of citizenship at the complex intersection of rights and responsibilities, where the provision of rights by both the U.S. government and institutions of higher education is crucial in allowing the students to undertake educational opportunities in the United States while, at the same time, using those opportunities to develop a notion of engaged citizenship.

At our next destination, exploring university life in the context of globalization led us to the University of Buenos Aires (UBA) in Argentina, where the context of our study was rooted in intense political upheaval responding to the 2001 collapse of the Argentine economy. Many attributed this collapse to mistaken policies advanced by the country's then political leaders and supranational organizations such as the International Monetary Fund (IMF). As countless students and faculty at UBA joined the movement against neoliberalism, they expressed their reactions in the form of intellectual support, political organizing, and active involvement in street demonstrations. As their participation deepened, the students and faculty did no less than accentuate the university's powerfully important role as a driving force of societal transformations, even when that role entailed opposition to the hegemony of neoliberalism and the "masters of the universe," as the political and economic elites who "rule" the world have been facetiously described.[19]

On the one hand, the actions of university actors as citizens centered on the relationship of Argentina to the neoliberal agenda of the IMF and World

Bank and their power to shape social and economic policy. Recognizing the deleterious effects of structural adjustment policies on the national economy, at the heart of citizenship enacted by these social actors is the fundamental question of the role of the modern university in the broader national context. Within that national context, the closeness of local communities and the university played an especially important role in responding to the challenges of neoliberalism and creating the kind of practical action capable of building more permanent coalitions between community and university activists.

On the other hand, the reach of citizenship also included a recognition of the university-level repercussions of neoliberal policies, highlighting the increasing privatization of the Argentine university, growing pressures to portray institutions of higher education as tools in economic development, and refashioning Argentine universities in the increasingly prominent model of academic capitalism.[20] In doing so, UBA students and faculty stressed the continuing relevance of the Argentine national project—in Santos's terms[21]—and the importance of university actors in critically examining, even actively opposing, mainstream neoliberal policy mandates.

Our journey through global cities and universities came to an end in Budapest, at Central European University (CEU) in Hungary, a privately funded, U.S.-affiliated graduate institution, whose establishment in 1991 was a direct consequence of a group of intellectuals' beliefs in the significant role of academic institutions in societal transformation. Indeed, the idea for CEU was born amid the transition from communism to capitalism in the late 1980s and early 1990s, a process representing some of the most momentous political changes in the region of Central and Eastern Europe and Central Asia. Reflecting the overwhelming influence of this transition, CEU's very existence was built upon the goal to strengthen the development of open societies in the region by training a new elite whose education was to be rooted to a significant extent in Western academic traditions and values. Reflecting these normative orientations, current CEU faculty members focus much of their teaching on topics, research, and pedagogies from the West, while highlighting the local and national realities of the postcommunist region.

During its first two decades of existence, CEU underwent two distinct phases of development. The primary focus in the first phase was on issues of regional importance, addressing the key societal changes that accompanied the shift from communism to capitalism. In the second phase, however, the university's actions were increasingly shaped by a strong recognition of a more global environment, where competition, entrepreneurial activities, revenue generation, and quality control were beginning to play especially important roles. In essence, CEU, as it became more established as a university, experienced the larger trends associated with academic capitalism, whose related policies and practices are becoming the building blocks of university functioning in virtually every part of the world today.

As a university model targeting new, globally relevant challenges and opportunities began to take shape at CEU, the faculty continued their work in an academic environment that supported their socially engaged teaching, research, and policy-related activities. At this point in the history of CEU, however, the focus of faculty work was no longer solely the postcommunist region. Instead, students at CEU today arrive from a widening range of countries, and the university has adopted a mission to address issues of societal transition in democratizing countries anywhere in the world. These developments represent a young university's response to the realities of social and economic transformation and the importance that scholarly work can play in charting a course for the twenty-first century. Yet, important to recognize is that CEU's response also harbors a commitment to its past mission of addressing issues of democratization and the development of open societies, even if in a modified form. The continuing emphasis on this mission has framed CEU's identity as a regionally and, later on, a globally engaged university providing key contexts for the expression of citizenship by its faculty.

All four of the universities in our study provide important insights into the changing context of higher education and the need to rethink notions of citizenship in a global era. What is clear from our case studies is that universities and their key actors face complex and challenging circumstances linked to the powerful influence of globalization. Relatedly, the most pressing issues of our time increasingly depend on global solutions and the ability of citizens to align their actions with the needs and interests of diverse individuals in many parts of the world. From our perspective, the crises of the twenty-first century increasingly will need to be confronted by individuals consciously thinking and acting as global citizens.

GLOBAL CRISES "HERE? THERE? SOMEWHERE?"

In the aftermath of September 11, 2001, former Secretary of Defense Donald Rumsfeld was asked where he intended to search for Osama Bin Laden. His famous response was, "Here? There? Somewhere?" which, as it has been pointed out, essentially amounts to everywhere.[22] In subsequent months, and in light of the fact that finding Bin Laden proved more difficult than the George W. Bush administration could have imagined, the effort became more broadly defined as a search to destroy terrorists wherever they may be found and at whatever stage they may be in plotting against U.S. interests. Hence, the reach of the U.S. military in its fight against global terrorism was to be unlimited in scope and preemptive in nature. This of course led many to point out that one person's terrorists are another's friends and neighbors; it seems terrorists and terrorism are harder to define than many in Washington, D.C. are willing to admit. The easy solution is simply to define terrorism as "what *they* carry out against *us*"[23] and ignore the vast array of historic, economic, and cultural complexities as to why one group takes up arms against another. But despite the shortcomings of the Bush administration's strategy against global terrorism, the one fact that was clear in the thinking of the time was that human conflict could no longer be considered in the same manner as in the past. Indeed, globalization was changing the very nature of both hatred and war.

Today, we see the influence of heightened global tensions, increased conflict, and crises—of both the violent and nonviolent kind—virtually everywhere in the world. The reduction of time and space has contributed to increased conflict by bringing greater and greater numbers of diverse peoples into everyday contact. At the same time, globalization has also presented gateways to further cooperation and understanding among a diversity of countries and regions. Indeed, there is now a heightened sense that global crises can be resolved only through collaborative efforts crossing national and regional boundaries. Globalization, in essence, provides the very tools that can aid in resolving the conflicts and crises that have crisscrossed national boundaries. And although a variety of actors can be involved in global solutions, our proposition in this book is that the role of universities—and the students and faculty who populate them—is crucial in addressing the problems of our times.

The continuing impact of global crises is difficult to dispute. The first decade of the twenty-first century has been marked by major economic calamity, where few places of the world have escaped the repercussions of the financial meltdown. The collapse of the real estate market and the troubles of financial institutions and other major corporations, coupled with rising unemployment rates, were just a few manifestations of an economic crisis that served as perhaps the most significant reminder of the interconnections that shape the lives of people in all parts of the planet. Although countries engaged in intense efforts to avoid major catastrophes, some of the most frightening statistics called attention to the scope of the global economic crises: According to data published by the United Nations Food and Agriculture Organization (FAO), in the year 2009, the number of people "on the brink of starvation" was likely to reach the historical record of 1.02 billion. As Jacques Diouf, director-general of FAO, warned: "A dangerous mix of the global economic slowdown combined with stubbornly high food prices in many countries has pushed some 100 million more people than last year into chronic hunger and poverty."[24] Undoubtedly, inequality, poverty, and hunger on a global plane remain the most perplexing and difficult-to-solve problems in today's global environment. Underscoring the key importance of worldwide cooperation in reversing this situation, Josette Sheeran, executive director of the UN World Food Programme, noted: "The world must pull together to ensure emergency needs are met as long term solutions are advanced."[25]

Other powerful examples of the global reach of crises are easy to find. In July 2009, the media reported the life sentence of Milan Lukic, the Serbian mass murderer, for severe crimes against humanity committed during the Bosnian war in 1992. Sredoje Lukic, his cousin and accomplice in the crimes, received a thirty-year prison sentence. Their victims are estimated to be over 130 Muslim men, women, children, and elderly in a three-week period.[26] The crimes of the Lukic cousins represent just minuscule incidents in the larger picture of past and continuing ethnic conflict, at times with sectarian undertones. According to some estimates, between 1946 and 2001, the world witnessed approximately fifty instances of major ethnic conflict, from Rwanda through the former Yugoslavia to Indonesia and Sri Lanka.[27] Although many of these conflicts have been resolved, the emergence of new conflicts and continuing efforts to understand the horrific crimes of the past remain constant reminders of the violence inflicted by humans on other human beings. As Stefan Wolff explained in his book on ethnic conflict:

People who die in ethnic conflict are more than just statistics. They often die horrible deaths. They leave behind grieving and frequently vengeful families who have to try to survive amid continuing violence that gradually but surely destroys the very social, political, and economic foundations of their lives. Yet, human beings are not only the passive, innocent, and unfortunate victims of torture, rape, looting, and killing in ethnic conflicts. They are also the ones who commit these very atrocities, leading others (by example) and following often too willingly. The accounts of victims and perpetrators often provide disturbing testimony to the depths to which human beings can sink.[28]

In a more positive tone, and stressing the importance of people not only understanding but also learning from and acting upon their knowledge of past ethnic conflict, Wolff continued: "Yet if there is anything optimistic in the realization that ethnic conflict is not a natural but a man-made disaster, it is the fact that human beings are able to learn—not only about how to kill and torture more effectively, but also about tools to resolve ethnic conflicts and help the societies in which they occur to rebuild and embark on a road towards sustainable peace and development."[29]

Instances of far-reaching conflict are also apparent in acts of terrorism and the global fight against it. During George W. Bush's administration, terrorism was thrown into an almost all-encompassing focus of U.S. foreign policy. The ongoing, worldwide hunt for Osama Bin Laden and present and future terrorists remains a reality that will most likely determine the relationship among a range of countries in the Western and Muslim worlds. In fact, Carlos Alberto Torres and Robert Rhoads identified the "global fight against terrorism" as one of five major manifestations of globalization, impacting international relations, activism, and world peace.[30]

The term *global* is also a frequent attribute of crises seemingly having little to do with terrorism or ethnic and sectarian conflict. Melting glaciers, shrinking coastlines, and gloomy images of polar bears losing their habitat have spawned numerous posters of the devastating environmental impact of global warming. Dangerous increases in the level of atmospheric carbon dioxide in the Arctic and Antarctic regions, a phenomenon that scientists have linked to worldwide climate change, may also lead to disturbing global effects. As Chris Rapley, head of the British Antarctic Survey, warned: "The crucial point is that you can't look at the Arctic and Antarctic in isolation. . . . What happens there has profound consequences for the rest of the planet."[31] As the effects of climate change in the Arctic can be readily felt in Africa and Asia, the importance of global collaboration in confronting the looming environmental crisis cannot be stressed enough. Such was the conclusion of a United Nations General Assembly conference held in 2008. Assembly President Srgjan Kerim noted in his closing remarks: "The actions necessary to address climate change are so intertwined that they can only be tackled through combined efforts."[32]

The rapid spread of infectious diseases has also become a reality of our time. In a recent case in point, the 2009 threat of the H1N1 flu prompted the World Health Organization (WHO) to raise its pandemic alert to 6—the highest level of alert and referencing a health crisis with global reach. Although the longer-term impact of the H1N1 flu was difficult to predict at the time, the spread of global reaction and fear called for global action, where the WHO took a central role in shaping the approaches taken by the governments of individual countries.

The global economic crisis, ethnic and sectarian conflict, terrorism, climate change, and pandemics are just some of the most widely recognized challenges crossing the boundaries of nation-states today. As these and other crises have reached global proportions, numerous organizations and individuals have taken it upon themselves to offer both action-oriented and philosophical responses with the goal of crisis mitigation. One such organization, Vision of Humanity, a collection of initiatives centering on issues of global peace, summarized well the importance of global cooperation in fighting the challenges of an increasingly interconnected world: "It is impossible to accurately portray the devastating effects that global challenges such as climate change, lack of fresh water, ever decreasing bio-diversity and overpopulation, will have on all nations unless global unified action is taken. These global challenges call for global solutions and these solutions will require co-operation on a global scale unparalleled in history."[33] A range of other organizations have also adopted similar goals, from Greenpeace through Genocide Watch and the

United Nations to Mercy Corps, each with its own agenda centering on challenges with an identifiable global reach.

Organizations with an explicit emphasis on addressing challenges of a global nature, however, do not stand alone. As higher education institutions adopt the internationalization of their student bodies, curriculum, and co-curriculum as their goals, the challenges of globalization are becoming increasingly apparent, shaping the very functioning of a growing number of universities around the world. Indeed, global challenges have not been absent from the lives of universities, their faculty, and students. To highlight one striking example, universities in the United States have suffered major setbacks as a result of the global financial crisis. Our own universities, UMass Boston and UCLA, were forced to accept considerable budget cuts in recent years—cuts that will no doubt significantly reshape the institutions' ability to implement their mission of teaching, research, and public service.

As universities continue to be critiqued for turning to commercialized values and norms and adopting an academic capitalist mentality in their approaches to globalization, their responses to global challenges in health care, politics, culture, conflict resolution, and a range of other issues often go unnoticed in the larger literature on the functioning of institutions of higher education in this age of globalization. Our goal in this book was to offer a more optimistic assessment of the twenty-first century university, an assessment that acknowledges the impact of crisis on university life, takes account of its academic capitalist responses, and explores the important role of university actors as citizens who actively react and respond to global challenges as well as opportunities. Using Santos's terms,[34] our book has explored both mercantilistic and emancipatory applications of the knowledge created by students and faculty at universities in four diverse regions of the world. As countless organizations have stressed the importance of global action in response to crises of a global nature, the role of faculty and students as globally informed citizens at the cusp of knowledge production cannot be stressed enough.

CONCEPTIONS OF CITIZENSHIP AND GLOBAL CITIZENSHIP

In today's world, citizenship is frequently conceptualized with reference to issues that reach beyond the boundaries of individual nation-states. Although the recognition of citizenship's strong international implications has a long history, recent years have brought heightened emphasis to the importance of considering citizenship in the context of the global, international, and transnational. In fact, the meaning of citizenship in a global world has attracted such widespread attention that it has led to perhaps one of the most provocative debates of our time, with opposing parties arguing about the very possibility of conceiving and enacting rights, responsibilities, and commitments in the context of a range of issues holding relevance beyond traditionally conceived national borders.[35] Another key aspect of the controversy concerns the necessity for global government—or, at least, strong global institutions—in providing the tools for the practice of global citizenship. Some have argued that in the absence of a widely developed network of such institutions and world government, global citizenship remains a hollow concept, while others have promoted the view that not only are global citizens actively engaged in existing institutions with global ties, but they also forge new institutions as well as social movements to further their aims.[36]

Within this continuing debate, we position ourselves as supporters of the possibility of developing a form of global citizenship that may involve conceptualizing and enacting rights and responsibilities in a global sphere of existence, in the economic/occupational, political/civic, and social/cultural dimensions. It may also refer to developing an awareness and mastery of globally relevant issues, skills, and phenomena and using such understandings in approaching and enacting citizen rights and responsibilities in a local, national, regional, or global context. Such notions of global citizenship were at the center of the views and actions of many of our participants in all four case studies. In addition, our book has provided evidence of the variety of ways in which universities provide an important context for the expression of global citizenship among students and faculty. As such, we see universities and, especially, globally engaged universities as key institutions in supporting the conception and expression of global citizenship.

The findings of the four case studies presented in this book speak directly to the relevance of global citizenship in the lives of students and faculty at globally engaged universities in diverse world regions. Globalization was significant in determining the ways in which students and faculty perceived their rights and responsibilities in the economic/occupational, social/cultural, and political/civic dimensions of citizenship. But global citizenship entails more than simply being informed by global understandings in one's views and actions. It is also powerfully shaped by a commitment to collectivist concerns that focus on the wider community within a local, national, regional, or global geographic sphere. According to this conceptualization, global citizenship can be thought of as one quadrant of a broader citizenship model consisting of two intersecting continua. One continuum represents the dimension of locally informed to globally informed, referring to the extent to which an individual's thoughts and actions are framed by local as opposed to global understandings. The other continuum ranges from individualist to collectivist and encompasses the enactment of rights and responsibilities across a host of issues ranging from those tied to themselves and their immediate families to broader collectivities of individuals and groups (Figure 6.1, repeated from Figure 1.2 in Chapter 1, depicts this model of citizenship).

Based on the four quadrants formed by the intersection of these two continua, four types of citizenship emerge: (1) locally informed collectivist, (2) globally informed collectivist, (3) locally informed individualist, and (4)

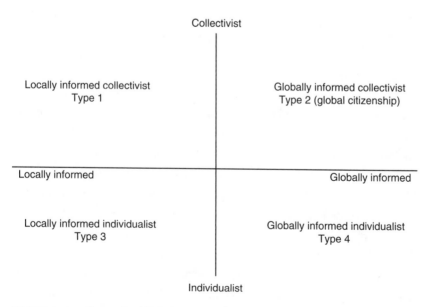

FIGURE 6.1. Citizenship/Global Citizenship Typology

globally informed individualist. Type 2 in this model (globally informed collectivist) encompasses our criteria for global citizenship, embodied in its globally informed and collectivist qualities. Importantly, our model does not specify the geographic scope of citizen thoughts and actions. Instead, it stipulates that expressions of citizenship can be focused on concerns addressing a range of geographic locales, from local to global. Our model proposes that even local action may be considered a form of global citizenship as long as that action is informed by global understandings and concerns. In a simple example, an individual who is committed to polluting less and minimizing energy usage in her or his daily localized life but whose actions are driven by considerations for global environmental degradation could be considered to have significant attributes of global citizenship. However, local action informed solely by local concerns does not embody the notion of global citizenship delineated here. Quite obviously, citizen thoughts and actions expressed in a global plane of existence, for example, volunteering for a charity that fights hunger worldwide and doing so with a strong concern for the reduction of global inequalities, also evidence attributes of global citizenship. This model of citizenship builds on the framework we previously proposed in an article reporting our findings from Chapter 3, our case study on international graduate students at UCLA.[37] The modified model presented in this book is built on the experiences of a wider range of students and faculty at four universities in four diverse world regions, outlining a more sophisticated analysis of citizenship and of global citizenship.

Importantly, the majority, if not all, of the participants in our study were overwhelmingly informed by global understandings as they formulated and enacted their rights and responsibilities. In this regard, their citizen views and actions were very much in line with Type 2 (globally informed collectivist) and Type 4 (globally informed individualist) in our model of citizenship. However, few of our participants represented clear-cut examples of any one type of citizenship, but instead displayed multifaceted aspects of citizenship. For example, the majority of the students and faculty in the four case studies displayed a combination of certain patterns of views and behaviors in the economic/occupational, political/civic, and social/cultural dimensions of citizenship. To be clearer, although the global quality of the forms of citizenship enacted by the students and faculty came across loud and clear, they also evidenced a diversity of views about citizenship reflecting the importance of context-specific thought and action. In other words, even someone strongly committed to addressing collective concerns and embracing global understandings will at other times be more self- and locally oriented. The key for us is the ability to recognize that many concerns call forth global solutions and strategies and that citizens must possess the capacity to think and act at times as global citizens. Hence, for us, global citizenship is not so much a static identity as it is an ability, disposition, or commitment (perhaps it is all of these). Furthermore, it is also important to acknowledge that, unavoidably, empirical research is only able to capture participants' views and perceptions at a limited number of points in time. As such, it is inevitable that our participants' conceptions of citizenship might take at least slightly different forms depending on the specific contexts in which the participants find themselves in their daily lives.

ELABORATING THE FOUR TYPES OF CITIZENSHIP

To bring greater clarity to our citizenship typology, we turn to offering more concrete examples of the four types of citizenship. Because the central focus of this book concerns expressions of global (or globally informed) citizenship, the majority of the discussion emphasizes Types 2 and 4 in our citizenship model. Indeed, the four universities in our case study chapters are powerful representations of the globally engaged university, where the economic, political, and social aspects of students' and faculty's lives are considerably shaped by global understandings. For this reason, our findings from the case studies will be used to illustrate Types 2 and 4 in our model. Because of the lack of significant representations of Types 1 and 3 of citizenship in our empirical findings, the examples we present for these two types of citizenship are drawn from the field of higher education in general and are offered only for the purpose of clarifying our typology.

In Type 1 of our citizenship model, *locally informed collectivism*, individuals' notions of rights and responsibilities are shaped primarily by local concerns. In other words, globalization and issues of global significance have little to do with this conception of citizenship that focuses, instead, on the local and national community as the principal point of reference. The local and national are also the geographic regions from where these individuals draw their knowledge and skills in the economic/occupational, political/ civic, and social/cultural realms. Collectivist action expressed as responsibilities, however, forms an important part of this type of citizenship, guiding significant engagement in issues and concerns affecting the local and national community. At colleges and universities, students and faculty embracing locally informed collectivist forms of citizenship might be involved in community-based efforts to support disadvantaged populations in gaining access to and succeeding in college. Individuals enacting this type of citizenship rely on the knowledge and skills that they gained in their U.S.-based education and work with disadvantaged youth, with a strong focus on collectivist action. In other examples, the actions of a college student who participates in community service aiming to deliver services to the elderly living in the neighborhood surrounding the university or a faculty member who commits significant time and energy to gaining institutional support for a new co-curricular program can also be considered examples of locally informed collectivism.

An essential quality of the globally informed collectivist approach to citizenship (Type 2) involves the heightened importance these individuals attach to understanding and considering the broader global context. Like the locally informed collectivist approach to citizenship, globally informed collectivist forms also place great emphasis on giving back to some larger collective, be that their local communities, nation-states, regions, and in some cases, the global community/environment. The focus in this conception of citizenship is overwhelmingly on responsibilities, although rights remain important in the sense of providing citizens the necessary globally relevant tools and privileges, enabling them both to live a personally satisfying life and to make important contributions to local, national, regional, or global concerns.

Although localism and nationalism seem rather self-evident in terms of the geographic locale to which they refer, the idea of regionalism may be a little murky. For our purposes, regionalism may reference a large geographic area within a particular nation, such as the western part of China where the Uighurs are predominantly found, as well as geographic locales that span nations, such as Eastern Europe or Southeast Asia. Thus, regionalism is evidenced when particular Brazilian students studying at UCLA referenced strengthening Latin America, or when some faculty members at CEU high-lighted the research they do to strengthen the former communist bloc coun-tries including, but not limited to, Hungary.

In our case studies, the most evident representation of globally informed collectivism focusing on local and national concerns was among faculty and students at UBA and their serious engagement in collectivist action directed at solving problems affecting Argentina. In doing so, they brought their un-derstanding of financial problems believed to be induced by neoliberalism and the role of powerful supranational organizations such the IMF to the resolution of local and national crises. In a similar, although less radical, fashion and focusing on national as well as regional concerns, a number of faculty members at CEU embraced their role in bringing their knowledge of international or Western curricula, research, pedagogical tools, and method-ologies to their ever-globalizing university. Their actions represented efforts to promote democratic development on the local level in a range of countries, through enriching the learning of their students, many of whom not only brought their home country experiences to the classroom but also returned to their homelands upon graduation. Also, many of the students and faculty at GDUFS spoke of using their knowledge of global economics and geopolitical affairs to strengthen China and its place in an increasingly global arena. These students and faculty saw themselves as deeply indebted to their "moth-erland" but took seriously their pursuit of knowledge related to and inform-ing complex global processes.

Several international graduate students in our study at the University of California, Los Angeles (UCLA) also displayed important qualities of glob-ally informed collectivism, reflected in their intention to learn from the foreign academic environment and then take back their globally informed knowledge and skills to their homelands. At the heart of their intentions lay the desire to address and resolve societal problems in their countries of ori-gin. Oftentimes for these students, local and national problems provided profound inspiration for undertaking graduate studies in the United States in the first place. The importance of possessing individual rights was especially pronounced in the lives of international graduate students. Indeed, it was through the granting of a set of basic rights—most significantly, rights to cross-border movement and educational and professional opportunities in the United States—that these graduate students were able to become globally informed in their views and actions.

When globally informed collectivists have a stronger focus on global concerns, they use their global understandings and knowledge to benefit the broader global environment, centering their conceptualizations of citizenship on a strong responsibility to a community that is larger than their local, national, and regional surroundings. They cast their eyes on a broader sphere of existence, recognizing and confronting problems that reach beyond the boundaries of individual nation-states and world regions. Their ideas of citizenship are rooted in recognition and hope that collective action, linking individuals, organizations, and movements from around the world, has the potential to effectively bring about change in the interest of solving globally relevant problems. In a sense, they not only stress the existence of a world community but also emphasize aspects of their identity that are inextricably linked to membership in that community. Individual rights remain important in this conception of citizenship; however, their significance is inseparable from enabling the fulfillment of responsibilities in a global sphere. In other words, although these individuals strive to advance in their professional and social circles, they often see individual success in close relationship to their ability to make broader societal contributions.

Such examples of globally informed collectivism were reflected especially well in our case studies related to UCLA and CEU. At UCLA, many of the international graduate students expressed their interest in global collectivist action by stressing the importance of making professional contributions with relevance to a broad range of issues worldwide, including protecting the environment in their work and everyday life, participating in organizations with a global mission, such as Amnesty International, and promoting a strongly multicultural view of citizenship. A number of faculty at CEU also embraced a global collectivist notion of citizenship. For some professors, this orientation was reflected in efforts to make available research findings to both local and global communities, recognizing the importance of highlighting issues in a variety of geographic contexts. Others spoke of their engagement in international policy organizations. Virtually all CEU faculty discussed the role they played in the classroom, an environment centered on critically considering and evaluating sometimes controversial and contradictory knowledge claims with students arriving from an ever-diversifying range of countries from around the world.

In Type 3 of our citizenship model, *locally informed individualism*, rights and opportunities attained and practiced in a local/national sphere of existence come to the fore with a strong focus on the attainment of individual rights and little consideration for a global sphere of existence. The attainment of knowledge and skills in this type of citizenship also takes place within the context of local and national orientations. In this sense, this type of citizenship remains locally informed as reflected, for example, in a college curriculum that has not heeded recent calls for internationalization. Collectivist action is also largely absent from locally informed individualism, with the primary focus placed on individual advancement in one's professional and social circles. A student who goes to college to attain a bachelor's degree with the goal of becoming a successful employee and achieving high levels of professional prestige on the basis of forms of knowledge rooted in the local or national context and whose considerations and actions tend to center on self-advancement evidences Type 3 forms of citizenship. Among faculty members, locally informed individualism might be reflected in a commitment to advancing one's career at a particular university, advancing in the institutional hierarchy, while drawing on the knowledge and skills gained at that university. No moral judgment is made here, because many factors and forces go into shaping one's choices in the world. However, an individual who only thinks and acts in terms of Type 3 forms of citizenship has little potential to contribute to broader concerns and issues, including those operating at a global level.

Type 4 in our citizenship model is *globally informed individualism*, a form of citizenship that includes citizens who are informed by global understandings but enact them in their self-interest and, by extension, in the interest of their immediate families, on a local or global stage. In other words, globally informed individualists focus on taking advantage of opportunities and skills linked to global understandings with the purpose of furthering their individual rights. This approach to citizenship was reflected in the thoughts and comments of a small number of undergraduates at GDUFS, who stressed the importance of gaining familiarity with the processes of globalization, with Western culture, with China's place in the world, and, importantly, with the

English language, in the interest of their own economic/occupational advancement. For these participants, then, mastering forms of knowledge tied to globalization was key to the professional success that they hoped to achieve, whether that be within their local communities or within the context of another country. Again, we do not make a moral judgment here, nor do we seek to cast the views and experiences of these students in a negative light. The fact is that most of the Chinese students who discussed globalization and its opportunities through a focus on individual rights seek to be as financially successful as possible in order to support their families, including providing for their parents, as part of the extended family structure common to China. Indeed, this is a major element of the economic and occupational planning of young people in China, given the tradition of the extended family, combined with a very weak social support system for the elderly.

In some cases, globally informed individualism stresses an expanded geographic scope, where the emphasis is on seeking to advance one's own interests on a global stage. These individuals focus on their advancement in occupational and economic spheres, oftentimes leaving the confines of their home countries and taking advantage of their existence as global jet-setters. Chapter 3 on international graduate students at UCLA presented examples of this conception of citizenship, whereby several students engaged in international educational opportunities at the graduate level with the specific purpose of turning their globally acquired knowledge and skills into individual gain and professional prestige, without much concern for the potential contributions of their work to community concerns, whether such communities were locally or globally rooted. In this sense, these individuals took personal advantage of the global market of knowledge, cultural forms, social connections, and economic networks.

From our perspective, of the four types of citizenship described in our framework, Type 2, globally informed collectivism, represents global citizenship. Indeed, conceptions of citizen views and actions that are informed by an understanding of globally relevant phenomena and concerned with expressing and enacting responsibilities in a collectivist fashion form the basis of what we consider the essential attributes of global citizenship. Our model brings together a focus on rights and responsibilities within one comprehensive framework of citizenship, where Type 1 (locally informed collectivism) and Type 2 (globally informed collectivism) foreground responsibilities, while also acknowledging the importance of certain rights in individuals' ability to live a personally satisfying life while making possible globally relevant citizen action. By contrast, Type 3 (locally informed individualism) and Type 4 (globally informed individualism) are primarily rights-based notions of citizenship. In this regard, our model departs from many existing conceptualizations of citizenship in higher education that underscore the crucial role of civic responsibilities.[38] Rather, our model recognizes the importance of both rights and responsibilities. Without a range of rights, citizens are in fact quite limited in their ability and opportunity to enact responsibilities.

Dominant models of citizenship in today's world have also placed overwhelming emphasis on the global as the geographic sphere of citizenship, focusing on views, actions, and commitments that, as their central focus, involve the crossing of national boundaries and extend to the sphere of the global.[39] This emphasis is readily apparent in our model of global citizenship as well. However, the explicit global component of our framework focuses more on the context of one's knowledge and understandings brought to bear on considerations and actions as a citizen, and not on the particular geographic stage upon which one acts. From our perspective, local action may still be seen as consistent with global forms of citizenship, if such action is globally informed.[40] The global nature of our model of citizenship thus lies in the act of developing an understanding of global issues and processes and applying knowledge and skills in a variety of geographic spheres, including the local, national, regional, and global. The inverse of our model would be represented by forms of citizenship ill-informed by global issues and processes, whether such forms are enacted on the basis of individualist or collectivist aims. We see such notions of citizenship, when advanced as a dominant modality, as foolhardy in today's world, given the prevalence of large-scale globally oriented problems. Furthermore, we see models of global citizenship (Type 2) as requiring a serious collectivist orientation; again, the nature of contemporary global problems leads us to such a conviction. Thus for us, global citizenship suggests a model of citizen thought and action relevant to the nature of today's global concerns. Consequently, we opt to turn our attention to the ideal of *global citizenship*—and specifically, to the role that universities play in advancing it.

THE ROLE OF UNIVERSITIES

We chose to study issues of global citizenship at universities because students and faculty are in unique and privileged positions with regard to their access to knowledge. Indeed, a large body of work in the United States highlights the role professors and students play in applying their knowledge to the benefit of society as a form of citizenship, with most of this literature focusing on the domestic implications of citizenship.[41] In many ways, the primary emphasis of this literature has much in common with Type 1 in our citizenship model, focusing on locally informed collectivism. Whether in a domestic or global context, one might speak of students and faculty, through the privilege they gain from their involvement in the production, management, and application of knowledge, potentially as "empowered citizens." In essence, our study sought to make sense of how students and faculty, as citizens, utilize their privileged roles in the production, management, and application of knowledge at globally engaged universities.

One of the assumptions underlying our study from its inception was that given the strength of globalization and the key role of higher education in a global world, a serious university must in some manner or form derive elements of its vitality from the globally informed endeavors of its students and professors. All four of the universities included in our study were in fact selected on the basis that we believed them to be globally engaged. Our assumption played out for the most part, and what we learned along the way adds complexity to understanding global citizenship and engagement. For example, our case studies reveal that citizenship in the context of global engagement sometimes takes a more reactionary form, as when global processes are seen to be acting on an institution. Forms of citizenship at globally engaged universities must therefore reflect sophisticated elements involving interpretation and meaning making of global events and processes. Here, we turn to some of the senior faculty at GDUFS who interpreted facets of globalization—namely, cultural globalization—to be potentially harmful to the campus in particular and to China in general. Similarly, although many of our participants saw global capitalism as a positive force in the lives of their universities and nations, students and faculty acting as citizens at UBA rejected the idea that global capitalism must have a free rein over societies. These students and faculty were not opposed to globalization and the engagement of university actors in global concerns. However, they were opposed to a particular variety of globalization described as neoliberalism.

Additionally, students and faculty working at globally engaged universities must advance thinking and lines of action that are more than simply reactionary; they must actively engage in developing their awareness and understanding of global processes and phenomena, an awareness and understanding that enable them to enact their citizen rights and responsibilities in a range of geographic locales. We found this to be the case among many of the students and faculty at all four universities. For example, many of the faculty at CEU used their knowledge of globally relevant phenomena (i.e., democratization and the growing relevance of open societies) in shaping the nature of societal transitions across nations around the world. Students and faculty at UBA sought to define and shape globalization in a manner consistent with a value orientation placing workers and local community needs over the free flow of capital. Several of the international students with whom we spoke at UCLA envisioned using their knowledge to refashion forms of social life in a global age. Many of the students and faculty at GDUFS saw themselves using their knowledge to influence the way China interacts with the outside world, thus playing a key role in shaping their nation's geopolitical participation in the global arena.

A key question to consider relative to our model of citizenship is, should universities promote certain types of citizenship among students and faculty, or should they avoid making value judgments regarding the nature of citizenship? From the perspective of universities, does it matter if a faculty member uses his or her locally or globally informed knowledge to address problems of local as opposed to global relevance? What are the implications of a student's turning his or her globally informed skills into personal professional gain, in an individualistic manner, rather than focusing on global collectivist action?

The answers to these questions are no doubt complicated. Most importantly, the expression of citizen behavior depends on more than an individual's decision to enact rights and responsibilities in the interest of a particular cause, be that cause related to individual or collectivist action in a local, national, regional, or global sphere of existence. Indeed, societal standing and circumstances play an enormous role in shaping the kinds of citizen behaviors in which a person engages. The types of citizen action that individuals adopt, then, are rooted in the desire to enact rights and responsibilities in a certain way, but also, to a considerable degree, their choices to follow particular lines of action are tied to their social and environmental context. For example, it is possible that some of our participants whose notions of citizenship focused on individualism simply did not have the means to engage in broadly relevant collectivist action given their social standing and substantial responsibilities toward their immediate families. For these participants, focusing on individual advancement, perhaps at the expense of collectivist action, thus remained a central goal.

To consider our point further, it is perhaps helpful to step away from the higher education context. For example, it would be difficult to expect a single, unemployed mother of five living in an impoverished community to aspire to enact forms of global citizenship. In such a case, the local and individual frames of reference remain focused on vital, life-saving concerns, perhaps with an emphasis on gaining locally based skills for a family's economic survival. In higher education, such examples generally are not as pronounced, partly because the ability to be affiliated with a university, as a student or as a faculty member, in almost every country of the world, harbors considerable privilege. Of course, this is not to say that many university students and faculty do not have economic hardships that at times limit their capacity to direct their attention to broader concerns. We think of the many undocumented students in the United States and the limited resources at their disposal. We also recall stories of faculty at African universities having to raise chickens in their apartments in order to survive, given their limited salaries. Many of the faculty at UBA had to maintain full-time professional careers, envisioning their teaching at the university as a form of missionary work. Certainly, Maslow's needs hierarchy comes to mind when we think about citizen action and who has the ability as well as the opportunity to focus on a broader, more collectivist agenda.

As the examples in our book demonstrate, an individual's life circumstances have a substantial role to play in the adoption of particular types of citizenship among students and faculty in higher education. Given the complexity of the nature of citizen behavior in a global age, is it even desirable for universities to promote preferred types of citizenship? Our answer to this question is affirmative, with qualifications underscoring the importance of remaining sensitive to the facets of one's individual circumstances, including one's social standing, economic resources, and the broader sociopolitical context. Most significantly, our view is rooted in a belief that the increasingly global context that we live in demands collective action on the part of citizens. In fact, the successful resolution of societal crises hinges not only on the cooperation of people living in diverse parts of the world but also on individuals becoming globally informed citizens, gaining knowledge and skills in a global sphere of existence, and in turn applying them at the local or global level. For these reasons, we recommend that universities intentionally support the development of globally informed collectivist citizens, Type 2 in our model of citizenship.

At the same time, we acknowledge the continuing role of higher education institutions in supporting students' and faculty's goals in individual societal advancement, in terms of more individualist expressions of citizenship. We do not, in any way, suggest that this role should be abandoned in the interest of solely promoting collectivist action. We recognize that the process of obtaining knowledge at universities is inextricably tied to the satisfaction of individual professional goals that may or may not be accompanied by collectivist ideals and action. In a very real sense, this role of higher education institutions is not only an essential aspect of societal success but also an indispensable cornerstone of the expression of individual responsibilities.

We do, however, emphasize the importance of strengthening the focus that universities can and, we believe, should place on the promotion of collectivist citizen action among students and faculty. Our view is grounded in intensifying accounts in the literature depicting higher education as following a business model more than ever before, where students increasingly attend college for personal professional and financial gain, where faculty entrepreneurial action is becoming the norm, especially in academic fields in closer proximity to the market, and where universities are more and more intent on pursuing revenue-generating activities, oftentimes at the expense of their traditional mission to promote the public good and to create and apply knowledge with emancipatory aims.[42]

This is not to say that the public good and a focus on emancipatory knowledge application are completely absent from the contemporary university. In fact, the literature highlights not only the possibility but also real and convincing examples of citizen responsibilities enacted at universities, reflected in studies of service learning, community outreach, faculty service, and a range of other aspects of university life.[43] What we propose is that universities, especially globally engaged universities, put even greater emphasis on the promotion of citizen action, building on their growing role in the globally informed production, management, and application of knowledge.

Our emphasis on the global sets this work apart from many existing accounts of citizenship in higher education, the majority of which highlight a strong focus on the domestic applications of citizenship, as in Type 1 of our citizenship model, without much emphasis on the increasing relevance of globally informed knowledge and skills enacted in both domestic and global spheres.[44] In essence, what is clear from our research is that citizenship at globally engaged universities extends various conceptions of the role students and faculty play in the production, management, and application of knowledge. We are in no way suggesting that local or regional issues and concerns no longer matter, but instead argue that such issues may be better addressed by citizens acting on the basis of more informed global understandings. But how can universities go about supporting the engagement of students and faculty in ways that reflect greater understanding of the global context and the problems befitting an increasingly interdependent world? In other words, how can universities as institutions engaged in the production, management, and application of knowledge promote engagement in more globally informed ways with a greater concern for the collective good? In what follows, we offer specific examples and ideas for encouraging globally informed citizenship on the part of students and faculty and organize our discussion around the production, management, and application of knowledge.

UNIVERSITIES AND THE PRODUCTION OF KNOWLEDGE

The production of knowledge plays a central role at any university, where knowledge is continually created in the form of research endeavors on the part of professors, graduate students, and, to a lesser extent, undergraduates participating in faculty research. Knowledge is also produced in the classroom, where students and faculty engage in conversations about the nature of empirical data, methods, discoveries, and theories related to their academic fields of study. The key distinguishing factor of knowledge production at globally engaged universities, however, is apparent in the geographic spheres where knowledge takes shape, characterized by the repeated crossing—either literally or figuratively—of traditionally conceived national boundaries by those engaged in knowledge creation. In this realm, we believe that universities should place an increased emphasis on these border crossings, bringing a global emphasis to knowledge production. Two primary efforts stand out as perhaps the most significant, with the first focusing on interactions and collaboration among students and faculty across a diverse range of countries and the second involving the identification of research problems harboring clear global or international relevance.

The first effort involves transnational and international collaboration, where faculty and student participants contribute to the same intellectual project, often bringing their own theoretical, conceptual, and methodological frameworks for understandings of locally or globally relevant phenomena. Such international collaboration in science and engineering fields, often referred to as "global science," has received particular attention in the literature, inspiring studies that seek to understand the nature of international scientific collaboration. Recognizing the potential of global science for the resolution of both locally and globally relevant problems, bringing scientists together in collectivist action, international scientific networks have spawned both organically and as a result of formal policy measures instituted by national governments.[45] Although fields other than the sciences and engineering have been less explored in terms of international collaboration, the potential of such interactions is strong in virtually any academic field of study, from the humanities through the social sciences to education and medicine.

Study abroad programs, including international service learning, and international student and scholarly exchange can also provide fertile ground for the globally informed production of knowledge by university actors. Forming some of the most important elements of colleges' and universities' efforts to internationalize their campuses,[46] these efforts support the creation of an international atmosphere of learning, as well as scholarly collaboration. Our chapters on international graduate students studying at UCLA and faculty work at CEU provide significant examples of knowledge creation in an international context within universities that host thousands of international students every year. In such an environment, knowledge is created in the presence of knowledge claims that sometimes conflict and at other times coalesce, giving rise to a climate where a diversity of ideas circulate. Importantly, the knowledge created in such a way also holds the strong potential to increase the ease of international communication and understanding among people from a diversity of backgrounds, thereby holding implications for all three dimensions of citizenship.

The second area of globally informed knowledge production relates to the identification of global problems in research and academic study, putting local issues in a global context, or stressing a focus on globally relevant phenomena. Examples might include addressing a health issue from a global perspective, such as UCLA's AIDS Institute described in Chapter 3, or a research emphasis on the global impact of environmental degradation, both of these examples reflecting a strong emphasis on collectivist action. In other instances, scholars who conduct research on concerns faced by marginalized groups in a specific country might bring a global emphasis to their research by adding a comparative dimension, focusing on similar issues faced by marginalized populations in other countries. Examples of such approaches to the study of marginalization are increasingly easy to find in the field of comparative education. A recently published book on the education of girls from underrepresented minority backgrounds across several nation-states exemplifies this emphasis. As the title, *Inexcusable Absence: Why 60 Million Girls Still Aren't in School and What to Do about It*,[47] suggests, the authors' primary concern relates to the underrepresentation of girls in education all over the world. Addressing the issue from a global and a local perspective at the same time—by comparing the situation in countries as diverse as Canada, New Zealand, the United States, Brazil, India, Malaysia, and Japan—allows the authors not only to assess the global ramifications of the issue of girls' education but also to make policy recommendations, keeping local as well as global realities in mind.

In their engagement in globally relevant knowledge production, faculty and students benefit from international training experiences and an exposure to international issues in the curriculum at various levels of education. Internationalizing the curriculum thus holds special relevance in this regard.[48] In the field of higher education, this might involve teaching a "Diversity in Higher Education" class with an emphasis on issues of diversity in other countries as well as the United States, highlighting similarities and differences across various national contexts. What the students might take away from this experience is recognition of the importance of considering research topics and developing policy implications from a domestic as well as international perspective. Although some of these issues might appear most immediately relevant in the social sciences, the importance of globally informed knowledge production with a collectivist orientation cannot be disputed in science, technology, and engineering fields, especially when researchers make the ever-important linkages to societal implications.

UNIVERSITIES AND THE MANAGEMENT OF KNOWLEDGE

Universities, the most multifaceted forms of higher education institutions in existence today,[49] have had to contend with the management of the knowledge they produce for many years. The full-fledged functioning of departments, academic programs, and research and administrative units, coordinated by a multitude of professional staff, pay tribute to this key function. Although a variety of administrative structures established for this purpose exist at all universities, at globally engaged universities, knowledge management is shaped to a significant extent by the global implications of knowledge production, necessitating the existence of modified as well as new organizational arrangements.

Perhaps most importantly, the global context surrounding issues in each academic field of study needs to be reflected in the organization of majors, degree programs, and coursework at both the undergraduate and graduate levels. Lending a global flavor to these structures not only underscores the significance a university attaches to the globally informed creation and management of knowledge but also makes available increasingly crucial opportunities for students and faculty to center their efforts of knowledge creation and acquisition on issues and skills holding global and collective significance that, in turn, can be applied to a variety of geographic contexts. The establishment of global studies programs, such as the one described at UCLA in Chapter 3, is a notable undertaking that is gaining increased popularity at university campuses. Such programs add innovative curricular arrangements to a university's academic offerings. Interdepartmental programs focusing on a set of issues from a global perspective also hold special relevance in this regard. Beyond these overarching programs that provide an academic home for a globally active subsection of the student and faculty population, it is important to recognize the key role played by individual academic departments in providing the necessary space for globally informed knowledge. The establishment of intradepartmental program areas focusing on globalization, hiring faculty with teaching and research expertise in globally relevant issues, and making a conscious effort to support the academic experiences of students (both domestic and international) with an interest in strengthening their global expertise and collectivist action all require significant participation on the part of individual academic departments. Consequently, gaining the commitment of individual academic departments to advancing global curricular endeavors is a key priority in advancing globally engaged universities.

Besides curricular offerings, offices of international, transnational, or global affairs provide a more overarching structure for the management of globally informed knowledge at universities. These administrative units can play a key role in pulling together a university's resources related to globalization, organizing international programs for students and faculty, providing easy access to databases that present opportunities for the globally informed production of knowledge, and representing the public face of the university in terms of its global engagement. Libraries and offices of institutional technology also play a significant role in this regard. In fact, these two organizational structures at globally engaged universities play major roles in both housing knowledge and managing knowledge transfer and exchange across international borders.

UNIVERSITIES AND THE APPLICATION OF KNOWLEDGE

Besides producing and managing knowledge, universities also play a crucial role in its application. In fact, this area of university functioning has received significant attention in recent years, leading to new conceptualizations of teaching and learning, as well as student and faculty life. The image of the engaged professor has been depicted in models of the scholarship of engagement,[50] a framework that forms the core of our discussion of citizenship among students and faculty at globally engaged universities. This framework harbors a clear shift from the primary responsibility of universities, students, and faculty to simply produce and manage knowledge. Instead, the main focus of this model stresses that these roles need to be accompanied by a strong emphasis on societal engagement, bringing knowledge closer to forms of application in solving real social problems. This shift in understanding the role of universities has also been described by Boaventura de Sousa Santos as the emancipatory application of pluriversity knowledge, a type of knowledge recognizable by its proximity to societal concerns.[51]

Considering the application of knowledge at globally engaged universities, relative to our notion of global citizenship, we stress the importance of including a clearly defined global emphasis. The central issue in shaping the globally informed application of knowledge thus concerns specific ways in which universities can encourage faculty and students to apply their knowledge and expertise in a manner that is globally informed. In essence, we believe that globally engaged universities should make available a variety of tools for the practice of globally informed citizenship that include opportunities for collectivist applications of knowledge by students and faculty. One example involves support for the creation and long-term functioning of international service and service learning programs, where students and faculty can put into practice their globally informed skills and knowledge about marginalized populations, and issues of poverty and development in an international context. Formally recognizing the value of such programs is apparent in the awarding of academic credit for student participation and considering faculty engagement in promotion and tenure decisions.

Institutional support for academic freedom in knowledge application, even when it involves taking a critical stance on the impact of globalization in a given context, is also crucial to encouraging globally informed collectivist action. Chapter 4 on UBA faculty involvement in the fight against neoliberalism in Argentina is a key example in this regard. Faculty at major universities such as UBA must in some manner or form function as a social conscience, and this is likely to involve adopting unpopular or even oppositional stances at times. Universities must be spaces where such forms of opposition thrive, as part of the necessary challenge and questioning they provoke in contrast to the hegemony of dominant systems of thought such as neoliberal versions of global capitalism.

Strengthening support structures for distributing the findings of globally informed knowledge production in a wide array of national and international contexts, including promoting publication of results in countries that stand to benefit the most from such global research, is another important facet to global knowledge application. This latter example raises important concerns relating to reward structures for student and faculty work at universities. In fact, we believe that the global application of knowledge should receive an especially important role in promotion and tenure decisions in faculty work and student efforts should be rewarded by academic credits. Just as some universities now give credit to faculty as part of their review process for contributions to diversity, the same type of considerations could be given to faculty on the basis of global contributions. This is not simply about whether or not professors have international standing, a feature that many universities already incorporate into the highest levels of faculty review, but it speaks to the very nature of the problems and issues addressed by professors in their research and teaching.

We recognize that many of the aforementioned strategies for the globally informed production, management, and application of knowledge can be accomplished in a multitude of ways, with varying levels of relevance in the promotion of student and faculty citizenship and collectivist action. The internationalization of the student body of a university or the introduction of study abroad programs, for example, can be driven by strong financial, profit-driven goals, rather than the objective of strengthening the global, international environment for the acquisition and application of knowledge and skills.[52] Similarly, it is important to make a key distinction between global research cooperation driven by competitive, profit-driven as opposed to non-competitive aims. In this regard, we share Michael Peters's concern, cautioning that the scale of global science is increasingly tipped in a competitive direction:

Universities encourage both competitive and non-competitive forms of international collaboration but increasingly with the historic downturn in state funding of higher education in the U.S. and the development of nearly 200 science research parks nationwide, with an emphasis on venture capital funding of spin-off companies, patents of university discoveries, and the attraction of leading multinationals on campus, the latter is giving way to the former as institutions struggle to diversify their funding bases.[53]

Recognizing these concerns, and based on our model of citizenship, we advocate for the important role of international collaboration, student and faculty international experiences, curricular internationalization, and a host of other strategies in the globally informed production, management, and application of knowledge, especially when these endeavors foreground the public good. Clearly, we see a more globally informed, collectivist model of citizenship as critical to meeting the needs of the twenty-first century and for advancing universities with the capacity and wherewithal to better serve the diverse needs of a constantly changing world.

CONCLUDING THOUGHTS

In July of 2009, U.S. President Barack Obama suggested that the relationship between the United States and China "will shape the 21st century."[54] Although we certainly acknowledge the importance of these two economic giants, we see a whole host of countries and regions of the world holding the potential to shape this century. From our perspective, *global relations* broadly defined will shape the twenty-first century. Hence, the move from "the once elite club of rich industrial nations known as the Group of 7" to the much broader and diverse Group of 20 symbolized the kind of expansive thought needed in this global age.[55] More players must be brought to the table, as we struggle collectively to address global problems and build stronger global ties. Whether or not expansion of key economic decision makers from seven (actually eight, given that Russia was added to this group) to twenty will result in better global relations remains to be seen, although supporters of the shift claim that "emerging nations, and the huge slice of the world's population that they represent, must have a seat at the table to debate not only economic issues, but also environmental issues like climate change."[56] And so the question confronting all of us, and most specifically for our purposes, universities around the world, is—what is to be the nature of global relations in the coming years? Will our grandchildren and their children look back at the twenty-first century and fondly characterize it as a period of peace and global cooperation? Or will they, with great remorse, recall times of conflict, famine, and environmental degradation in which we as a global community failed to work across national boundaries to resolve worldwide crises?

From our perspective, we are at a point in world history where nationalism can no longer be the primary source of identity as citizens. The great problems of the age will require boundary-spanning thought and action. The transnational nature of conflict, famine, and environmental problems will require citizens acting on the basis of broader geographic points of reference than their own nation, their own region, or their own city or countryside. We are not suggesting that localism has no place in the twenty-first century—but only that it must exist in combination with increasing global awareness. Certainly there are many parts of the world where local issues and concerns must be the priority. But working toward the resolution of localized problems in the coming years will increasingly require knowledge and understanding of complex global processes.

The question for us then is: How do we promote globally informed forms of local and global thought and action, with a focus on collectivism? Of course, we see universities as critical to this mission, given the significant role they play in the production, management, and application of knowledge. Although university administrators certainly play key roles in these areas, in this book we specifically turned our attention to faculty and students, whom we see as occupying the front lines of the university knowledge industry. And make no mistake about this, it is indeed a knowledge industry, but complex questions about whose interests will be served by this mega-industry remain highly contentious. We believe that collectivist perspectives coinciding with service to the broader public good ought to be at the core of the knowledge industry, and so our vision of citizenship places great emphasis on advancing public good concerns at both the local and global levels. Hence, we believe universities ought to be in the business of promoting and encouraging globally informed collectivists among their faculty and students and within the broader society in general. Certainly, individualism in the form of both the local and global may produce social, political, and economic enhancements for communities and societies, but the ideal of service to the collective good resonates more with us than the potential trickle-down benefits spawned by service to oneself.

Findings from our case studies of GDUFS, UCLA, UBA, and CEU offer some important ideas for how universities might better position themselves as contributors to the development and encouragement of globally informed citizens acting in service to the broader collective good. We do not see them as models for other universities to follow, but instead refer to their attributes as a means to highlight global engagement and to better understand the potential for advancing globally informed collectivist citizens—or simply, global citizenship. The real value of these four universities for us was the blending of our findings and the synthesis they, in their totality, produced about what it means to be a global citizen. There are many other universities we could have selected, but these four institutions served our needs quite nicely and helped us grapple with the complex issues of global citizenship and the role of the university. Consequently, the typology we presented reflects the greater complexity and sophistication inspired by our field work and analysis. In this regard, we are grateful to all the interview subjects and research participants who served as trail guides for a sojourn of sorts to four distinctive corners of the world. Their thoughts and comments are reflected in our work and helped us to advance a more complete and thorough understanding of global citizenship and the contemporary university.

REFERENCE MATTER

NOTES

1. GLOBALIZATION, CITIZENSHIP, AND THE UNIVERSITY

Portions of this chapter borrow from the article by Katalin Szelényi and Robert A. Rhoads, "Citizenship in a Global Context: The Perspectives of International Graduate Students in the United States," *Comparative Education Review*, 51(1), 2007, pp. 25–47. Copyright © 2007 by University of Chicago Press. Used with permission. All rights reserved.

1. Said 1993, xxv.
2. Said 1993.
3. Wright 1991.
4. Fanon 1963, 15.
5. Fanon 1963, 15.
6. Fanon 1963, 15.
7. Vidal 2002; Harvey 2003.
8. Harvey 2003, 11.
9. Said 1993, 20.
10. Rizvi 2009, 5.
11. Barber 1995; Ritzer 1993.
12. Rizvi and Walsh 1998, 8.
13. Luke and Luke 2000, 283.
14. Luke and Luke 2000, 276.
15. See Tomlinson 1999, 2003.
16. Frammolino 2004. For a similar discussion of the globalization of rap music (in this case its emergence in the Middle East), see Daragahi and Fleishman 2009.
17. Luke and Luke 2000, 276.
18. Frammolino 2004, A23.

19. Chomsky 2006.

20. Marginson 2010.

21. Portions of this book borrow from Rhoads and Szelényi (2009). From the article: Rhoads, Robert A., and Katalin Szelényi. "Globally Engaged Universities and the Changing Context of Academic Citizenship." *Education and Society* 27, no. 2 (2009): 5-26. Copyright © 2009 JAMES NICHOLAS PUBLISHERS, Melbourne, Australia. Used with permission. All rights reserved.

22. See Fay 1987 for a rich discussion of critical social science and its emancipatory aims.

23. Geertz 1973, 20.

24. Geertz 1973, 5.

25. FitzGerald 1987, 24.

26. Giddens 1990, 64.

27. Held 1991.

28. Held 1990, 192.

29. Chua 2004, 8.

30. Chua 2004, 8.

31. Burbules and Torres 2000; Chomsky 1999, 2006; Rhoads and Liu 2009; Stiglitz 2002; Torres and Rhoads 2006.

32. Held 1990, 193.

33. Apple 2000. See Rhoads, Saenz, and Carducci 2005 for a detailed example of the conservative restoration at work—in the form of opposition to affirmative action.

34. See Kellner 1995. In this book Kellner discussed a number of films that reflected—and perhaps helped to manufacture—the "angry white male" trope (described at times by Kellner as "white male paranoia" [p. 65]), including *First Blood* (the first appearance of "Rambo") with Sylvester Stallone. The film *Falling Down* with Michael Douglas may be the quintessential "angry white male" film.

35. Bakan 2004, 60.

36. Bakan 2004, 69.

37. See for example Held 1990.

38. Harvey 2003, 26.

39. Harvey 2003, 26–27.

40. Harvey 2003, 27.

41. Calderone and Rhoads 2005.

42. Rizvi 2004.

43. For additional reading on the impact of globalization in the areas of politics, economics, and culture see Held and McGrew 2003; Held, McGrew, Goldblatt, and Perraton 1999.

44. Dahl 1995.

45. Soysal 1994, 6.

46. Soysal 1994, 6.

47. Soysal 1994, 7.

48. Guarasci 1997.

49. Guarasci 1997, 20.

50. Rhoads 1997, 1998b, 2000; Torres 1998, 2002.

51. In China, for example, Google, one of the world's leading Internet search engines, has had to limit access to various materials and sources of information deemed problematic by the ruling Chinese Communist Party. For instance, a search of the phrase "Tiananmen Square" yields different results depending on whether the search is initiated in the United States or in China (more photos of the student-led democratic movement of 1989 come up with the U.S.-originating search).

52. Boyer 1990, 1996; Colbeck and Michael 2006; Rice 2002; Ward 2003.

53. Eyler and Giles 1999; Kezar and Rhoads 2001; Rhoads 1997, 1998a, 2003, 2009; Rhoads and Howard 1998; Rhoads and Rhoades 2005; Vogelgesang and Rhoads 2003.

54. Dower 2002.

55. Heater 2002.

56. Burbules and Torres 2000; Chomsky 1999; Stiglitz 2002.

57. Castells 1997; Touraine 1988.

58. Quoted in Hall and Held 1990, 174.

59. Heater 2002, 11–12.

60. Heater 2002, 12.

61. Falk 1993.

62. Miller 2002.

63. Miller 2002, 85.

64. Miller 2002.

65. Calhoun 2002.

66. McGrew 1997, 231.

67. See, in particular, Archibugi and Held 1995; McGrew 1997.

68. Archibugi and Held 1995, 13.

69. Held 1995.

70. Calhoun 2002.

71. Calhoun 2002; Miller 2002.

72. Calhoun 2002.

73. Miller 2002.

74. Burbules and Torres 2000; Chomsky 1999; Rhoads and Torres 2006b.

75. Joppke 1998b.

76. Brubaker 1992.

77. Calhoun 2002, 279.

78. Bakan 2004, 163.

79. Santos 2006.

80. Santos 2006, 62.

81. Santos 2006, 62.

82. Santos 2006, 62.

83. Santos 2006, 63.

84. Santos 2006, 64.

85. Aronowitz 2000; Bok 2003; Clark 1998; Giroux and Giroux 2004; Gould 2003; Marginson and Considine 2000; Slaughter and Leslie 1997; Slaughter and Rhoades 2004; Soley 1995; Washburn 2005.

86. Geiger 1986, 1993.

87. Geiger 1986, 233–34.

88. Geiger 1986, 175.

89. Geiger 1986, 257.

90. Geiger 1986, 264.

91. Harding 1991.

92. Harding 1991, 2–3.

93. Bennis and Movius 2006.

94. Slaughter and Leslie 1997.

95. Slaughter and Rhoades 2004.

96. Slaughter and Rhoades 2004, 305.
97. Slaughter and Rhoades 2004, 29.
98. Slaughter and Rhoades 2004, 29.
99. Slaughter and Rhoades 2004, 20.
100. Aronowitz 2000.
101. Kerr 1963.
102. Aronowitz 2000, 32.
103. Aronowitz 2000, 32.
104. See Apple 2000; Rhoads, Saenz, and Carducci 2005.
105. Giroux 2002.
106. Giroux 2002, 426.
107. Giroux 2002, 426.
108. Giroux 2002, 431.
109. Giroux 2002, 432.
110. Washburn 2005, 2.
111. Washburn 2005, 2.
112. Washburn 2005, 3.
113. Washburn 2005, 4.
114. Washburn 2005, 4.
115. Buchbinder and Newson 1990; Clark 1998; Marginson 1993, 1995; Smyth 1995.
116. Rhoads and Torres 2006b.
117. Mok1997b, 2002; Yang 2004.
118. Said 1993, 19–20.
119. Said 1993, 17.
120. Bakan 2004.
121. Santos 2006, see in particular pages 78–91.
122. See Gramsci 1971; Rhoads and Mina 2001.
123. J. Jacobson 2005, A9.
124. J. Jacobson 2005.
125. Santos 2006.

2. "ONE COIN HAS TWO SIDES"

Portions of this chapter borrow from the article by Robert A. Rhoads and Xuehong Liang, "Global Influences and Local Responses at Guangdong University of Foreign Studies," *World Studies in Education,* 7(2), 2006, pp. 23–53. Copyright © by James Nicholas Publishers, Melbourne, Australia. Used with permission. All rights reserved.

Portions of one section borrow from the article by Robert A. Rhoads and Katalin Szelényi, "Globally Engaged Universities and the Changing Context of Academic Citizenship," *Education and Society,* 27(2), 2009, pp. 5–26. Copyright © 2009 by James Nicholas Publishers, Melbourne, Australia. Used with permission. All rights reserved.

1. The empirical data forming the basis for this chapter involved extended site visits to Guangdong University of Foreign Studies, conducted mostly during 2005 and 2006. In all, twenty-five professors and twenty students were formally interviewed and hundreds of hours of participant observation were conducted.

2. Throughout this chapter we use the term *professor* in a generic sense to signify any member of the faculty at GDUFS, although only a small percentage hold the formal title of "professor."

3. All names of the GDUFS students and professors identified in this chapter are pseudonyms.

4. Magnier 2005f.

5. Magnier 2005f.

6. "One coin has two sides" may be translated to Chinese Pinyin as *"fǎn shì yǒu liǎng mìan."* "Seek harmony out of the differences" may be translated as *"qíu tóng cún yì."* Pinyin (*Pīnyīn*) is the most commonly used Romanization of Chinese Mandarin.

7. Magnier 2005g, A1.

8. Magnier 2005f.

9. Deng Xiaoping was never the official head of state of China, but his power and influence amounted to his serving more or less as the nation's supreme leader.

10. S. Zhao 2004, 210.

11. S. Zhao 2004, 210–11.

12. S. Zhao 2004, 211.

13. Nathan 2001.

14. Nathan 2001, xliv.

15. Pieke 1998.

16. See National Security Agency 2005; "Sino Mania" 2005; Spence 1990.

17. Boren 2001, 213.

18. Boren 2001, 213.

19. Wasserstrom 1991, 298.

20. Boren 2001, 214.

21. Christensen 1996, 37.

22. See Yardley 2008.

23. See for example Mooney 2005a, 2005c.

24. See French 2005b; Magnier 2005a.

25. Jacobs 2008.

26. Tabuchi 2010.

27. Magnier 2005d, A3.

28. Magnier 2005d, A3.

29. D. Zhao 2002.

30. Pierson 2005.

31. D. Lee 2005, A11.

32. Lee and Ni 2005, A1.

33. Hiltzik 2008.

34. See Rhoads and Torres 2006b; Slaughter and Leslie 1997; Slaughter and Rhoades 2004.

35. See Torres and Rhoads 2006.

36. Slaughter and Leslie 1997.

37. Slaughter and Rhoades 2004.

38. Clark 1998, 2000.

39. Boron 2006; Boron and Torres 1996; Mollis 2001, 2006; Santos 2006.

40. Giddens 1990; Held 1991.

41. Rhoads and Torres 2006a; Said 1993.

42. Vaira 2004.

43. Altbach 2003.

44. Mok 1997a, 46.

45. Mok 2005.

46. Cheng 1990; Hayhoe 1996; Lin 1999; Mok 1997a, 1997b, 2000, 2001; Yang 2004; Zha 2001.
47. Mok 1997b.
48. Cheng 1990; Yin and White 1994.
49. Zha 2001, 11–12.
50. Mok 1997a, 47.
51. Mok 1997a, 48.
52. Mok 1997a, 55.
53. Julius 1997.
54. Mok 2000.
55. French 2005a.
56. Wei 1996.
57. Luke and Luke 2000, 276.
58. Mok 1997a, 54.
59. This finding was somewhat supported by a 2005 survey conducted in China and reported in the *Los Angeles Times* by Magnier 2005e.
60. Mazzetti 2005, A1.
61. Magnier 2005c, A3.
62. Magnier 2005b, A8.
63. Friedman 2001.
64. D. Lee 2005; Lee and Ni 2005.
65. Lee and Douglass 2005.
66. Barboza 2005.
67. Barboza 2005.
68. Richter 2005, C1.
69. For a more complete discussion of this social trend see Ross 1993.
70. Slaughter and Leslie 1997.
71. Slaughter and Rhoades 2004.
72. Fairweather 1996, 2005; Fairweather and Rhoads 1995; Lee and Rhoads 2004.
73. Whyte Jr. 1956.
74. Foucault 1978.
75. Castells 1997.
76. Touraine 1988.
77. Huhua 2004.
78. Huhua 2004, vii.
79. Huhua 2004, vii.
80. Huhua 2004, 17.
81. Riesman, Glazer, and Denney 1950.
82. Tönnies 1957.
83. Szelényi and Rhoads 2007.
84. Mooney 2005b.
85. Said 1993, 58.
86. Luke and Luke 2000, 283.
87. Slaughter and Leslie 1997; Slaughter and Rhoades 2004.

3. PLURIVERSITY KNOWLEDGE IN A MOBILE WORLD

Portions of this chapter borrow from the article by Katalin Szelényi and Robert A. Rhoads, "Citizenship in a Global Context: The Perspectives of International Graduate Students in the United

States," *Comparative Education Review,* 51(1), 2007, pp. 25–47. Copyright © 2007 by University of Chicago Press. Used with permission. All rights reserved.

1. Foxman 2005.

2. UCLA International Institute, "Interdepartmental Programs, Global Studies," UCLA International Institute, http://www.international.ucla.edu/idps/globalstudies/.

3. Abu-Lughod 1999; Horvath 2004.

4. Horvath 2004, 93.

5. Klein 1999,189.

6. Malone, Baluja, Costanzo, and Davis 2003.

7. Institute of International Education 2009.

8. Brint, Douglass, Thomson, and Chatman 2010.

9. UCLA International Institute, "Outreach," UCLA International Institute, http://www.international.ucla.edu/outreach/.

10. UCLA International Institute, "UCLA Student Activists Make News with Sudan Divestment," news release, March 29, 2006.

11. C. Lee 2007.

12. University of California, Los Angeles, "Driving Innovation to Market," http://www.spotlight.ucla.edu/impact/2007/11/01/driving-innovation-to-market/#more-166.

13. University of California, Office of Intellectual Property, *UCLA Invents* (2009), http://oip.ucla.edu/publications/UCLAInvents2009.pdf.

14. Silverstein 2006.

15. Torres and Rhoads 2006.

16. Santos 2006.

17. Santos 2006, 75.

18. Santos 2006, 73–74.

19. Interesting to note here is the fact that the recent literature on university transformation focuses overwhelmingly on the mercantile side of knowledge application. For prime examples of this literature, see Slaughter and Leslie 1997; Slaughter and Rhoades 2004. Although these authors, in their discussions of academic capitalism, acknowledge the coexistence of public good and academic capitalist knowledge/learning regimes, their emphasis remains on academic capitalism, without fully examining the present functioning of the public good knowledge/learning regime and, perhaps even more importantly, the ways in which the two regimes coexist and intersect.

20. The findings discussed in this study are part of a qualitative project based on interviews with thirty Brazilian, Chinese, and Italian students. However, because four of the thirty students had visa statuses other than the student visa (two held green cards, one held an H1-B (specialty worker) visa, and one recently had become a U.S. citizen), this chapter relies on data from interviews with twenty-six participants. This focus allows for a more in-depth exploration of the implications of holding a student visa by international graduate students in the United States.

21. Rizvi 2000.

22. Knight 2004, 11.

23. Santos 2006.

24. Dower and Williams 2002; Falk 2002; Nussbaum 2002; Ong 1999; Soysal 1994.

25. Miller 1999; Neff 1998.

26. Dower 2000.

27. Dower 2000, 60.

28. For key proponents of this argument, see D. Jacobson 1996; Soysal 1994.

29. Brubaker 1992, 23.

30. Brubaker 1992, 28.

31. Joppke 1998a.

32. Joppke 1999, 632–33.

33. For notable examples, see Bringle, Games, and Malloy 1999; Kezar, Chambers, and Burkhardt 2005.

34. Santos 2006.

35. The literature on international service learning is a notable exception to this trend. See, for example, Kiely 2004; Monard-Weissman 2003; Porter and Monard 2001.

36. Dower 2000.

37. Ong 2004, 65.

38. Ong 1999, 6.

39. Santos 2006.

40. Brubaker 1992.

41. Joppke 1999; Soysal 1994.

42. Institute of International Education 2009.

43. *Open Doors Report on International Educational Exchange* is a yearly publication and online resource concerning international students residing in the United States and U.S. students studying abroad. It presents data on places of origin, financial aid, fields of study, academic characteristics, and the impact of international students on the U.S. economy. For more information, please see http://opendoors.iienetwork.org/.

44. Institute of International Education 2009.

45. Selingo 2004.

46. Gravois 2004.

47. Arnone 2004.

48. Bollag 2005.

49. See, for example, Stromquist 2007.

50. Institute of International Education 2009.

51. Borjas 2002. Borjas's report did receive considerable attention in the media, prompting the critical response of the Institute of International Education (IIE) as well. For press clipping and IIE's response, see http://opendoors.iienetwork.org/?p=29517.

52. Slaughter and Rhoades 2004.

53. Lee, Rhoades, and Maldonado-Maldonado 2006, 558.

54. See Barker 2000; Lengyel 1947; NAFSA: Association of International Educators 2003a; UNESCO 1974.

55. UNESCO 1974, 5.

56. NAFSA: Association of International Educators 2003b, 1.

57. NAFSA: Association of International Educators 2003a, p. iv.

58. Dolby 2004, 173.

59. Alves and Caminada 2008; Amman 2003.

60. Colitt 2008.

61. United Nations Development Programme 2008.

62. United Nations Development Programme 2008.

63. Amyot 2004, 94.

64. Dell'Olio 2005.

65. Although the People's Republic of China's overall GDP is considerable, in per capita terms, the country was ranked eighty-sixth in 2005. China's HDI placed the country at eighty-first in the same year. See United Nations Development Programme 2008.

66. Giddens 1990, 64.

67. Torres and Rhoads 2006.

68. This idea was conveyed to us by Liang, a Chinese graduate student in electrical engineering.

69. All student names used in this chapter are pseudonyms.

70. Brubaker 1992.

71. In the case of international graduate students who, during their university education, are socialized to become members of specific professional fields (e.g., economics, engineering, and art), the words *occupational* and *professional* are both used to describe this dimension of rights and responsibilities. There were instances, for example, in which international graduate students did not see themselves as parts of particular occupations, but preferred to refer to their professional aspirations and their roles in various professions. Other times, however, occupational considerations were more relevant to the students' experiences.

72. Findings from the same students related to migratory decision-making are explored in Szelényi 2006.

73. UNESCO 2009.

74. Borjas 2002; McMurtrie 2001; Zakaria 2004.

75. For such studies on international students, see Al-Sharideh and Goe 1998; Zhao, Kuh, and Carini 2005.

76. Santos 2006.

77. Ong 1999.

78. In the case of UCLA, these aspects of the foreign student experience are formally outlined in a document entitled *F-1 Student Handbook and Summary of Visa Regulations,* referring to visa procedures, reporting requirements, enrollment patterns, changes in educational status, traveling abroad, the availability of health insurance, and employment options both during and after a student's course of study. For more information, see University of California, Los Angeles. *F-1 Student Handbook and Summary of Visa Regulations.* University of California, Los Angeles (2008), http://www.internationalcenter.ucla.edu/files/pdf/F1Handbook.pdf.

79. Academic student employees at the University of California are represented by UAW Local 2865. The UAW Web site states that "[i]nternational scholars have the same rights as US citizens to join and participate in the Union. In many years of representing international student workers at UC and elsewhere, no one has reported any complications in their status from unionizing." UAW Local 2865. *Frequently Asked Questions.* (n.d.). http://www.uaw2865.org/about/faq.php.

80. The policy climate toward transnational movement in the aftermath of September 11, 2001 is discussed in detail in Rizvi 2004.

81. Soysal 1994.

4. RESISTANCE TO NEOLIBERALISM

This chapter borrows from and advances earlier work from Jenée Slocum and Robert A. Rhoads, "Faculty and Student Engagement in the Argentine Grassroots Rebellion: Toward a Democratic and Emancipatory Vision of the University," *Higher Education: The International Journal of Higher Education and Educational Planning,* 51(1), 2009, pp. 85–105. Copyright © 2008 by Springer Science+Business Media B. V. With kind permission from Springer Science+Business Media.

Portions of one section borrow from the article by Robert A. Rhoads and Katalin Szelényi, "Globally Engaged Universities and the Changing Context of Academic Citizenship," *Education and Society,* 27(2), 2009, pp. 5–26. Copyright © 2009 by James Nicholas Publishers, Melbourne, Australia.

1. Pimentel 2004.

2. See Morduchowicz 2004. In this review essay, Morduchowicz estimates that Argentine workers reclaimed some two hundred factories, involving over fifteen thousand workers.

3. Morduchowicz 2004.

4. Pimentel 2004.

5. The *piquetero* movement actually dates back to the 1990s when the nation's unemployment rate soared as a consequence of the privatization of public programs and services throughout Argentina.

6. We conducted eighteen formal and informal interviews with professors and students during our two visits to UBA. These data were later combined with twenty additional interviews conducted by a doctoral student and colleague, Jenée Slocum. Hence, data from thirty-eight interviews form the thrust of the personal narratives incorporated into this chapter.

7. We must convey our gratitude to friend and colleague Carlos Alberto Torres for his kind help in connecting us with several of his colleagues from UBA and for joining Professor Rhoads in conducting several of the interviews in Spanish.

8. The following works all offer evidence of the growing engagement of universities in various manifestations of neoliberal globalization, including the push toward privatization, commercialization, and corporatization: Clark 1998, 2004; Giroux 2002; Marginson 2004; Marginson and Considine 2000; Newson and Buchbinder 1988; Rhoads and Liu 2009; Rhoads and Torres 2006b; Slaughter and Leslie 1997; Slaughter and Rhoades 2004; Washburn 2005.

9. Hopkins 2002.

10. Hopkins 2002.

11. Hopkins 2002.

12. Burbach 2002.

13. *"Que se vayan todos"* was the Spanish-spoken slogan for "Everyone has to be thrown out."

14. Burbach 2002.

15. Burbach 2002.

16. Pseudonyms are used for the names of professors and students who participated in the study forming the basis of this chapter. Also, the term *professor* is used generically throughout this chapter and may represent an individual holding the position of instructor, adjunct, assistant, associate, or full professor.

17. Oppositional movements, which have been most visible at meetings of global economic leaders, including those held by the WTO, IMF, and G-8, typically are framed as anti-globalization protests when in fact few involved in such struggles are opposed to globalization. Their biggest concern is the antidemocratic manner by which global economic policies are established, leaving many key players out of the decision-making process (i.e., unions, environmentalists, leaders from developing nations, and so forth).

18. Chomsky 2006, 55. This is an edited version of his World Social Forum speech.

19. de Jonquières 2001, 18.

20. Chomsky 2006, 55.

21. See Stiglitz 2002.

22. Rhoads and Torres 2006a, 322–23.

23. International Monetary Fund 2003, 63.

24. Again, for a rich and informed discussion of this sort of criticism, see Stiglitz 2002.

25. Collins and Rhoads 2008, 2010.

26. Menem actually outpolled Kirchner in the initial election but failed to win enough of the vote to capture the presidency. Menem then faced Kirchner in a runoff but decided to withdraw just before the election was to take place in light of his poor showing in published polls.

27. This North-South characterization obviously does not hold across the board, but in the case of Argentina certainly major external influences on its national policies have come and continue to derive from nations to the north, including the United States and members of the European Union.

28. See Mollis 2006.

29. Pujadas 2000.

30. Torres and Rhoads 2006.

31. Mollis and Marginson 2002 (this point is specifically drawn from pages 325–26).

32. Castells 1997, 1–2.

33. Slaughter and Rhoades 2004.

34. Rhoads 2007.

35. Santos 2006, 70.

36. Rhoades 1998.

37. Boron 2006, 144.

38. Santos 2006, 70.

39. Santos 2006, 67.

40. Mollis 2006, 204.

41. Mollis 2006, 204.

42. See Rhoades and Slaughter 2006; Slaughter and Leslie 1997; Slaughter and Rhoades 2004.

43. Mollis 2006, 204.

44. Newson and Buchbinder 1988.

45. Kerr 1963.

46. Schugurensky 2006.

47. See, for example, Aronowitz 2000; Bok 2003; Giroux and Giroux 2004; Gould 2003; Soley 1995; Washburn 2005.

48. Schugurensky 2006, 303.

49. For a discussion of student activism in the United States, including a summary of the 1960s, see Rhoads 1998a.

50. See Rhoads and Mina 2001.

51. Minerva is the Roman goddess of wisdom and is sometimes cast as a "protector of wisdom," or even the protector of a "wise city," as is the case with Guadalajara, Mexico, where a great statue of Minerva serves as the city's guardian.

52. Szelényi and Rhoads 2007.

53. Schugurensky 2006, 315.

54. Schugurensky 2006, 315.

55. Santos 2006, 76.

56. Santos 2006, 77.

57. Santos 2006, 76–77.

58. Altbach 1999.

59. Altbach 1999.

60. Altbach 1999.

61. Movements of unemployed workers is expressed in Spanish as *movimientos trabajadores desocupados,* hence the abbreviation MTD.

62. Gaudin 2005.

63. Gaudin 2005.

64. Gaudin 2005.

65. Gaudin 2005.

66. See Argentina Autonomista Project, http://www.autonomista.org/.

67. Huff-Hannon 2003.

68. We use the singular term *movement* here, but once again we want to stress that the struggle that goes on in Argentina (and has gone on for some time now) is in effect the coming together of many social movements.

69. Harvey 2003, 68–69.

70. "Picket, frying pan, the fight is one and the same" is our translation of *"Piquete, cacerola, la lucha es una sola."*

71. Mollis 2003.

72. Mollis 2003.

73. Mollis 2003.

74. Mollis 2002.

75. Women's Human Rights Net 2002.

76. Women's Human Rights Net 2002.

77. Women's Human Rights Net 2002.

78. Giddens 1998, 8.

79. Giddens 1998, 12–13.

80. Slaughter and Rhoades 2004, 20.

81. Slaughter and Rhoades 2004, 29.

82. Mander 2006.

83. Slaughter and Rhoades 2004, 305.

84. Santos 2006, 82.

85. Santos 2006, 82.

86. Santos 2006, 74.

87. Santos 2006, 75.

88. Santos 2006, 80.

89. Santos 2006, 80.

5. POSTCOMMUNISM, GLOBALIZATION, AND CITIZENSHIP

Portions of this chapter borrow from the article by Robert A. Rhoads and Katalin Szelényi, "Globally Engaged Universities and the Changing Context of Academic Citizenship," *Education and Society,* 27(2), 2009, pp. 5–26. Copyright © 2009 by James Nicholas Publishers, Melbourne, Australia.

1. For an English-language description of Szoborpark, see the park's Web site at http://www.szoborpark.hu/index.php?Lang=en.

2. Light 2000, 168.

3. Light 2000.

4. In the end, while forty-two statues, monuments, and plaques were placed in Szoborpark, other statues were left in their original settings, some were stripped of communist symbols, some were destroyed, and some were placed in cemeteries. For a detailed description of these processes, see Boros 2001.

5. Statue Park. http://www.szoborpark.hu/index.php?Content=Szoborpark&Lang=en.

6. Musil 2002.

7. Central European University, "An Introduction to CEU." http://web.ceu.hu/introduction.html#2.

8. This quotation appeared in a 2006 interview with István Teplán. "Akár a Holdon is" 2006.

9. Lewin 2001.

10. Soros Alapítvány 1990.

11. Musil 2002.

12. This quotation is from George Soros. See Lewin 2001.

13. Musil 2002.

14. Musil 2002, 17.

15. Musil 2002, 17.

16. Musil 2002, 17.

17. Soros Alapítvány 1990.

18. For literature referring to this statement by Radio Free Europe, refer to Kuran 1991, 7.

19. Eley 2002.

20. Kenney 2003.

21. Eley 2002.

22. Tismaneanu 1999.

23. Tismaneanu 1999, 72.

24. Sandole 1999.

25. Tismaneanu 1998, 4.

26. All names of faculty members participating in interviews are pseudonyms. In addition, the gender of some faculty members was changed in order to further protect confidentiality. Because the language of instruction at CEU is English, all faculty members were entirely fluent in English. For this reason, English was the language of all interviews.

27. Yehuda Elkana, *Rector's Report No. 2.* (Budapest, Hungary: Central European University, 2000), 1. http://web.ceu.hu/rectors_report.html.

28. This syllabus can be found at http://web.ceu.hu/crc/Syllabi/IRES/Tur_Privatiz.W96IR.v2 .html.

29. This syllabus can be found at http://web.ceu.hu/crc/Syllabi/Leg/Dim_ConstFed.F95Leg .v2.html.

30. Central European University, "An Introduction to CEU." http://web.ceu.hu/introduction .html#2.

31. Central European University, *Student Profile 2006/2007.* http://cio.ceu.hu/admissions_ profile.html.

32. "Between Past and Future: March 26–28, 1999" 1999.

33. Central European University, *Why CEU?* http://www.ceu.hu/about.

34. For more information on CEU Center for EU Enlargement Studies, see the center's Web site at http://web.ceu.hu/cens/.

35. Yehuda Elkana, *Rector's Report 5* (Budapest, Hungary: Central European University, 2001), 12. http://web.ceu.hu/rectors_report.html.

36. Yehuda Elkana, *Rector's Report 6* (Budapest, Hungary: Central European University, 2002). http://web.ceu.hu/rectors_report.html.

37. Elkana, *Rector's Report 8* (Budapest, Hungary: Central European University, 2002), 14. http://web.ceu.hu/rectors_report.html.

38. Elkana, *Rector's Report 6,* 15.

39. Elkana, *Rector's Report 5* (Budapest, Hungary: Central European University, 2002), 14. http://web.ceu.hu/rectors_report.html.

40. Central European University, *Financial Aid.* (Budapest, Hungary: Central European University, 2008). www.ceu.hu/admissions/financialaid.

41. Elkana, *Rector's Report No. 2,* 1.

42. Slaughter and Leslie 1997, 11.

43. Torres and Rhoads 2006.

44. Stromquist 2002.

45. Guilhot 2007, 466.

46. Slaughter and Rhoades 2004.

47. Central European University, *Why Choose CEU Business School?* http://www.ceubusiness
.org/why-choose-ceu-business-school.

48. Slaughter and Rhoades 2004, 15.

49. Slaughter and Rhoades 2004.

50. Central European University, *CEU Strategic Plan 2003-2013.* www.cio.ceu.hu/downloads/
strategic_plan_ceu.doc.

51. Elkana, *Rector's Report 8,* 3–4.

52. Central European University, *CEU Strategic Plan 2003–2013,* 3.

53. For major works related to the theoretical and practical understandings of the globalization of culture, see Appadurai 1996; Ritzer 1993; Robertson 1992; Tomlinson 1999.

54. Tomlinson 1999.

55. Tomlinson 1999, 6.

56. Tomlinson 1999, 8.

57. For such accounts of the intersections of local and global realities in the context of globalization, see Luke and Luke 2000; Robertson 1992. The term *glocalization* was coined by Robertson.

58. Tomlinson 1999.

59. Boyer 1990.

60. One of the most scathing critiques of the disengaged faculty was represented in Bok 1990.

61. Boyer 1990, 16.

62. For discussions of Boyer's *Scholarship Reconsidered* and the scholarship of engagement, see
Boyer 1996; Colbeck and Michael 2006; Rice 2002; Ward 2003.

63. Gibbons et al. 1994.

64. Gibbons et al. 1994.

65. Gibbons et al. 1994.

66. Mohrman, Ma, and Baker 2008.

67. For more information on the university's current mission, see Central European University, *Mission and History,* http://www.ceu.hu/about/missionhistory.

68. Slaughter and Rhoades 2004, 28.

69. Boyer 1990; Gibbons et al. 1994.

6. GLOBAL CITIZENSHIP AND CHANGING TIMES FOR
   UNIVERSITIES

1. Pierson 2008.

2. Pierson 2008.

3. Passel 2004.

4. Los Angeles Unified School District, "Los Angeles Unified School District Profile,"
LAUSD Research Report. http://search.lausd.k12.ca.us/cgi-bin/fccgi.exe.

5. Los Angeles Unified School District, "R30 Language Census Report." Research Report,
Planning and Assessment Division, LAUSD (Spring 2009).

6. We choose to focus on the examples of Los Angeles and Boston for the simple reason that
we reside in these cities. The fact is that we could have picked just about any U.S. city to highlight
the growing impact of cultural globalization and the implications for universities and the conceptualization of citizenship.

7. Listed here are the languages most commonly spoken at home in households where a language other than English is primarily used. Boston Redevelopment Authority, Research Division. *New Bostonians 2005.* http://www.bostonredevelopmentauthority.org/PDF/ResearchPublications// New%20Bostonians%20No.%20609.pdf.

8. Bluestone and Stevenson 2000.

9. Boston Redevelopment Authority, *New Bostonians 2005.*

10. Boston Redevelopment Authority, *New Bostonians 2005.*

11. Thang 2009.

12. Boston High School Valedictorians. http://www.boston.com/news/education/k_12/ gallery/valedictorians/.

13. Boston High School Valedictorians.

14. University of Massachusetts Boston, *UMass Boston Renewal: Building the Student-Centered, Urban Public University of the New Century* (Boston: University of Massachusetts Boston, n.d.). http://www.umb.edu/strategic_plan/.

15. NAFSA: Association of International Educators 2005.

16. Appadurai 1996; Luke and Luke 2000; Ritzer 1993; Robertson 1992; Tomlinson 1999.

17. Luke and Luke 2000.

18. Santos 2006.

19. Chomsky 2006; de Jonquières 2001.

20. Slaughter and Rhoades 2004.

21. Santos 2006.

22. Rhoads 2007; Vidal 2002.

23. Chomsky 2006.

24. UN Food Agency 2009.

25. UN Food Agency 2009.

26. Traynor 2009.

27. Wolff 2006.

28. Wolff 2006, 8.

29. Wolff 2006, 8.

30. Torres and Rhoads 2006.

31. McKie 2006.

32. McKie 2006.

33. More information on Vision of Humanity is available at http://www.visionofhumanity .org/about/about.php.

34. Santos 2006.

35. Dower 2000; Miller 1999; Neff 1998.

36. Castells 1997; Dower 2000; Rhoads and Torres 2006a.

37. Szelényi and Rhoads 2007.

38. Bringle, Games, and Malloy 1999; Kezar, Chambers, and Burkhardt 2005.

39. See for example Falk 1993; Nussbaum 2002.

40. The relevance of the local in considerations of cosmopolitanism is also underscored by Fazal Rizvi, who noted that "we need to ask how we might teach about issues of global interconnectivity so that they are locally relevant, but are equally compatible with global concerns. This requires an educational vocabulary that transcends the binary between the global and the local, while promoting an understanding of global interconnectivity that is both empirically grounded and ethically informed." This quotation is from Rizvi 2008, 21.

41. See, for example, Bringle, Games, and Malloy 1999; Eyler and Giles 1999; Kezar, Chambers, and Burkhardt 2005; Ward 2003.

42. Aronowitz 2000; Newson and Buchbinder 1988; Schugurensky 2006; Slaughter and Rhoades 2004; Washburn 2005.

43. Eyler and Giles 1999; Kezar, Chambers, and Burkhardt 2005; Rhoads 1997; Rhoads and Howard 1998; Vogelgesang and Astin 2000; Ward 2003.

44. Important exceptions to this general trend are found in the relatively novel field of international service learning. For discussions of international service learning, see Grusky 2000; Porter and Monard 2001.

45. Georghiou 1998; Peters 2006.

46. Knight 2004; Siaya and Hayward 2003.

47. Lewis and Lockheed 2006.

48. Knight 2004.

49. Wide recognition of the multitude of functions fulfilled by universities has led to identification of universities as "multiversities," reflected most significantly in Kerr 1963.

50. Boyer 1990.

51. Santos 2006.

52. Lee, Rhoades, and Maldonado-Maldonado 2006; Stromquist 2007.

53. Peters 2006.

54. BBC News 2009.

55. Andrews 2009.

56. Andrews 2009.

BIBLIOGRAPHY

Abu-Lughod, Janet L. 1999. *New York, Chicago, Los Angeles: America's Global Cities.* Minneapolis: University of Minnesota Press.

"Akár a Holdon is – Dr. Teplán István, a Central European University Rektorhelyettese (On the Moon, if Need Be: Dr. István Teplán, the Central European University's Executive Vice President)." 2006. *Magyar Narancs* 18(20). http://www.narancs.hu/index.php?gcPage =/public/hirek/hir.php&id=13138.

Al-Sharideh, Khalid A., and W. Richard Goe. 1998. "Ethnic Communities Within the University: An Examination of Factors Influencing the Personal Adjustment of International Students." *Research in Higher Education* 39(6): 699–725.

Altbach, Philip G. 1999. "The University of Buenos Aires Model for the Future of Higher Education: A Neglected Perspective." *International Higher Education* (Winter). http://www. bc.edu/bc_org/avp/soe/cihe/newsletter/News14/text3.html.

Altbach, Philip G. 2003. "Globalization and the University: Myths and Realities in an Unequal World." *Current Issues in Catholic Higher Education* 23: 5–25.

Alves, Fabio, and Carlos Caminada. 2008. "Brazilian Debt Raised to Investment Grade by S&P." *Bloomberg.com,* April 30. http://www.bloomberg.com/apps/news?pid=newsarchive&sid=a86v4f6_W2Jg.

Amman, Edmund. 2003. "Economic Policy and Performance in Brazil Since 1985." In *Brazil Since 1985: Politics, Economy and Society* (pp. 107–37), Maria D'Alva Kinzo and James Dunkerley, eds. London: Institute of Latin American Studies, University of London.

Amyot, Grant. 2004. *Business, the State and Economic Policy: The Case of Italy.* London: Routledge.

Andrews, Edmund L. 2009. "Global Economic Forum to Expand Permanently." *New York Times,* September 24. http://www.nytimes.com.

Appadurai, Arjun. 1996. *Modernity at Large: Cultural Dimensions of Globalization.* Minneapolis: University of Minnesota Press.

Apple, Michael W. 2000. "Between Neoliberalism and Neoconservatism: Education and Conservatism in a Global Context." In *Globalization and Education: Critical Perspectives* (pp. 57–77), Nicholas C. Burbules and Carlos Alberto Torres, eds. New York: Routledge.

Archibugi, Daniele, and David Held. 1995. "Editors' Introduction." In *Cosmopolitan Democracy: An Agenda for a New World Order* (pp. 1–16), Daniele Archibugi and David Held, eds. Cambridge, MA: Polity Press.

Arnone, Michael. 2004. "New Survey Confirms Sharp Drop in Applications to U.S. Colleges from Foreign Graduate Students." *Chronicle of Higher Education, Today's News,* March 4. http://chronicle.com.

Aronowitz, Stanley. 2000. *The Knowledge Factory: Dismantling the Corporate University and Creating True Higher Learning.* Boston: Beacon Press.

Bakan, Joel. 2004. *The Corporation: The Pathological Pursuit of Profit and Power.* New York: Free Press.

Barber, Benjamin. 1995. *Jihad vs. McWorld: How Globalism and Tribalism Are Shaping the World.* New York: Ballantine Books.

Barboza, David. 2005. "Chinese Company Ends Unocal Bid, Citing Political Hurdles." *New York Times,* August 2. http://www.nytimes.com.

Barker, Carol M. 2000. *Education for International Understanding and Global Competence.* New York: Carnegie Corporation of New York.

BBC News. 2009. "U.S.-China Ties 'to Shape Century.'" *BBC News,* July 27. http://news.bbc.co.uk/go/pr/fr/-/2/hi/business/8169869.stm.

Bennis, Warren, and Hallam Movius. 2006. "Opinion: Why Harvard Is So Hard to Lead." *Chronicle of Higher Education, Today's News,* March 8. http://chronicle.com.

"Between Past and Future: March 26–28, 1999." 1999. *CEU Gazette: The Chronicle of Central European University* 8(4). http://web.ceu.hu/downloads/CEU_Gazette_vol8_no4.pdf.

Bluestone, Barry, and Mary Huff Stevenson. 2000. *The Boston Renaissance: Race, Space, and Economic Change in an American Metropolis.* New York: Russell Sage Foundation.

Bok, Derek. 1990. *Universities and the Future of America.* Durham, NC: Duke University Press.

Bok, Derek. 2003. *Universities in the Marketplace: The Commercialization of Higher Education.* Princeton, NJ: Princeton University Press.

Bollag, Burton. 2005. "Graduate-School Applications from Overseas Decline Again, Survey Finds." *Chronicle of Higher Education, Today's News,* March 10. http://chronicle.com.

Boren, Mark Edelman. 2001. *Student Resistance: A History of the Unruly Subject.* New York: Routledge.

Borjas, George J. 2002. *An Evaluation of the Foreign Student Program.* Washington, DC: Center for Immigration Studies. http://www.cis.org/ForeignStudentProgram.

Boron, Atilio A. 2006. "Reforming the Reforms: Transformation and Crisis in Latin American and Caribbean Universities." In *The University, State, and Market: The Political Economy of Globalization in the Americas* (pp. 141–163), Robert A. Rhoads and Carlos Alberto Torres, eds. Stanford, CA: Stanford University Press.

Boron, Atilio A., and Carlos Alberto Torres. 1996. "The Impact of Neoliberal Restructuring on Education and Poverty in Latin America." *Alberta Journal of Educational Research* 42(2): 102–14.

Boros, Géza. 2001. "Budapesti emlékmű-metamorfózisok: 1989–2000 (Metamorphosis of Budapest's Monuments: 1989–2000)." *Budapesti Negyed* 9(2–3). http://epa.oszk.hu/00000/00003/00025/boros.html.

Boyer, Ernest L. 1990. *Scholarship Reconsidered: Priorities of the Professoriate.* Princeton, NJ: The Carnegie Foundation for the Advancement of Teaching.

Boyer, Ernest L. 1996. "The Scholarship of Engagement." *Journal of Public Service and Outreach* 1(1): 11–20.

Bringle, Robert G., Richard Games, and Edward A. Malloy, eds. 1999. *Colleges and Universities as Citizens*. Needham Heights, MA: Allyn and Bacon.

Brint, Steven, John Aubrey Douglass, Gregg Thomson, and Steve Chatman. 2010. *Engaged Learning in a Public University: Trends in the Undergraduate Experience*. Berkeley: University of California, Berkeley, Center for Studies in Higher Education. http://cshe.berkeley.edu/publications/docs/SERU_EngagedLearningREPORT_2010.pdf.

Brubaker, Rogers. 1992. *Citizenship and Nationhood in France and Germany*. Cambridge, MA: Harvard University Press.

Buchbinder, Howard, and Janice Newson. 1990. "Corporate-University Linkages in Canada: Transforming a Public Institution." *Higher Education* 20(4): 355–79.

Burbach, Roger. 2002. "The Argentine Rebellion." *ZNet*, February 20. http://www.zmag.org/content/LatinAmerica/BurbachArgentina.cfm.

Burbules, Nicholas C., and Carlos Alberto Torres. 2000. "Globalization and Education: An Introduction." In *Globalization and Education: Critical Perspectives* (pp. 1–26), Nicholas C. Burbules and Carlos Alberto Torres, eds. New York: Routledge, 2000.

Calderone, Shannon, and Robert A. Rhoads. 2005. "The Mythology of the 'Disappearing Nation-State': National Competitive Advantage Through State-University Collaboration." *Education and Society* 23(1): 5–23.

Calhoun, Craig. 2002. "Constitutional Patriotism and the Public Sphere: Interests, Identity, and Solidarity in the Integration of Europe." In *Global Justice and Transnational Politics: Essays on the Moral and Political Challenges of Globalization* (pp. 275–312), Pablo De Greiff and Ciaran Cronin, eds. Cambridge, MA: MIT Press.

Castells, Manuel. 1997. *The Power of Identity* (Vol. II). Oxford, UK: Blackwell Publishers.

Cheng, K. M. 1990. "Financing Education in Mainland China: What Are the Real Problems?" *Issues and Studies* 3: 54–75.

Chomsky, Noam. 1999. *Profit over People: Neoliberalism and Global Order*. New York: Seven Stories Press.

Chomsky, Noam. 2006. "A World Without War." In *The University, State, and Market: The Political Economy of Globalization in the Americas* (pp. 39–59), Robert A. Rhoads and Carlos Alberto Torres, eds. Stanford, CA: Stanford University Press.

Christensen, Thomas. 1996. "Chinese Realpolitik." *Foreign Affairs* 73(5): 37–52.

Chua, Amy. 2004. *World on Fire: How Exporting Free Market Democracy Breeds Ethnic Hatred and Global Instability*. New York: Anchor Books.

Clark, Burton R. 1998. *Creating Entrepreneurial Universities: Organizational Pathways of Transformation*. Oxford, UK: Pergamon Press.

Clark, Burton R. 2000. "Creating Entrepreneurialism in Proactive Universities: Lessons from Europe." *Change*, January/February: 10–19.

Clark, Burton R. 2004. *Sustaining Change in Universities: Continuities in Case Studies and Concepts*. Berkshire, UK: SRHE & Open University Press.

Colbeck, Carol L., and Patty Wharton Michael. 2006. "The Public Scholarship: Reintegrating Boyer's Four Domains." In *Analyzing Faculty Work and Rewards: Using Boyer's Four Domains of Scholarship* (New Directions for Institutional Research, no. 129) (pp. 7–19), John M. Braxton, ed. San Francisco: Jossey-Bass.

Colitt, Raymond. 2008. "Sleeping Giant Brazil Wakes, but Could Stumble." *Reuters*, May 13. http://www.reuters.com/article/managerViews/idUSNOA3328932008 0513.

Collins, Christopher S., and Robert A. Rhoads. 2008. "The World Bank and Higher Education in the Developing World: The Cases of Uganda and Thailand." In *The Worldwide Transformation of Higher Education* (pp. 177–221), David P. Baker and Alexander W. Wiseman, eds. Oxford, UK: Emerald.

Collins, Christopher S., and Robert A. Rhoads. 2010. "The World Bank, Support for Universities, and Asymmetrical Power Relations in International Development." *Higher Education: The International Journal of Higher Education and Educational Planning* 59(2): 181–205.

Dahl, Robert. 1995. "Participation and the Problem of Civic Understanding." In *Rights and the Common Good: The Communitarian Perspective* (pp. 261–70), Amitai Etzioni, ed. New York: St. Martin's Press.

Daragahi, Borzou, and Jeffrey Fleishman. 2009. "Mideast Rappers Take the Mic." *Los Angeles Times*, April 7. http://www.latimes.com.

Dell'Olio, Fiorella. 2005. *The Europeanization of Citizenship: Between the Ideology of Nationality, Immigration and European Identity*. Aldershot, UK: Ashgate.

Dolby, Nadine. 2004. "Encountering an American Self: Study Abroad and National Identity." *Comparative Education Review* 48(2): 150–73.

Dower, Nigel. 2000. "The Idea of Global Citizenship: A Sympathetic Assessment." *Global Society* 14(4): 553–67.

Dower, Nigel. 2002. "Global Citizenship: Yes or No?" In *Global Citizenship: A Critical Introduction* (pp. 30–40), Nigel Dower and John Williams, eds. New York: Routledge.

Dower, Nigel, and John Williams, eds. 2002. *Global Citizenship: A Critical Introduction*. New York: Routledge.

Eley, Geoff. 2002. *Forging Democracy: The History of the Left in Europe, 1850–2000*. Oxford, UK: Oxford University Press.

Eyler, Janet, and Dwight E. Giles. 1999. *Where Is the Learning in Service Learning?* San Francisco: Jossey-Bass.

Fairweather, James S. 1996. *Faculty Work and Public Trust: Restoring the Value of Teaching and Public Service in American Academic Life*. Boston: Allyn and Bacon.

Fairweather, James S. 2005. "Beyond the Rhetoric: Trends in the Relative Value of Teaching and Research in Faculty Salaries." *Journal of Higher Education* 76(4): 401–22.

Fairweather, James S., and Robert A. Rhoads. 1995. "Teaching and the Faculty Role: Enhancing the Commitment to Instruction in American Colleges and Universities." *Educational Evaluation and Policy Analysis* 17(2): 179–94.

Falk, Richard. 1993. "The Making of Global Citizenship." In *Global Visions: Beyond the New World Order* (pp. 39–50), Jeremy Brecher, John Brown Childs, and Jill Cutler, eds. Boston: South End Press.

Falk, Richard. 2002. "An Emergent Matrix of Citizenship: Complex, Uneven, and Fluid." In *Global Citizenship: A Critical Introduction* (pp. 15–29), Nigel Dower and John Williams, eds. New York: Routledge.

Fanon, Frantz. 1963. *The Wretched of the Earth*. New York: Grove Press.

Fay, Brian. 1987. *Critical Social Science*. Ithaca, NY: Cornell University Press.

FitzGerald, Frances. 1987. *Cities on a Hill*. New York: Simon and Schuster.

Foucault, Michel. 1978. *Discipline and Punish: The Birth of the Prison*. Translated by Alan Sheridan. New York: Vintage Books.

Foxman, Adam. 2005. "Globalization Hits UCLA." *Daily Bruin*, February 8. http://www.daily bruin.com/articles/2005/2/8/globalization-hits-ucla/.

Frammolino, Ralph. 2004. "You Can't Get a Bad Rap Here." *Los Angeles Times*, November 12, A1, A23.

French, Howard W. 2005a. "China Luring Foreign Scholars to Make Its Universities Great." *New York Times*, October 28. http://www.nytimes.com.

French, Howard W. 2005b. "Chinese Pressing to Keep Village Silent on Clash." *New York Times*, December 17. http://www.nytimes.com.

Friedman, Thomas L. 2001. "Foreign Affairs; One Nation, 3 Lessons." *New York Times*, April 13, A17.

Gaudin, Andres. 2005. "Occupying, Resisting, Producing: Argentine Workers Take Over Abandoned Factories." *Third World Traveler* (retrieved December 25, 2005; originally published with *Dollars and Sense Magazine*, March/April 2004, 29–33). http://www.thirdworld traveler.com/ South_America/Occupy_Resist_Argentina.html.

Geertz, Clifford. 1973. *The Interpretation of Cultures*. New York: Basic Books.

Geiger, Roger. 1986. *To Advance Knowledge: The Growth of American Research Universities, 1900–1940*. New York: Oxford University Press.

Geiger, Roger. 1993. *Research and Relevant Knowledge: American Research Universities Since World War II*. New York: Oxford University Press, 1993.

Georghiou, Luke. 1998. "Global Cooperation in Research." *Research Policy* 27(6): 611–26.

Gibbons, Michael, Camille Limoges, Helga Nowotny, Simon Schwartzman, Peter Scott, and Martin Trow. 1994. *The New Production of Knowledge: The Dynamics of Science and Research in Contemporary Societies*. London: Sage.

Giddens, Anthony. 1990. *The Consequences of Modernity*. Stanford, CA: Stanford University Press.

Giddens, Anthony. 1998. *The Third Way: The Renewal of Social Democracy*. Cambridge, UK: Polity.

Giroux, Henry A. 2002. "Neoliberalism, Corporate Culture, and the Promise of Higher Education: The University as a Democratic Public Sphere." *Harvard Educational Review* 72(4): 425–64.

Giroux, Henry A., and Susan Searls Giroux. 2004. *Take Back Higher Education: Race, Youth, and the Crisis of Democracy in the Post-Civil Rights Era*. New York: Palgrave Macmillan.

Gould, Eric. 2003. *The University in a Corporate Culture*. New Haven, CT: Yale University Press.

Gramsci, Antonio. 1971. *Selections from the Prison Notebooks of Antonio Gramsci*. Edited and translated by Quintin Hoare and Geoffrey Nowell Smith. New York: International Publishers.

Gravois, John. 2004. "Graduate Admissions for Foreign Students Continue a Post-2001 Decline, Report Says." *Chronicle of Higher Education, Today's News*, September 9. http://chronicle.com.

Grusky, Sara. 2000. "International Service Learning: A Critical Guide from an Impassioned Advocate." *American Behavioral Scientist* 43(5): 858–67.

Guarasci, Richard. 1997. "Community-Based Learning and Intercultural Citizenship." In *Democratic Education in an Age of Difference: Redefining Citizenship in Higher Education* (pp. 17–49), Richard Guarasci, Grant H. Cornwell, and Associates, eds. San Francisco: Jossey-Bass.

Guilhot, Nicolas. 2007. "Reforming the World: George Soros, Global Capitalism and the Philanthropic Management of the Social Sciences." *Critical Sociology* 33: 447–77.

Hall, Stuart, and David Held. 1990. "Citizens and Citizenship." In *New Times: The Changing Face of Politics in the 1990s* (pp. 173–88), Stuart Hall and Martin Jacques, eds. London: Verso.

Harding, Sandra. 1991. *Whose Science? Whose Knowledge: Thinking from Women's Lives*. Ithaca, NY: Cornell University Press.

Harvey, David. 2003. *The New Imperialism*. Oxford, UK: Oxford University Press.

Hayhoe, Ruth. 1996. *China's Universities, 1985–1995: A Century of Cultural Conflict*. New York: Garland.

Heater, Derek. 2002. *World Citizenship: Cosmopolitan Thinking and Its Opponents*. London: Continuum.

Held, David. 1990. "The Decline of the Nation State." In *New Times: The Changing Face of Politics in the 1990s* (pp. 191–204), Stuart Hall and Martin Jacques, eds. London: Verso.

Held, David. 1991. "Editor's Introduction." In *Political Theory Today* (pp. 1–22), David Held, ed. Stanford, CA: Stanford University Press.

Held, David. 1995. *Democracy and the Global Order: From the Modern State to Cosmopolitan Governance*. Stanford, CA: Stanford University Press.

Held, David, and Anthony McGrew, eds. 2003. *The Global Transformation Reader: An Introduction to the Globalization Debate* (2nd ed.). Cambridge, UK: Polity Press.

Held, David, Anthony G. McGrew, David Goldblatt, and Jonathan Perraton. 1999. *Global Transformations: Politics, Economics and Culture*. Stanford, CA: Stanford University Press.

Hiltzik, Michael A. 2008. "Bailouts: Too Big a Crutch?" *Los Angeles Times*, September 17. http://www.latimes.com.

Hopkins, Alfred. 2002. "Running Out of Patience." *World Press Review*, February 27. http://www.worldpress. org/Americas/380.cfm.

Horvath, Ronald J. 2004. "The Particularity of Global Places: Placemaking Practices in Los Angeles and Sydney." *Urban Geography* 25(2): 92–119.

Huff-Hannon, Joseph. 2003. "East Coast Autonomista Caravan." argentina autonomísta project Web site (retrieved December 27, 2005). http://www.autonomista.org/joznet.htm.

Huhua, Ouyang. 2004. *Remaking of Face and Community of Practice: An Ethnography of Local and Expatriate English Teachers Reform Stories in Today's China*. Beijing: Peking University Press.

Institute of International Education. 2009. "Record Numbers of International Students in U.S. Higher Education." News release. http://opendoors.iienetwork.org/?p=150649.

International Monetary Fund. 2003. *Lessons from the Crisis in Argentina*. Washington, DC: International Monetary Fund.

Jacobs, Andrew. 2008. "Too Old and Frail to Re-Educate? Not in China." *New York Times*, August 21. http://www.nytimes.com.

Jacobson, David. 1996. *Rights Across Borders: Immigration and the Decline of Citizenship*. Baltimore, MD: Johns Hopkins University Press.

Jacobson, Jennifer. 2005. "What Makes David Run." *Chronicle of Higher Education*, May 6, A8–A12.

de Jonquières, Guy. 2001. "Power Elite at Davos May Be Eclipsed by Protesters." *Financial Times*, January 24, 18.

Joppke, Christian. 1998a. *Challenge to the Nation-State: Immigration in Western Europe and the United* States. Oxford, UK: Oxford University Press.

Joppke, Christian. 1998b. "Immigration Challenges the Nation-State." In *Challenge to the Nation-State: Immigration in Western Europe and the United States* (pp. 5–48), Christian Joppke, ed. Oxford, UK: Oxford University Press.

Joppke, Christian. 1999. "How Immigration Is Changing Citizenship: A Comparative View." *Ethnic and Racial Studies* 22(4): 629–52.

Julius, Daniel J. 1997. "Will Chinese Universities Survive an Emerging Market Economy?" *Higher Education Management* 9(1): 141–56.

Kellner, Douglas. 1995. *Media Culture: Cultural Studies, Identity and Politics Between the Modern and the Postmodern*. London: Routledge.

Kenney, Padraic. 2003. *A Carnival of Revolution: Central Europe 1989*. Princeton, NJ: Princeton University Press.

Kerr, Clark. 1963. *The Uses of the University*. Cambridge, MA: Harvard University Press.

Kezar, Adrianna J., Anthony C. Chambers, and John C. Burkhardt, eds. 2005. *Higher Education for the Public Good: Emerging Voices from a National Movement*. San Francisco: Jossey-Bass.

Kezar, Adrianna, and Robert A. Rhoads. 2001. "The Dynamic Tensions of Service-Learning in Higher Education: A Philosophical Perspective." *Journal of Higher Education* 72(2): 148–71.

Kiely, Richard. 2004. "Chameleon with a Complex: Searching for Transformation in International Service-Learning." *Michigan Journal of Community Service Learning* 10(2): 5–20.

Klein, Norman M. 1999. "The Outline of Global Los Angeles." *Emergences* 9(2): 189–206.

Knight, Jane. 2004. "Internationalization Remodeled: Definition, Approaches, and Rationales." *Journal of Studies in International Education* 8(1): 5–31.

Kuran, Timur. 1991. "Now Out of Never: The Element of Surprise in the East European Revolution of 1989." *World Politics* 44(1): 7–48.

Lee, Cynthia. 2007. "Deep Impact." *UCLA Magazine,* October 1. http://www.magazine .ucla.edu/features/economic-impact-report_2007/.

Lee, Don. 2005. "China Faces Challenges on Currency." *Los Angeles Times,* July 23, A11.

Lee, Don, and Elizabeth Douglass. 2005. "Chinese Drop Takeover Bid for Unocal." *Los Angeles Times,* August 3, C1, C16.

Lee, Don, and Ching-Ching Ni. 2005. "In a Significant Shift, China Raises Value of Its Currency." *Los Angeles Times,* July 22, A1, A4.

Lee, Jenny J., Gary Rhoades, and Alma Maldonado-Maldonado. 2006. "The Political Economy of International Student Flows: Patterns, Ideas, and Propositions." *Higher Education: Handbook of Theory and Research* 21: 545–90.

Lee, Jenny J., and Robert A. Rhoads. 2004. "Faculty Entrepreneurialism and the Challenge to Undergraduate Education at Research Universities." *Research in Higher Education* 45(7): 739–60.

Lengyel, Emil. 1947. "International Education as an Aid to World Peace." *Journal of Educational Sociology* 20(9): 562–70.

Lewin, Tamar. 2001. "Soros Gives $250 Million to University in Europe." *New York Times,* October 14. http://www.nytimes.com.

Lewis, Maureen A., and Marlaine E. Lockheed. 2006. *Inexcusable Absence: Why 60 Million Girls Still Aren't in School and What to Do About It.* Washington, DC: Center for Global Development.

Light, Duncan. 2000. "Gazing on Communism: Heritage Tourism and Post-Communist Identities in Germany, Hungary and Romania." *Tourism Geographies* 2(2): 157–76.

Lin, Jing. 1999. *Social Transformation and Private Education in China.* Westport, CT: Praeger Publishers.

Luke, Allan, and Carmen Luke. 2000. "A Situated Perspective on Cultural Globalization." In *Globalization and Education: Critical Perspectives* (pp. 275–97), Nicholas C. Burbules and Carlos Alberto Torres, eds. New York: Routledge.

Magnier, Mark. 2005a. "China Detains Police Official." *Los Angeles Times,* December 12, A3.

Magnier, Mark. 2005b. "China OKs Law Aimed at Taiwan." *Los Angeles Times,* March 14, A8.

Magnier, Mark. 2005c. "China Seeks to Allay U.S. Fears as Summit Nears." *Los Angeles Times,* August 26, A3.

Magnier, Mark. 2005d. "China's Cadres Sent to School." *Los Angeles Times,* July 8, A3.

Magnier, Mark. 2005e. "Chinese Urbanites Are of Two Minds on U.S., Poll Finds." *Los Angeles Times,* March 4, A5.

Magnier, Mark. 2005f. "Driven to Be Made in China." *Los Angeles Times,* July 11. http://www .latimes.com.

Magnier, Mark. 2005g. "Flip Side to Fame in China." *Los Angeles Times,* March 14, A1, A8.

Malone, Nolan, Kaari F. Baluja, Joseph M. Costanzo, and Cynthia J. Davis. 2003. *The Foreign-Born Population: 2000*. Washington, DC: U.S. Department of Commerce, Economics and Statistics Administration, U.S. Census Bureau. http://www.census.gov/prod/2003pubs/c2kbr -34.pdf.

Mander, Jerry. 2006. "Introduction: Globalization and the Assault on Indigenous Resources." In *Paradigm Wars: Indigenous People's Resistance to Globalization* (pp. 3–10), Jerry Mander and Victoria Tauli-Corpuz, eds. San Francisco: Sierra Club Books.

Mander, Jerry, and Victoria Tauli-Corpuz, eds. 2006. *Paradigm Wars: Indigenous People's Resistance to Globalization*. San Francisco: Sierra Club Books.

Marginson, Simon. 1993. *Education and Public Policy in Australia*. Cambridge, UK: Cambridge University Press.

Marginson, Simon. 1995. "Markets in Higher Education: Australia." In *Academic Work: The Changing Labour Process in Higher Education* (pp. 17–39), John Smyth, ed. London: Open University Press.

Marginson, Simon. 2004. "Doing Somersaults in Enschede: Rethinking and Inverting Public/Private in Higher Education amid the Winds of Globalization." Keynote paper presented at the Consortium of Higher Education Researchers (CHER) Conference, Enschede, The Netherlands, September.

Marginson, Simon. 2007. "Globalisation, the 'Idea of a University,' and Its Ethical Regimes." *Higher Education Management and Policy* 19(1): 19–34.

Marginson, Simon. 2010. "The Rise of the Global University: 5 New Tensions." *Chronicle of Higher Education* (May 30). http://chronicle.com.

Marginson, Simon, and Mark Considine. 2000. *The Enterprise University: Power, Governance, and Reinvention in Australia*. Cambridge, UK: Cambridge University Press.

Mazzetti, Mark. 2005. "Chinese Arms Threaten Asia, Rumsfeld Says." *Los Angeles Times*, June 4, A1.

McGrew, Anthony. 1997. "Democracy Beyond Borders? Globalization and the Reconstruction of Democratic Theory and Politics." In *The Transformation of Democracy? Globalization and Territorial Democracy* (pp. 231–66), Anthony McGrew, ed. Cambridge, UK: Polity Press.

McKie, Robin. 2006. "Pollution Soaring to Crisis Levels in Arctic." *Guardian.co.uk*, March 12. http://www.guardian.co.uk/environment/2006/mar/12/science.climatechange.

McMurtrie, Beth. 2001. "Foreign Enrollments Grow in the U.S., but So Does Competition from Other Nations." *Chronicle of Higher Education, International*, November 16. http://chronicle .com.

Miller, David. 1999. "Bounded Citizenship." In *Cosmopolitan Citizenship* (pp. 60–80), Kimberly Hutchings and Roland Dannreuther, eds. London: Macmillan.

Miller, David. 2002. "The Left, the Nation-State and European Citizenship." In *Global Citizenship: A Critical Introduction* (pp. 84–91), Nigel Dower and John Williams, eds. New York: Routledge.

Mohrman, Kathryn, Wanhua Ma, and David Baker. 2008. "The Research University in Transition: The Emerging Global Model." *Higher Education Policy* 21(1): 5–27.

Mok, Ka Ho. 1997a. "Private Challenges to Public Dominance: The Resurgence of Private Education in the Pearl River Delta." *Comparative Education* 33(1): 43–60.

Mok, Ka Ho. 1997b. "Retreat of the State: Marketization of Education in the Pearl River Delta." *Comparative Education Review* 41(3): 260–76.

Mok, Ka Ho. 2000. "Marketizing Higher Education in Post-Mao China." *International Journal of Educational Development* 20(2): 109–26.

Mok, Ka Ho. 2001. "From State Control to Governance: Policy of Decentralization and Higher Education in Guangdong, China." *International Education Review* 47(1–2): 123–49.

Mok, Ka Ho. 2002. "Policy of Decentralization and Changing Governance of Higher Education in Post-Mao China." *Public Administration and Development* 22(3): 261–73.

Mok, Ka Ho. 2005. "Globalization and Educational Restructuring: University Merging and Changing Governance in China." *Higher Education: The International Journal of Higher Education and Educational Planning* 50(1): 57–88.

Mollis, Marcela. 2001. *La Universidad Argentina en Tránsito: Ensayo para jóvenes y no tan jóvenes (The Argentine University in transition: An essay for the young and not so young).* Buenos Aires: Fondo de Cultura Económica.

Mollis, Marcela. 2002. "Argentine Higher Education in Transition." *International Higher Education* (Winter). http://www.bc.edu/bc_org/avp/soe/cihe/newsletter/News26/ text013. htm.

Mollis, Marcela. 2003. "A Decade of Higher Education Reform in Argentina." *International Higher Education* (Winter). http://www.bc.edu/bc_org/avp/soe/cihe/newsletter/News30/ text 012.htm.

Mollis, Marcela. 2006. "Latin American Identities in Transition: A Diagnosis of Argentine and Brazilian Universities." In *The University, State, and Market: The Political Economy of Globalization in the Americas* (pp. 203–20), Robert A. Rhoads and Carlos Alberto Torres, eds. Stanford, CA: Stanford University Press.

Mollis, Marcela, and Simon Marginson. 2002. "The Assessment of Universities in Argentina and Australia: Between Autonomy and Heteronomy." *Higher Education* 43(3): 311–30.

Monard-Weissman, Kathia. 2003. "Fostering a Sense of Justice through International Service-Learning." *Academic Exchange Quarterly* 7(2): 164–69.

Mooney, Paul. 2005a. "China Abruptly Cancels Scholarly Meeting on Democratization." *The Chronicle of Higher Education, Today's News*, May 19. http://chronicle.com.

Mooney, Paul. 2005b. "Chinese Students Line Up for First Undergraduate Gay-Studies Course." *Chronicle of Higher Education, Today's News*, August 23. http://chronicle.com.

Mooney, Paul. 2005c. "Peking U. Fires Professor Who Assailed China's Crackdown on Free Speech." *Chronicle of Higher Education, Today's News*, March 31. http://chronicle.com.

Morduchowicz, Daniel. 2004. "*The Take*: A Review." *ZNet*, September 20. http://www.zcommunications.org/the-take-by-daniel-morduchowicz-1.

Musil, Jiři. 2002. "A Squandered Opportunity: How Prague Lost the Chance to Host the Central European University." *The New Presence: The Prague Journal of Central European Affairs* 4: 16–17.

NAFSA: Association of International Educators. 2003a. *Securing America's Future: Global Education for a Global Age*. Washington, DC: NAFSA: Association of International Educators. http://www.nafsa.org/uploadedFiles/NAFSA_Home/Resource_Library_Assets/Public_Policy/securing_america_s_future.pdf?n=3894.

NAFSA: Association of International Educators. 2003b. *Toward an International Education Policy for the United States: International Education in an Age of Globalism and Terrorism*. Washington, DC: NAFSA: Association of International Educators. http://www.nafsa.org/content/PublicPolicy/USIntlEdPolicy/NIEP2003 updateFINAL.pdf.

NAFSA: Association of International Educators. 2005. *Internationalizing the Campus 2005: Profiles of Success at Colleges and Universities*. Washington, DC: NAFSA: Association of International Educators. http://www.nafsa.org/_/File/_/itc2005.pdf.

Nathan, Andrew J. 2001. "Introduction: Documents and Their Significance." In *The Tiananmen Papers* (pp. xxxv–lxv), Andrew J. Nathan and Perry Link, eds. (compiled by Zhang Liang). New York: Public Affairs.

National Security Agency. 2005. *Tiananmen Square, 1989: The Declassified History* (National Security archive electronic briefing book, retrieved July 14, 2005). http://www.gwu.edu/~nsarchiv/NSAEBB/NSAEBB16/documents/.

Neff, Stephen C. 1998. "International Law and the Critique of Cosmopolitan Citizenship." In *Cosmopolitan Citizenship* (pp. 105–19), Kimberly Hutchings and Roland Dannreuther, eds. London: Macmillan.

Newson, Janice, and Howard Buchbinder. 1988. *The University Means Business: Universities, Corporations, and Academic Work*. Toronto: Garamond Press.

Nussbaum, Martha C. 2002. *For Love of Country?* (edited by Joshua Cohen). Boston: Beacon Press.

Ong, Aihwa. 1999. *Flexible Citizenship: The Cultural Logics of Transnationality*. Durham, NC: Duke University Press.

Ong, Aihwa. 2004. "Higher Learning: Educational Availability and Flexible Citizenship in Global Space." In *Diversity and Citizenship Education: Global Perspectives* (pp. 49–70), James A. Banks, ed. San Francisco: Jossey-Bass.

Passel, Jeffrey. 2004. "Mexican Immigration to the US: The Latest Estimates." Research Report, Migration Policy Institute, Washington, DC. http://www.migrationinformation.org/usfocus/display.cfm?ID=208.

Peters, Michael A. 2006. "The Rise of Global Science and the Emerging Political Economy of International Research Collaborations." *European Journal of Education* 41(2): 225–44.

Pieke, Frank N. 1998. "The 1989 Chinese People's Movement in Beijing." In *Student Protest: The Sixties and After* (pp. 248–63), Gerard J. DeGroot, ed. London: Longman.

Pierson, David. 2005. "Change in China, Change in L.A." *Los Angeles Times*, June 4, B1, B14.

Pierson, David. 2008. "New Chinatown Grows in Far East San Gabriel Valley." *Los Angeles Times*, June 19. http://www.latimes.com.

Pimentel, Lester. 2004. "*The Take*." *PopMatters*, October 8. http://www.popmatters.com/film/reviews/t/take-2004.shtml.

Porter, Maureen, and Kathia Monard. 2001. "'Ayni' in the Global Village: Building Relationships of Reciprocity Through International Service Learning." *Michigan Journal of Community Service Learning* 8(1): 5–17.

Pujadas, Carlos. 2000. "Higher Education Reform in Argentina." *International Higher Education* (Winter). http://bc.edu/bc_org/avp/soe/cihe/newsletter/News03/textcy4.html.

Rhoades, Gary. 1998. *Managed Professionals: Unionized Faculty and the Restructuring of Academic Labor*. Albany: State University of New York Press.

Rhoades, Gary, Judy Marquez Kiyama, Rudy McCormick, and Marisol Quiroz. 2007. "Local Cosmopolitans and Cosmopolitan Locals: New Models of Professionals in the Academy." *Review of Higher Education* 31(2): 209–35.

Rhoades, Gary, and Sheila Slaughter. 2006. "Academic Capitalism and the New Economy: Privatization as Shifting the Target of Public Subsidy in Higher Education." In *The University, State, and Market: The Political Economy of Globalization in the Americas* (pp. 103–40), Robert A. Rhoads and Carlos Alberto Torres, eds. Stanford, CA: Stanford University Press.

Rhoads, Robert A. 1997. *Community Service and Higher Learning: Explorations of the Caring Self*. Albany: State University of New York Press.

Rhoads, Robert A. 1998a. *Freedom's Web: Student Activism in an Age of Cultural Diversity*. Baltimore, MD: Johns Hopkins University Press.

Rhoads, Robert A. 1998b. "In the Service of Citizenship: A Study of Student Involvement in Community Service." *Journal of Higher Education* 69(3): 277–97.

Rhoads, Robert A. 2000. "Democratic Citizenship and Service Learning: Advancing the Caring Self." In *Teaching to Promote Intellectual and Personal Maturity: Incorporating Students' Worldviews and Identities into the Learning Process* (New Directions for Teaching and Learning, No. 82) (pp. 37–44), Marcia B. Baxter Magolda, ed. San Francisco: Jossey-Bass.

Rhoads, Robert A. 2003. "Globalization and Resistance in the United States and Mexico: The Global Potemkin Village." *Higher Education: The International Journal of Higher Education and Educational Planning* 45(2): 223–50.

Rhoads, Robert A. 2007. "The New Militarism, Terrorism, and the American University: Making Sense of the Assault on Democracy 'Here, There, Somewhere.'" *InterActions* 3(1): article 2. Electronic journal. http://escholarship.org/uc/gseis_interactions.

Rhoads, Robert A. 2009. "Learning from Students as Agents of Social Change: Toward an Emancipatory Vision of the University." *Journal of Change Management* 9(3): 309–21.

Rhoads, Robert A., and Jeffrey P. F. Howard, eds. 1998. *Academic Service Learning: A Pedagogy of Action and Reflection.* (New Directions for Teaching and Learning, no. 73). San Francisco: Jossey-Bass.

Rhoads, Robert A., and Xuehong Liang. 2006. "Global Influences and Local Responses at Guangdong University of Foreign Studies." *World Studies in Education* 7(2): 23–53.

Rhoads, Robert A., and Amy Liu. 2009. "Globalization, Social Movements, and the American University: Implications for Research and Practice." *Higher Education: Handbook of Theory and Research* 24: 273–315.

Rhoads, Robert A., and Liliana Mina. 2001. "The Student Strike at the National Autonomous University of Mexico: A Political Analysis." *Comparative Education Review* 45(3): 334–53.

Rhoads, Robert A., and Gary Rhoades. 2005. "Graduate Employee Unionization as Symbol of and Challenge to the Corporatization of U.S. Research Universities." *Journal of Higher Education* 76(3): 243–75.

Rhoads, Robert A., Victor Saenz, and Rozana Carducci. 2005. "Higher Education Reform as a Social Movement: The Case of Affirmative Action." *Review of Higher Education* 28(2): 191–220.

Rhoads, Robert A., and Katalin Szelényi. 2009. "Globally Engaged Universities and the Changing Context of Academic Citizenship." *Education and Society* 27(2): 5–26.

Rhoads, Robert A., and Carlos Alberto Torres. 2006a. "The Global Economy, the State, Social Movements, and the University: Concluding Remarks and an Agenda for Action." In *The University, State, and Market: The Political Economy of Globalization in the Americas* (pp. 321–51), Robert A. Rhoads and Carlos Alberto Torres, eds. Stanford, CA: Stanford University Press.

Rhoads, Robert A., and Carlos Alberto Torres, eds. 2006b. *The University, State, and Market: The Political Economy of Globalization in the Americas.* Stanford, CA: Stanford University Press.

Rice, R. Eugene. 2002. "Beyond *Scholarship Reconsidered*: Toward an Enlarged Vision of the Scholarly Work of Faculty Members." In *Scholarship in the Postmodern Era: New Venues, New Values, New Visions* (New Directions for Teaching and Learning, no. 90) (pp. 7–17), Kenneth J. Zahorski, ed. San Francisco: Jossey-Bass.

Richter, Paul. 2005. "More U.S.-China Battles Are Likely." *Los Angeles Times*, August 3, C1, C5.

Riesman, David, Nathan Glazer, and Reuel Denney. 1950. *The Lonely Crowd: A Study of the Changing American Character.* New Haven, CT: Yale University Press.

Ritzer, George. 1993. *The McDonaldization of Society.* Thousand Oaks, CA: Pine Oaks Press.

Rizvi, Fazal. 2000. "International Education and the Production of Global Imagination." In *Globalization and Education: Critical Perspectives* (pp. 205–26), Carlos Alberto Torres and Nicholas C. Burbules, eds. New York: Routledge.

Rizvi, Fazal. 2004. "Debating Globalization and Education after September 11." *Comparative Education* 40(2): 157–71.

Rizvi, Fazal. 2008. "Epistemic Virtues and Cosmopolitan Learning." *Australian Educational Researcher* 35(1): 17–35.

Rizvi, Fazal. 2009. "Globalization and Policy Research in Education." In *The SAGE International Handbook of Educational Evaluation* (pp. 3–18), Katherine E. Ryan and J. Bradley Cousins, eds. Thousand Oaks, CA: Sage.

Rizvi, Fazal, and Lucas Walsh. 1998. "Difference, Globalisation and the Internationalisation of Curriculum." *Australian Universities' Review* 41(2): 7–11.

Robertson, Roland. 1992. *Globalization: Social Theory and Global Culture.* London: Sage.

Ross, Heidi A. 1993. *China Learns English: Teaching Language and Social Change in the People's Republic.* New Haven, CT: Yale University Press.

Said, Edward W. 1993. *Culture and Imperialism.* New York: Vintage Books.

Sandole, Dennis J. D. 1999. *Capturing the Complexity of Conflict: Dealing with Violent Ethnic Conflicts of the Post–Cold War Era.* London: Pinter.

Santos, Boaventura de Sousa. 2006. "The University in the 21st Century: Toward a Democratic and Emancipatory University Reform." In *The University, State, and Market: The Political Economy of Globalization in the Americas* (pp. 60–100), Robert A. Rhoads and Carlos Alberto Torres, eds. Stanford, CA: Stanford University Press.

Schugurensky, Daniel. 2006. "The Political Economy of Higher Education in the Time of Global Markets: Whither the Social Responsibility of the University?" In *The University, State, and Market: The Political Economy of Globalization in the Americas* (pp. 301–20), Robert A. Rhoads and Carlos Alberto Torres, eds. Stanford, CA: Stanford University Press.

Selingo, Jeffrey. 2004. "Applications from Foreign Graduate Students Decline, Survey Finds." *Chronicle of Higher Education, Today's News,* February 26. http://chronicle.com.

Shafir, Gershon, ed. 1998. *The Citizenship Debates: A Reader.* Minneapolis: University of Minnesota Press.

Siaya, Laura, and Fred M. Hayward. 2003. *Mapping Internationalization on U.S. Campuses.* Washington, DC: American Council on Education.

Silverstein, Stuart. 2006. "UCLA Breaks Fundraising Record." *Los Angeles Times,* February 16. http://www.latimes.com.

Sino Mania. 2005. "Tiananmen Square Uprising: A Perspective" (retrieved July 14, 2005). http://sinomania.com/CHINANEWS/tiananmen_perspective.htm.

Slaughter, Sheila, and Larry L. Leslie. 1997. *Academic Capitalism: Politics, Policies, and the Entrepreneurial University.* Baltimore, MD: Johns Hopkins University Press.

Slaughter, Sheila, and Gary Rhoades. 2004. *Academic Capitalism and the New Economy: Markets, State and Higher Education.* Baltimore, MD: Johns Hopkins University Press.

Slocum, Jenée, and Robert A. Rhoads. 2009. "Faculty and Student Engagement in the Argentine Grassroots Rebellion: Toward a Democratic and Emancipatory Vision of the University." *Higher Education: The International Journal of Higher Education and Educational Planning* 57(1): 85–105.

Smyth, John, ed. 1995. *Academic Work: The Changing Labour Process in Higher Education.* London: Open University Press.

Soley, Lawrence C. 1995. *Leasing the Ivory Tower: The Corporate Takeover of Academia.* Boston: South End Press.

Soros Alapítvány. 1990. "Soros Alapítvány Évkönyv 1990 (The 1990 Yearbook of the Soros Foundation." http://www.adata.hu/_soros/Soros_evkonyvek.nsf/11fcbf9d3d07 fd42c1256d3600346085 /549ca0e75400ec1fc1256dc5002dfeba?OpenDocument#K%C3%96Z%C3%89PEUR%C3%93 PAI%20EGYETEM%20(CEU).

Soysal, Yasemin. 1994. *Limits of Citizenship: Migrants and Postnational Membership in Europe*. Chicago: Chicago University Press.

Spence, Jonathan. 1990. *Children of the Dragon*. New York: Collier Books.

Stiglitz, Joseph E. 2002. *Globalization and Its Discontents*. New York: W. W. Norton.

Stromquist, Nelly P. 2002. *Education in a Globalized World: The Connectivity of Economic Power, Technology, and Knowledge*. Lanham, MD: Rowman and Littlefield.

Stromquist, Nelly P. 2007. "Internationalization as a Response to Globalization: Radical Shifts in University Environments." *Higher Education* 53: 81–105.

Szelényi, Katalin. 2006. "Students Without Borders? Migratory Decision-Making Among International Graduate Students in the U.S." In *The Human Face of Global Mobility* (pp. 181–209), Michael Peter Smith and Adrian Favell, eds. New Brunswick, NJ: Transaction Press.

Szelényi, Katalin, and Robert A. Rhoads. 2007. "Citizenship in a Global Context: The Perspectives of International Graduate Students in the United States." *Comparative Education Review* 51(1): 25–47.

Tabuchi, Hiroko. 2010. "Chinese Honda Strike a Wake-Up Call for Japan." *New York Times*, June 1. http://www.nytimes.com.

Thang, M. 2009. "16 of 37 Valedictorians of Boston Public Schools Not Born in US." *New England Ethnic News*, June 3. http://www.ethnicnewz.org/en/16-37-valedictorians-boston-public -schools-not-born-us.

Tismaneanu, Vladimir. 1998. *Fantasies of Salvation: Democracy, Nationalism, and Myth in Post-Communist Europe*. Princeton, NJ: Princeton University Press.

Tismaneanu, Vladimir. 1999. "Reassessing the Revolutions of 1989." *Journal of Democracy* 10(1): 69–73.

Tomlinson, John. 1999. *Globalization and Culture*. Chicago: University of Chicago Press.

Tomlinson, John. 2003. "Globalization and Cultural Identity." In *The Global Transformation Reader: An Introduction to the Globalization Debate* (2nd ed.) (pp. 269–77), David Held and Anthony McGrew, eds. Cambridge, UK: Polity Press.

Tönnies, Ferdinand. 1957. *Community and Society: Gemeinschaft and Gesellschaft*. Translated by Charles P. Loomis. New York: Harper and Row.

Torres, Carlos Alberto. 1998. *Democracy, Education, and Multiculturalism: Dilemmas of Citizenship in a Global World*. Lanham, MD: Rowman and Littlefield.

Torres, Carlos Alberto. 2002. "Globalization, Education, and Citizenship: Solidarity Versus Markets?" *American Educational Research Journal* 39(2): 363–78.

Torres, Carlos Alberto, and Nicholas C. Burbules, ed. 2000. *Globalization and Education: Critical Perspectives*. New York: Routledge.

Torres, Carlos Alberto, and Robert A. Rhoads. 2006. "Introduction: Globalization and Higher Education in the Americas." In *The University, State, and Market: The Political Economy of Globalization in the Americas* (pp. 3–38), Robert A. Rhoads and Carlos Alberto Torres, eds. Stanford, CA: Stanford University Press.

Touraine, Alain. 1988. *Return of the Actor: Social Theory in Postindustrial Society* (translated by Myrna Godzich). Minneapolis: University of Minnesota Press.

Traynor, Ian. 2009. "Serbian Warlord Gets Life for Crimes Against Humanity." *Guardian.co.uk*, July 20. http://www.guardian.co.uk/world/2009/jul/20/milan-lukic-life-sentence.

UN Food Agency. 2009. "Number of World's Hungry to Top 1 Billion This Year." *UN News Centre*, June 19. http://www.un.org/apps/news/story.asp?NewsID=31197&Cr=hunger&Cr1=#.

UNESCO. 1974. "Recommendation Concerning Education for International Understanding, Cooperation and Peace and Education Relating to Human Rights and Fundamental Freedoms."

New York: United Nations Educational, Scientific and Cultural Organization. http://www
.unesco.org/education/nfsunesco/pdf/Peace_e.pdf.

UNESCO. 2009. *Global Education Digest 2009: Comparing Education Statistics Across the World.*
Montreal: UNESCO Institute for Statistics.

United Nations Development Programme. 2008. *Human Development Report 2007/2008: Fighting
Climate Change: Human Solidarity in a Divided World.* New York: United Nations Development Programme.

Vaira, Massimiliano. 2004. "Globalization and Higher Education Organizational Change: A
Framework for Analysis." *Higher Education* 48(4): 483–510.

Vidal, Gore. 2002. *Dreaming War: Blood for Oil and the Cheney-Bush Junta.* New York: Thunder's
Mouth Press.

Vogelgesang, Lori J., and Alexander W. Astin. 2000. "Comparing the Effects of Service Learning
and Community Service." *Michigan Journal of Community Service Learning* 7: 25–34.

Vogelgesang, Lori J., and Robert A. Rhoads. 2003. "Advancing a Broad Notion of Public Engagement: The Limitations of Contemporary Service Learning." *Journal of College and Character* 2.
Electronic journal. www.collegevalues.org.

Ward, Kelly. 2003. *Faculty Service Roles and the Scholarship of Engagement.* ASHE-ERIC Higher
Education Report 29, no. 5. San Francisco: Jossey-Bass.

Washburn, Jennifer. 2005. *University Inc.: The Corporate Corruption of Higher Education.* New
York: Basic Books.

Wasserstrom, Jeffrey. 1991. *Student Protests in Twentieth-Century China: The View from Shanghai.*
Stanford, CA: Stanford University Press.

Wei, Feng. 1996. "The Great Tremors in China's Intellectual Circles: An Overview of Intellectuals
Floundering in the Sea of Commercialism." *Chinese Education and Society* 29(6): 7–104.

Whyte, William H., Jr. 1956. *Organizational Man.* New York: Simon and Schuster.

Wolff, Stefan. 2006. *Ethnic Conflict: A Global Perspective.* Oxford, UK: Oxford University Press.

Women's Human Rights Net. 2002. "An Interview with María José Lubertino." *WHRnet* (May).
http://www.whrnet.org/docs/interview-lubertino-0205.html.

Wright, Bobby. 1991. "The 'Untameable Savage Spirit': American Indians in Colonial Colleges." *The
Review of Higher Education* 14(4): 429–52.

Yang, Rui. 2004. "Openness and Reform as Dynamics for Development: A Case Study of Internationalisation at South China University of Technology." *Higher Education* 47: 473–500.

Yardley, Jim. 2008. "China's Leaders Try to Impress and Reassure the World." *New York Times,*
August 8. http://www.nytimes.com.

Yin, Qiping, and G. White. 1994. "The 'Marketisation' of Chinese Higher Education: A Critical
Assessment." *Comparative Education* 30(3): 217–37.

Zakaria, Fareed. 2004. "Rejecting the Next Bill Gates." *Washington Post,* November 23. http://www
.washingtonpost.com.

Zha, Qiang. 2001. "The Resurgence and Growth of Private Higher Education in China." Paper
presented at the Annual Meeting of the Canadian Society for the Study of Higher Education
(CSSHE), Quebec.

Zhao, Chun-Mei; George D. Kuh, and Robert M. Carini. 2005. "A Comparison of International
Student and American Student Engagement in Effective Educational Practices." *Journal of
Higher Education* 76(2): 209–31.

Zhao, Dingxin. 2002. "Student Nationalism in China." *Problems of Post-Communism* 49(6): 16–28.

Zhao, Suisheng. 2004. *A Nation-State by Construction: Dynamics of Chinese Nationalism.* Stanford,
CA: Stanford University Press.

INDEX